A Tame Colonial Girl

By Wendy Stanley

1. HOW THIS STORY CAME ABOUT

One day in 2009, thirteen years after I typed out my memories on a rather battered typewriter as "self-therapy" as described in the first Chapter, I was talking to Brian, one of the Professors we used to safari with. My friend described to me a fun story that he had recently read about Kenya, which he related to although it was "all fiction", because – quote – it "reminded him of the places he had visited on safaris with his students". I told him I had written a lot of "that sort of stuff about Kenya, but it is not fiction". Brian asked me to email my writings to him. That is when I took the time to go back through all the painful memories I had typed out, and transferred them to "digital", cutting out nearly - but not quite – all of the stuff about the monster.....Mike.

I emailed what was remaining to Brian, who sent back the message "Publish it!"

Initially I used all fake names, including my own, leaving out a lot of detail about family members and friends who would otherwise have been mentioned. However, each and every person who read the script was of the opinion I should write under my own name.

Therefore, years after changing my diary entries into story form, I decided to use my real name, leaving only a few changed names in order to protect people's privacy. However, putting real names brought about the problem of deleting many parts even though they were fact,.......!

Not wanting to offend anyone, and because I needed their feedback, I offered to send copies of my draft story to various family plus extended-family members, also to friends whose opinions I valued. Only one person unexpectedly refused my request, which was a pity as I needed her input; the rest sent back very useful and positive comments, all of which I have taken into account.

Now, to heck with it, I have done with hiding names, deleting, adding, cutting and pasting: I am leaving it as it is!

2. BACKGROUND

If you meet me, you will surely find me boring; that is, unless you are prepared to play Scrabble, or discuss my favourite hobby "the flora and fauna of Kenya", birds in particular. I am a very ordinary, everyday, run-of-the-mill woman, spending too much money on anti-wrinkle creams that don't work; continually dieting, but refusing to accept I will never have a Naomi Campbell figure. I am old-fashioned in that I like a man to give up his seat for me, and I consider it good manners for a man to open a door for me. I am a normal woman.

Hang on! What IS a "normal" woman? Normal by whose definition? Doesn't "normal" imply a boring, law-abiding woman, such as one who obeyed her parents' wishes by remaining a virgin until she married; who is faithful to her husband; whose "normal" husband is faithful to her? A woman who would not get involved with an abuser?

Correction: begin again. On average, I *was* a fairly normal woman. I think. Once....sometime prior to 1979, when I became entangled with an evil Monster.

It was on a certain day in December 199 that my memory was violently jogged to bring back to mind things that had taken place sixteen years previously: things my brain had totally and utterly blanked out. After this happened, I realised I needed help – that is, help in the form of counselling or therapy or whatever. However, *"counselling"* means pouring out your deepest secrets, hideous memories and overwhelming regrets to another person. There was no way I could do that.

Therefore, I decided instead, to try putting it all down *"on paper"*, which might be as good a form of therapy. At least it was effective in forcing me to face up to things, to attempt to put them in perspective, to try to make sense of the overall picture and to piece together the jigsaw as to why I allowed the things to happen, that happened..... Perhaps it helped to some degree. But then again, perhaps not. There are too many regrets, and too much guilt, remaining.

To begin with, my sole reason for writing this narrative, most of which was put down in diary form, was because I had allowed my whole being to be taken over by a warped individual called Mike. Mike was a serious chauvinistic abuser: a perverted freak who did his utmost to destroy my little family; who succeeded, to a certain extent, in destroying me. Events have taken place in my life that should have no place in the life of an ordinary, everyday, run-of-the-mill woman: these involve my relationship with this evil creature disguised in a human body.

This story relates events literally from my birth up to the time of my relationship with Mike, and events that occurred in my life *"after"* Mike. Yet, as explained in the Preface, the main Dear Diary entries which centred on him, the Monster – plus all the things I wanted but never dared to say to him – are almost entirely left out, having been cut and pasted elsewhere. For some inexplicable reason, much of what I fantasised about saying to Mike but never had the courage to, was recorded in my Diary in the form of poetry. Hidden away, I have a book of poems I wrote to Mike.

In complete contrast to the Mike issue, I feel what I have written here should be told: things bottled up inside me need to be let out, such as:-

- My naivety and total unpreparedness when I was faced with the Real World, having experienced a sheltered upbringing *"in the bush"*.....

- My private rebellion against *"Colonial Rules".....*

- The price I have paid for love in my life.....

But, above all, this is an attempt to describe what it was really like, to be brought up in the most amazing country in the world, in True Brit tradition.....

.....as a Colonial Girl.

3. MY PARENTS

I suppose my life started off fine although, as I later discovered, I was unwanted. My mother came from a warm, happy, English working-class family in Norfolk. My father was from North of the Border and brought up very strictly, in true Scottish tradition. I came to know his family very well but never understood the reasons for his family's snobbish attitude towards the attractive and vivacious young grey-eyed red-head that he took home for approval at Christmas-time, in 1943.

From a very early age, I knew that my mother had always been top of class and eventually top of school. She won a prized scholarship to High School she was unable to utilise because her folks could not afford the bus-fare to the school, which was on the other side of the County. Mum never got over this and I felt so bad whenever she related the sad story to me. She worked on the quay gutting fish, eventually becoming manager of the village fishmonger's shop, until she joined the Women's Air Force in 1943.

Dad was six feet two inches tall and devastatingly good-looking, with very dark, wavy hair and hazel eyes. At the time of the Second World War, he joined the Royal Air Force, which is how he met my mother.

Dad never swept a floor and, until the day he died, the only *"meal"* he ever cooked was cheese on toast, which involved slicing bread, slicing cheese, then placing them under a grill – making sure the cheese was on top. But he made the best pot of tea, and the best hot toddies, in the world.

Mum & Dad's rather "severe" Wedding
at Silloth

Royal visit to
the Airforce Base

11

My parents never discussed anything as hush-hush as contraception and dad never used any because that, like housework and cooking, was the woman's domain. From 1943-44, my mother thrived on Service Life. She intended to make a career of it. She was very popular, which is obvious from all the complimentary comments in her Autograph Book and the photographs from those days. Becoming an Officer in the Air Force would more than make up for not having gone to High School; she was well on the way and there would be no looking back. She had great ambitions.

My poor mother. She often related to me how, on the very week she was to attend an interview for a Commission, mum discovered to her indescribable horror that she was pregnant. She was utterly devastated. She bade farewell to her beloved Air Force, and went to live with Great Aunt Bess in Puddlesford-on-Mud until I was born, exactly nine months and thirteen days after their Wedding Day. Dad was delighted to be having a son; I was already named Michael. When mum telegraphed him in Aden in November 1944 saying "Wendy arrived last night", he telegraphed back querying "Wendy Who?"

On mum's side of the family, my birth meant that five generations were still living. I have a photograph of me with my mother, my mother's mother, my mother's mother's father and my mother's mother's father's mother. I do have vague memories of Great Grandad, for instance when he came stumbling down the stairs shouting that there were geese in his bed; there was a feather mattress on his bed and a seam had split! All I remember about my Grandmother's Grandmother is she was allowed to eat jelly marmalade as she had no teeth left, while I had to eat marmalade that was full of tough bits of orange skin.

FIVE GENERATIONS

Dad had spent much time abroad during the war years; he had learned what it means to feel warm right down to the marrow in one's bones. Back in Scotland after being de-mobbed, he huddled next to the fire-place in what he referred to as *"the last Winter I shall ever spend on this God-forsaken Island"*. He remained true to his word. Mum and dad set off on their epic overland trip to South Africa. On 13 October 1947, they left the bombed site in Folkestone where they had camped for the night, and took the ferry to Boulogne.

Without me.

Unhappily, my mother and I never became physically close. I cannot recall her ever putting an arm around me or cuddling me. Rightly or wrongly, I put this down to the fact that any physical contact between us was lost from the time they left me in UK for over a year when I was not yet three. Or perhaps it was simply that I had spoiled her chances of becoming a Commissioned Officer. Who knows? Mum's relationship with my young sister, was quite different. An incident from around 1958, stands out clearly in my mind. We were sitting in the back of a car when my sleepy sister laid her head on mum's shoulder and fell asleep; mum put her arm around Linda. What makes this incident so weird, was how totally flabbergasted I was at this brazen display of affection! It was *unthinkable* I should ever feel the kind of closeness to my mother that would allow me to put my head on her shoulder – let alone having mum put her arm around me!

Preparing to set off on their epic overland trip to Africa

Left behind in Britain, 1947-48, I was passed from one relative to the other, while my parents travelled overland to Africa in a convoy of two converted ex-Army ambulances; a small group of pioneers who had never met each other previously. The "Civilian Pioneers of the Sahara"!

4. OVERLAND TO AFRICA

Mother kept a diary throughout their overland trip. There was an entry, written when they travelled through the Apennines which she described as "beautiful scenery", at a time when food was scarce and "terribly expensive", describing how it was like a dream-come-true when a flock of ducks and turkeys wandered onto the truck. The person driving at the time quickly swerved towards them. Mother's diary states "Caught a duck; just missed turkey!" and "Old lady, looking exactly like witch" burst out of the bushes, screaming at them and waving a stick. She was still running after them brandishing her stick until she was left far behind in a cloud of dust and feathers.

Over the years mum was to regale me with many tales of their overland journey. They travelled with the 1939 Michelin Map, and had also been given an invaluable hand-drawn map of the desert with instructions such as "if you have not reached three identical sand-dunes to the left by 6.30 p.m., stop and make camp for the night". They re-fuelled from deposits left behind and buried by the British war-time forces, which were identified on the maps.

Although much tougher in terms of terrain, breakdowns, lack of spare parts, no roads and so on, this overland journey made seven decades ago, was in so many ways more enjoyable than similar journeys made today. They were enthusiastically welcomed at border posts, invited to take hot showers and meals at Ambassadorial Residences, where they dressed up in evening attire: jewellery, cufflinks and all, whilst dining at the residence of the local Commandant or Government Representative.

It is written in mum's diary that, on my third Birthday, they had camped in Guezzam, where they had their first "primitive shower" which mother defined as "delicious". I scoured the page for mention of me, her daughter turning three, but there was none.

They spent Christmas in Kano, *"British Nigeria"* where, according to mother's diary, "an unknown gentleman made us a present of a turkey and 100 eggs on Xmas Day – bless him!" They reached Uganda on 18 January 1948. They never made it to South Africa, having run out of money soon after arriving in Kenya. Mum and dad spent their fourth Wedding Anniversary at the Norfolk Hotel in Nairobi.

In Kenya, they sold the truck and their winter clothes. Via a certain Mr Jessop, dad was offered a managerial job with the infamous Groundnut Scheme, in Tanganyika. On 30 January 1948 they left Nairobi by train at 10 p.m., breakfasted the following morning at Nakuru, in the Great Rift Valley, and boarded the lake steamer at Kisumu at 6 p.m. that evening. Mother's diary states "lovely lazy trip! No cooking. Visited Musoma. Andy caught fish from boat with native's line".

They took a steam train from Mwanza to Urambo, their new home. On 4 February 1948, the very last entry in my mother's diary states simply "Watched from Mess whilst tent was erected for us".

I had always wanted Mum to write a book about their amazing adventure and in fact bought her a typewriter for her 71st Birthday, for this very purpose. But our mother died, cruelly whisked away from this world at least twenty years too soon, ten days before her 72nd Birthday, never having completed her story.

I have often asked you God, why, why, why did you take her so early?

Sunday October 12th. 1947.	Left Addlestone for Folkestone. Arrived evening parked on bombed site near quay.
Monday 13th.	Folkestone - Boulogne 2½ hours Boulogne - 16 kilos outside Abbeville. Parked in farmyard. (Eggs and Milk cost 300 fr.)
Tuesday 14th.	On to Paris. Stopped in Beauvais 1 hour. Paris - parked in Rue de Grande Armee just behind Arc de Triomph
Wednesday 15th.	Left Paris p.m. reached Obeuil parked in yard beside butcher's shop.
Thursday 16th.	Returned to Paris for new Piston Rod etc.
Friday 17th.	Pushed on through St.Lo and parked in woods.
Saturday 18th.	Made good going passed through Vichy and from there up into the hills. Parked in high pine woods - beautiful but very cold.
Sunday 19th.	Le Puy - St. Dedier - parked at farmhouse bought eggs and rabbit.
Monday 20th.	Through Appenines and beutiful scenery. Caught a duck (nr ile) just missed turkey. Arrived Marseilles 3.30.
Tuesday 21st.	Parked in Hotel Yard.
Wednesday 22nd.	Bathed in Med. Terrific storm later.
Thursday 23rd.	Very Warm.
Friday 24th.	Went into town shopping. Everything terribly expensive.
November 2nd.	Sailed from Marseilles in Ville D'Oran. Arrived Algiers following day.
Friday November 21st.	Left Algiers 9.30. (Hail storm) Passed through Blida Medea Lovardo Berrouaghia and Boghart. (Raided orange grove) Blida at the foot of Atlas Mountains. (Water tanks burst)
Saturday November 22nd.	... , drove the night until 4.30. Arr. El Golea 4.0 p.m.
Sunday 23rd.	Fete Day. No Petrol Available.
Monday 24th.	Filled up. Left El Golea 1 p.m.
Tuesday 25th.	Travelled overnight.
Wednesday 26th.	Delayed. Arr. InSalah 3.30 p.m. Very rough going.
Thursday 27th.	Left In Salah 9.0. Soft sand. Track varies from 1939 A.A. Book.
Friday 28th.	Travelled overnight. Reached Arak 11 a.m. Repaired rads. Left 4.30 p.m.
Saturday 29th.	Reached Tamanrasset 2 p.m. Stayed overnight.
Sunday 30th.	Left Tam. midday. Soft sand. Heavy going. Lost track and doubled back.
Monday 1st. December.	Very Slow. Stopped overnight.
Tuesday 2nd.	Up at 4 and off at 5.0. Stopped for breakfast 6.0. Big Ends gone. Laid up for repairs. Boiling hot - had to get out of trucks and lay under tarpaulins whilst men worked.
Wednesday 3rd.	Only 30 miles in today. Very hot. Rads boiling continuously. Every ½ hour stopping and turning against wind to cool.
Thursday 4th.	Slightly cooler. Arr. In Guezzam mid-afternoon. Two wireless operators. Had primitive shower - delicious.

5. JOINING MY PARENTS

Photo for my first Passport
prior to my 3 day flight
to join my parents.
I am told the photographer
said "Smile!" and I replied:
"I <u>is</u> a-smilin'"

I have little recollection of the year I was left behind in UK.

Apparently, my very loving but – at that time – typically stagnant relatives, were opposed to my being sent off to darkest Africa at such a tender age. I still have very vague memories of my flight to East Africa via BOAC Hermes, which took three days, stopping nightly to sit in baking hot, dusty rooms with ceiling fans stirring up damp heat and flies. My prickly-heat covered hands were bandaged. I remember finally walking down the ladder that had been wheeled to the door of the aircraft, to see a slim lady with golden hair and a beautiful smile reaching out for me. I even remember the pleated beige dress she wore, with padded shoulders and a pinched-in waist.

This was my Mother.

Apparently my parents had been travelling back and forth daily by steam train, between the airstrip and the camp where they lived, awaiting the arrival of my aeroplane. On this day, as on the two days previously, when it became too late for a plane to land, they had climbed back onto a railway coach and were returning to the camp. The local District Officer was shaving when he heard the aeroplane fly overhead. He dashed out to his Land Rover, shirtless and barefoot, with half his face covered in shaving foam, and drove like a demon to halt the train. This he managed to accomplish by driving alongside the train gesticulating madly at the engine driver, who obediently stopped and shunted back to the platform and waited for my parents to alight and collect me from the airstrip.

According to my mother, the trains had no corridors, just coaches with doors opening on either side. Years later I would laugh at Mum's description of this train journey. Friends in other coaches, upon hearing of my arrival, would clamber along the outside of the train, or sometimes on the roof Rambo-fashion, dropping in through our coach window clutching bottles of booze to celebrate! I was told the train moved so slowly that any lady desperate for a pee simply jumped off and hid behind a bush, climbing back on a few coaches further along. Men, of course, being blessed with such handy gadgets, did not need to leave the train when nature called.

After a two-hour journey, our steam train arrived at a wooden platform in the middle of the bush. This was the railway siding at the camp where my parents had settled, the place where 'The Browns' were to live for the next three and a half years.

6. CHILDHOOD MEMORIES OF TANGANYIKA

I have no memory of beautiful scenery in this part of the world. I remember only dusty, corrugated dirt roads in the dry season, then enormous muddy puddles in the wet season. The terrain as I recall it was flat; much of what I saw was being prepared for the planting of ground-nuts. There appeared to be a never-ending amount of large machinery, which I watched ploughing up the land and clearing wide expanses of trees and vegetation to create "tsetse belts". Tsetses are huge brown flies with a burning bite that can inflict trypanosomiasis or "sleeping sickness", which is an infection of the brain caused by a parasite carried by some of these flies. I gather that these clearings were created to destroy vegetation where the adult flies would rest and lay eggs; it also helped to prevent migration of these flies from one area to another.

We moved into a stone house with a thatched roof

HOME SWEET HOME

... large machinery clearing the bush for development & creating "tsetse belts"

Tsetses are huge brown flies .....

These were good days, initially living under canvas and eating in a large mess tent, eventually moving into a house with thatched roof on a brand new "housing estate". My mother was so excited when her new Singer sewing-machine arrived, with rolls and rolls of material. She spent hour's snip-snipping, sewing curtains, tablecloths and napkins. We still have her sewing-machine, which functions perfectly.

The term "Snip-snipping" brings back a vivid memory of a time I was happily snipping in the air with mum's scissors, when I accidentally cut a small nick at window-ledge height in one of our beautiful new floor-length curtains. Worried sick about what my parents would say, I proceeded to cut along the width of the curtain, in my childish wisdom believing they wouldn't notice anything if I cut all the way across. To my distress, my ayah appeared on the scene when I was cutting in a neat upward slope, only three-quarters of the way across the curtain. The ayah went ballistic, the whites of her eyes rolling around in their sockets. I was furious when she stopped me, honestly believing my parents would never had noticed if I had been left to cut the whole way across!

Of course, my mother simply could not understand it. I was always so well-behaved! She had to cut all the living-room curtains to the same window-ledge length. For a long time afterwards, Mother would look at me with puzzlement, not comprehending why her obedient little daughter had done something so wicked! It must have been about fifteen years later I was able to explain my action to my parents, who laughed when all was made clear! In later years, I tried to remember these incidents from my youth, when dealing with episodes of apparent delinquency involving my own children. There are usually quite reasonable explanations, but children cannot find the correct words.

I had arrived in Africa with a headful of bubbly golden curls. Within a few days, dad took me to have a haircut. I sat on a canvas chair under a mango tree, while an Indian barber razor-cut my hair, very short like a boy's; like the Michael that I wasn't. My curls fell to the ground all around the chair. This was how I was to wear my hair for the next seventeen years.

Nineteen-forty-something and the Groundnut Scheme, where the population of our little "township" in the bush was gradually increasing, meaning more and more children for me to play with. A school established; the teaching must have been good because I was reading fluently before I turned five.

Memories from those days! I recall causing problems for my mother when, for some inexplicable reason, she told me "Father *Christmas"* is really "daddy". I must have been far too young to learn this earth-shattering news, because it definitely changed my outlook on life. I was terribly disillusioned and immediately relayed the information to the first friends I saw at school, who skipped school to run home and find out if it was true. Poor mother was really in trouble with other parents.

In our family, the loo was always referred to as "the potty"; words such as "lavatory" and "toilet" were not uttered in our house. Our private parts were referred to as our "bottoms"; and we went to the "potty" to do our "business". Thus "bottom" and "business" were the rudest words in my vocabulary for years.

My best friend, Anne, and I used to play our own special version of "Doctors", until it went wrong. The patient lay with knees bent up to chest, while the doctor measured her temperature with a paintbrush – just the little brush in its metal holder, minus stick, balancing on the edge of her most private part. I was doctor at the time.

I said "Right my dear, it should be ready now". I went to remove the paintbrush only to discover that, horror of horrors, it had disappeared! In a panic, we searched the bed.

"It's gone up into my stomach and I'll die!" My patient let out a scream and tore out of the house, bawling all the way down the dirt track.

Mother came dashing through "What's wrong with Anne?" she asked, alarmed.

"She's got a headache" I said.

"Nonsense!" my mother was bustling out of the door in a vain attempt to catch up with my fleeing patient. I grabbed hold of my mother.

"She's got a paintbrush in her bottom", I explained.

Ann's mother took her to the real doctor, who said the paintbrush had obviously fallen out, and there was nothing to worry about. We never played that game again.

Uncle Bert, one of my favourite uncles, left UK and joined us in Tanganyika. He was a happy, carefree person, and such fun. Generally, I loved him very much. However I didn't love him on the day he looked at me quizzically and announced that my right ear stuck out further than my left. He motioned to my dad to come and have a look. They made me stand on a step turning this way and that, while studying me closely from all angles. They agreed that indeed it was so. I was six at the time, and a freak! For the next fifteen years, until I grew my hair which hid my deformity, I slept on my right side with my ear flat but, when sleeping on my left side, I folded my ear over. I consequently suffered a constant pain in the gristly part of my left ear. But now my hair remains longer, which hides this particular disfigurement.

Both parents were very heavy smokers. They never went to the loo without a cigarette. We grew up using long-drop toilets, "choos" in Swahili (pronounced "Ch-oh"), which didn't smell too good at the best of times. I could never differentiate between the smell of *choos* and the smell of cigarettes. To this day, cigarettes smell like long-drop toilets to me!

One day, a further twelve years down the line, mum decided to give up smoking. Therefore dad, deciding it was unfair to continue smoking while mother was quitting the habit, quietly put his fags aside and never touched another for the remaining thirty-three years of his life. Mum, meanwhile, lit up again the next day. Smoking was a major factor in her early death.

My very best memory of our Tanganyika days, was the birth of my little sister, Linda. Dad had named her "Ian" until she was born. Dad and I visited mother in the local *"hospital"*, and there was my little sister, sleeping innocently in a basket beside mum's bed. Incredulous, I asked my mother where she had found the baby, and was told she had come from a toy-shop. I couldn't understand it at all. We had very few shops in Urambo in any case, more like little kiosks selling matches, long bars of yellow washing-soap and straw baskets; even carvings of wananchi (local people) forming human chains to tug an unfortunate victim from the jaws of a crocodile. But I had never seen any babies for sale.

My sister and I, with our unusual upbringing in the bush, were in many ways close to nature. However, we led a very sheltered existence under the strict guidance of our Scottish father and subservient mother. In later years at Primary School I discovered that I was terribly naive as far as the *"ways of the world"* were concerned. A school friend used to bath with her dad and her description of his willy enthralled me; nothing like that ever happened in our home. Apart from occasional glimpses when a boy baby's nappy was being changed, the first time I really saw such a strange appendage on an adult male I could not fathom out how on earth he managed to hide it inside his trousers!

7. BUSH LIFE IN TANGANYIKA

There were very few dogs in Urambo, though we were given a cheeky young wire-haired terrier that we named "Patch". Patch died of tsetse-fly fever. I still shudder at the memory of him sitting on the verandah with my mother stroking and soothing him, while he held his little head up and howled and howled. Mum took him daily to our resident vet and he was well on the way to recovery when it was time for dad's "home leave". Patch was left in the care of a friend who did not keep up with his medication, which is why he died.

We had a number of free-range chickens running around the garden. I used to watch in disgusted horror when the cook chopped off a chicken's head, leaving the headless body to run around the yard spraying blood everywhere. What a different upbringing from that of a friend brought up in the centre of Glasgow, who was surprised to discover, upon seeing chickens running around free, that they only had two legs!

When clothes were washed, they were laid out on the grass to dry. The grass was full of mango flies which left their eggs in the clothes that were conveniently strewn around. The eggs somehow found their way under my skin, particularly around my tummy, where they grew into "mango worms", huge boil-like eruptions which itched like crazy. I now know that, when the worms are ready, all you need to do is to press the inflamed skin around the bump and the worms will pop straight out. My parents knew nothing of this. I have horrible memories of my father sitting on my legs, holding my arms down forcibly, while mum dug and squeezed and squeezed and squeezed while I was screaming in agony, until bits of unripe worm were forced out of my poor little tummy, leaving awful sores.

Then there were "Jiggers". Jiggers are tiny little flea-like insects which burrow their way into a person's skin mainly around and underneath toenails. Like mango worms, they itch uncontrollably. The first sign of the little beast is a tiny black dot which eats away happily, growing larger by the day. The secret is to wait until the Jigger looks like a pea-sized pus-ball under a toe-nail, then gradually poke around the sac with a needle until it is freed *intact*. This leaves a large hole which must be kept clean to avoid risk of infection. People who are ignorant about Jiggers, will most likely attempt to dig them out without due care, bursting the cyst which then re-seals and continues to grow.....and to itch, aaarh! As we used to go around barefoot most of the time (I still do) Jiggers were quite common. They don't jump very high, therefore toe-nails are the easiest prey. If you sleep on the ground for some time in a Jigger-infested area, they can penetrate your finger-nails and other delicious hideaways.

We came into frequent contact with wild animals. There were numerous snakes in the garden. One of the boys at school had a beautiful pet monkey. When it died, the boy's father cut off one of its hands, which he somehow manipulated by pulling tendons, making the fingers grip your arm. I put on a brave act but, actually, it was quite gross.

There was a troupe of baboons plaguing the labourers, until some bright spark came up with the idea of trapping one and painting him brilliant blue. The poor creature's gang-members ran away from him like crazy, occasionally slowing down to look back, only to put on an extra spurt of speed when they spotted the blue monster gaining on them. The last sight of any baboons for a long time, was of this big blue bewildered fellow taking off after his troupe, as they fled from him in terror over the horizon.

Apart from Patch, my pets were mainly dikdiks whose mothers had disappeared while the large machinery was clearing the bush. I was told their mothers had disappeared. I well recall collecting my first dikdik. Dad had asked me to meet him at the bar in the mess tent, where a lot of noisy men were guzzling beer. A bearded man with a huge belly and kindly red, smiling face, was seated at the bar with a dear little animal on his lap. My heart leapt; I ran over and hugged it. The man handed me a baby's bottle of milk and told me to feed the baby dikdik, which I did.

Then he said, "Take her. She's yours!"

"MINE?" I was overjoyed. I took my beautiful little pet home, and took good care of her. Gradually she began wandering into the bush, eventually staying away for nights at a time. She was the first of many such orphan pets that I nursed. They frequently came back to visit, standing cautiously on the boundary of our little garden. I believed they were bringing their babies for approval.

My pets were mainly dikdiks

The many workers who were earning money for the first time in their lives, had very little to spend their wages on. Therefore, when the first consignment of bicycles was railed in, hundreds of labourers were suddenly proud owners of transport. They learned to ride very quickly, but could not get the hang of braking and balancing feet on the ground without toppling off. Mother was learning to drive a car at that time, and she wasn't very good at braking either. Early evening after dad came home, was the time for mum's driving lesson. I would sit in the back of the Willy's Jeep while mum drove slowly up a track lined on both sides by bicycles; as the car approached, so each cyclist fell off his bicycle onto the road, laughing his head off, while dad reached over from the passenger seat to grip the steering wheel and negotiate a zigzag course down the track.

Of course it didn't take long before the workers discovered the delights of cigarette smoking, and "Centi Kumi" ("Ten Cent") cigarettes did a roaring trade in our little settlement, as did "Players Clipper" cigarettes, amongst the elite. Very soon, cheap petrol cigarette lighters were arriving in the local dukas. One of the first lucky owners of one of these modern gadgets went to fill his smart new lighter at the one and only petrol pump. He adjusted it to maximum flame, proudly flicking the wheel to display his new acquisition to the gathering crowd of onlookers, and the whole garage went up in flames with a great BOOM. I overheard dad recounting the incident to mum, describing it as absolutely horrific.

The rains always appeared to be overdue and very heavy when they arrived, immediately forming deep puddles where my friend Anne and I loved to "swim", until we were discovered up to our waists in thick mud, by dad driving home from work! When the rains abruptly ceased and the puddles dried up, the puddle-beds were full of little one-eyed fish, with which my ayah would make a delicious stew. I wonder how those funny little fish arrived in the puddles.

Mother was a marvellous ballroom dancer. She could dance the tango, the samba, the rumba and the quickstep. She and dad were experts at the old-fashioned waltz. Many a time I was left in the care of my ayah while dad, looking absolutely devastating in his dinner suit and bow tie, would escort mother out to the sparklingly clean Jeep. He would help mother into the Jeep, conscientiously arranging her long brocade skirt around her legs on the newly-scrubbed floorboards, before setting off for a dinner-dance at the Club-house. They would leave behind a cloud of dust and a waft of mum's perfume that came from one of her little spiral-shaped Goya bottles. This aroma was much headier than the smell of Yardley's English Lavender Water that mum liberally splashed all over her body before attending less important functions. Mother told me she never sat down at these dances, because women were few and far between and therefore much in demand at such events. She was very happy and laughed a lot in those days. She and dad were forever singing songs together, songs that were popular at the time: one I particularly remember is "East is East and the West is West, and the wrong one I have chose..."

Mum, Dad & I with the Willy's Jeep that mum learned to drive in

Linda & I on the
"Rhodesia Castle"

8. CRUISING TO BRITAIN & BACK TO TANGANYIKA

In 1952, when dad's contract came to an end, it was decided Mum, Linda and I should go back to UK while Dad stayed on in Africa to look for work. After a few days spent travelling on dusty roads, we took off from Kenya's Lake Naivasha in the Rift Valley, on what I believe was the last flight of the Sunderland flying-boat on this particular route. It was wonderful. As we sped along the Lake, I looked out of the window at all the little pixies in shuttlecocks grinning at me through the spray, while they bobbed up and down on the water. I saw them so clearly and accepted them for what they were. It was only when I had outgrown those wonderful fairy-tale childhood years, that I began questioning what the pixies might really have been; a line of buoys perhaps, marking our take-off path...how unromantic! The men and most of the women were standing around the aeroplane's bar when the pilot's voice once came over the speakers "Please will some of you return to your seats, the aircraft is starting to fly lop-sided!" I believe we landed on Lake Victoria at Entebbe and on the Nile at Khartoum, then the River Thames.

I enjoyed our few months on the "Isle of Uck" as UK was referred to, meeting all our cousins, second-cousins and cousins once or twice removed, and their cousins. We accompanied our relatives to windy, pebbled beaches, where they were crazy enough to dip their porcelain-like bodies into the icy waters. We travelled on the top of double-decker buses. One bus had a black conductor; happy to see a familiar sight in this unfamiliar land, I smiled at him and said "Jambo!" Probably Jamaican or West Indian, he glowered down at me. My mother nudged me and hissed at me not to be rude. I couldn't understand what I had done wrong.

Mum, Linda and I stayed with various relatives north and south of the border. Grandad in Scotland was a gentle soul, always telling jokes and teasing us as we sat where his lap should have been. Originally he had legs but they were injured in the War and gangrene gradually crept up and up until he had just stumps and then no legs left at all.

Then came the day when dad wrote to inform mum that he had been employed as a travelling salesman for an International Harvester Company, a job that would take him to various Central and East African countries.

We sailed back to East Africa on the "Rhodesia Castle", a six-week cruise that took us from Southampton via the Cape of Good Hope, to Dar-es-Salaam. Linda, a toddler, used to disappear frequently, more often than not to be found on the Captain's Bridge. The portholes in the cabins had two bars on them. I remember getting my head stuck between the bars. Mum had to apply much Vaseline in order to manoeuvre my head out of the bars, which left me with burning ears. At least she didn't have to call for a maintenance man with a metal saw!

I clearly recall mum's excitement when she spotted dad running along the quay in long strides, as the ship steered into Dar-es-Salaam harbour.

Riding on a rickshaw in DaresSalaam

Morogoro

We eventually moved into a dear little stone house on a hillside in a range of blue-green mountains

For a few days, we ran on the beaches, swam in the warm sea and rode in rickshaws: smart two-wheeled, canopied barrows, pulled by energetic, laughing young men. All too soon, we left the coast, to spend long, hot dusty days travelling on bumpy roads. All the roads were

heavily corrugated, bump-bump-bump-bump-bump; of course I knew nothing about corrugations and never asked about them, quite certain in my young mind that they were logs lying side-by-side across the road, covered with earth...what a tedious way of building roads!

En route to our new home-town, Morogoro, we stayed overnight in a colonial "dak-bungalow" next to a country railway stop. Upon arrival in Morogoro, we stayed for a few weeks in a wonderful wooden hotel managed by a European lady, slap in the middle of the tiny town; the hotel had a long verandah where we would sit looking straight onto the dirty, dusty, main street. We eventually moved into a dear little stone house, which was built on a hillside amongst natural springs in a range of blue-green mountains.

For the best part of a year we lived in this house, right next to a deep gully. Although there was no electricity, we did have running bath-water, heated in an oil-drum outside, and a *flush toilet!* During this time, I never had a single child to play with. I used to keep an eye on Linda, the seven-year gap in our ages seeming immense. Somehow, we managed to acquire a Cocker Spaniel called Bessy, from a South African couple residing in a ranch they had cultivated in the middle of nowhere.

Bessy and I spent hours exploring the dry gully and the nearby disused mica mine. When the rains came, we could hear the water starting in the far distance, roaring down the mountainside; it came down the gully like a solid wall, sweeping all before it: trees, animals, plus the occasional herder and sleeping drunkard caught unawares. In the evenings, we would sit with mum, watching hundreds of "fire-flies" dive-bombing the windows. Dad seemed to be away most of the time; it was very exciting when he came home. I would accompany him in his pick-up truck on day-trips to the surrounding Greek-owned sisal plantations, where we were more often than not, served a lunch of red beans and mashed potato. These friendly people, who were making fortunes from growing sisal, always gave us a warm welcome.

Dad's favourite trips were to Southern Rhodesia. When he described this wonderful country, it sounded like Utopia, "centuries ahead of the rest of Africa"! I am glad he is not around to see how this once-ultra-civilised country has been totally destroyed.

9. MOVE TO KENYA 1952

My father's job with the same Company eventually took us to Kenya, where we lived on a housing estate (ugh!) in a suburb of Nairobi, called "Woodley". I attended Nairobi Primary School, together with hundreds of other children. For the first time in Africa, we lived in a house with an occasionally-functioning telephone, sometimes-working electricity, and automatically heated bath-water. We were not happy. My parents couldn't bear living in such relative civilisation, dad was not enjoying his job, and I felt completely out-of-place in the huge school. I had trouble relating to the children of the neighbours: they would hold lighted matches to the bloated abdomens of spiders, causing them to burst. They would shoot Colie-Colies (Mousebirds) with airguns. I thought they were monsters and they considered me a wimp. Across the road from our house there was a vlei (Afrikaans?) where Bessy and I would spend our evenings and weekends exploring the land of witches and fairies. I can only describe a vlei as a field that is dry in the dry season and wet in the rainy season!

Uncle Bert followed us to Kenya and moved into our guestroom. My uncle socialised a lot. My parents often accompanied him to football games, which he and dad sometimes took part in. I would stay at home with Bessy, in charge of Linda. In the early evening, trailed by Bessy, I would take Linda down the road to the local "duka" (shop) to buy sweets. Can you imagine walking down the road in Nairobi these days – even during daytime – Heaven forbid! With dad out of the way, I would sometimes buy chewing-gum, which was forbidden in our house. I lived in fear of my intestines being glued together with gum, so many times did I have to swallow a lump of chewing-gum or bubble-gum, upon my father's sudden unexpected appearance. Linda once hid a piece of gum behind her ear; it took mum ages to cut it out of her hair.

One evening our parents and Uncle Bert arrived home from a football match, very excited about a discussion with an Englishman who was looking for somebody to manage his two plantations, one a coffee farm beyond Thika (as in "Flame Trees of" – though the farm Elspeth wrote about had jacarandas rather than flame trees, which wouldn't have sounded nearly so romantic) and the other a wheat farm many miles in the opposite direction, on the 'Kinangop' half-way up the escarpment of the Rift Valley in the midst of what had been the "Happy Valley", so-named because the 'Black Sheep' of the British aristocracy, who had been exported to Kenya in the 1920's, 30's and 40's, would gather in this area, living decadent lifestyles.

The following weekend, we dressed up in our Sunday Best and set off for the coffee plantation which was near a small mountain called "Donyo Sabuk" (which is Masaai for "Hill of the Buffalo"), some thirty miles outside Nairobi. How exciting, back to the bush again! Unobstructed views of so many hills and mountains. It was a wonderful journey along a dirt road that wound up and down hills, with many bridges crossing fast-flowing rivers of red water; beautiful forested areas and *hardly any people* – Heaven!

The house was pretty as a picture, double-storied with white walls & a green corrugated iron roof

♥ Kiboko ♥

With Dad & Linda in front of the house

Kiboko (Hippo) Farm as it was named, was perfect. One boundary was a loop in the Athi River which was teaming with crocodiles and hippo. The house was as pretty as a picture, double-storied with white walls and a green corrugated iron roof, set in a colourful garden with sweeping lawns and wonderful climbing trees. We moved out there almost immediately, while Uncle Bert took the job of managing the other farm, many miles away on the Kinangop.

Linda and I have nothing but fond memories of those days. Our nearest neighbours, the Izats, lived on a farm about ten miles away. Their daughter Bonnie became my close friend. Mother, with many "shamba-boys" (gardeners) at her disposal, established a flourishing vegetable garden and fruit orchard; she also bred chickens. The team of shamba-boys tended the flower-beds, looked after the fruit trees and vegetable plots, and spent hours cutting the lawns with ingeniously designed grass-slashers. With our home-grown veggies, fruit and chickens, and the guinea fowl, spurfowl and gazelle that dad shot, as well as the tilapia and trout that he caught, we were almost entirely self-sufficient. We lived very happily in these idyllic surroundings for some years. Under dad's stern supervision, I learned to drive the farm pick-up and was able to drive adequately by the age of nine, which was fairly normal for many kids brought up on farms in Kenya in that era.

I have few recollections of my mother cooking or, as dad put it "slaving over a hot stove the way my 'mither' did"! We always had somebody to cook our meals, clean the house, make the beds, polish our shoes, and do the laundry – which was in a steel tub in the back yard. Ironing was carried out perfectly with a wonderful heavy iron filled with hot charcoal. Food was cooked on a large iron stove heated by firewood. Saucepans were scoured clean by the cook, who took them to a sandpit, where he scrubbed them with sand under a garden tap until they were sparkling and shiny. Our house was always filled with the tantalising aroma of roasting coffee beans, emanating from the wood-fuelled kitchen stove.

Occasionally the water pumped out of the borehole contained curious algae which came out in foul-smelling clumps. Mum would wrap one of dad's socks around the tap, which would filter out the gunk but not the smell. Water was heated in a large oil drum on top of an open wood fire. Linda and I would collect maize on cobs, fresh from the garden, and cook them to a rich brown amongst the embers of the fire. Delicious!

Our telephone consisted of a huge box with a receiver on top and a handle on the side. We were on a "party-line" and each homestead had a different call sign: ours was one long followed by two short rings. In cases of emergency we would turn the handle in continual short bursts and everybody on the line would lift their receivers. One nosey neighbour would pick up her receiver whenever the phone rang, to listen in to everybody's conversations; we could hear her dogs barking in the background and sometimes she would give an involuntary cough or sneeze! To call further afield, we would give one l-o-n-g ring for the operator in the local post office who, if she/he happened to be awake, would answer and connect us via some kind of magic to the receiving party. Modern technology, amazing stuff!

A neat little guesthouse was situated amongst guava trees, beside the badminton court, in a corner of the garden. Here the gentlemanly owner would stay when paying one of his infrequent visits, occasionally accompanied by his beautiful upper-class wife and plain, snotty daughter.

Although a mile from the Athi River, we frequently spotted hippo prints in the garden in the mornings. I remember a herder rushing into the compound, screaming to dad that a crocodile had got hold of a calf that was on the river bank, drinking. Dad grabbed his gun and jumped into the car, but arrived too late. The croc was mid-river with calf's snout firmly between its jaws. He shot the croc, but the poor calf was very dead. Dad was quite obviously upset as evidenced when I heard him describing to mum, signs on the riverbank of the struggle the brave little calf had put up against the prehistoric creature. Crocodiles thrill me, as is the case with all wildlife, but I do not rate them high up on my list of favourites, purely because of the manner in which they kill – causing such unthinkable pain and suffering. Crocs are not far behind Wild "Cape Hunting Dogs" in this field.

Dad was occasionally called out to shoot a rogue buffalo. One such time was when a lone buffalo (always to be treated with suspicion) charged after three of our farm workers who were cycling across a vlei near the house. With the beast easily gaining on them, they leapt off their bicycles next to an acacia tree; they began climbing the tree, the long thorns piercing deep into their limbs. Ignoring the pain, two of the terrified men managed to climb high enough to be beyond the reach of the buffalo's horns, while the third was hooked out of the tree and tossed to the ground. The two were still sitting in the tree when dad went to rescue them three hours later, while the beast continued to stamp their unlucky friend into the ground.

Dad's workers were well housed and their wives were given food rations to be sure the family ate, even if the men spent most of their money on illegal intoxicating brews; the same applied to employees of any of our friends in the farming community. On the farms, schooling and medical treatment was free for the workers. The women sang as they picked coffee berries and lined up to collect their pay as they emptied their baskets into the coffee berry trough. Dad would always come home tired and happy, with stories to relate, such as that of a pregnant woman disappearing behind a coffee tree and reappearing with a baby tied around her waist, feeding at the breast, while the mother carried on happily singing and picking coffee.

On Christmas Day, the farm labourers would ask if they could perform their tribal dances for us on the lawn. Nowadays we become weary of the commercialised "tribal dancing" performed in tourist traps. The performances we were privileged to witness were the real thing. These friendly, fun-loving people genuinely wanted to entertain us and show-off their true customs. We were enthralled.

three hours later, the beast continued to stamp their unlucky friend into the ground

Christmas Day tribal dances on the lawn

We had a marvellous Pishi (Swahili – "Cook"). Every weekend our house was full of bachelors, many of whom are sadly no longer with us, such as: Peter Davey, Joe Cheffings, John Malcolm-Smith, Finn Aagaard, Alan

Tainton... and adventurous couples who were carving out a new life for themselves, often in rigorous conditions, on surrounding farms. Alan Delap, a huge outstandingly handsome man who hailed from South America, would frequently join us together with his petite French wife Janine and their three children. It was said that Alan "brought the Bougainvillea to Kenya"; when we met him he had developed a bright orange bloom which was named "Sylvia" after his daughter and he was in the process of developing a double-white which would be named "Alan Delap".

Partly to the long distances involved, partly due to the security situation when different factions of the Kikuyu tribe started killing each other in what was to become known as the "Mau Mau" movement, and also because they enjoyed the unaccustomed relaxing and downing of alcohol, many would stay over on Saturday night. The sound of laughter and the music of the Gay Gordons as our guests drank, chatted and danced to 78 LP records spinning on the wind-up gramophone, would continue into the early hours, as they anticipated gorging themselves on our pishi's famous Sunday Curry Lunch.

After lunch, our guests would loll around in the garden to the strains of Gigli and Tauber, awaiting their turn on the badminton court. One such lazy Sunday, Linda disappeared after being told off for crossing the badminton court whilst a game was in progress. We looked for her for over an hour, guests and staff searching through the vegetable garden, fruit orchard and amongst the coffee trees. It was always a worry that she might wander into the coffee and become hopelessly lost.

As I dashed through the lounge, I was astonished to discover that Linda had mysteriously reappeared and was sitting comfortably on a sofa!

48

"Where have you been?" I shrieked. "We thought you were lost. Everybody's been looking for you in the coffee!"

Looking disdainfully down her little button nose and glancing at the ever-bubbling coffee-percolator, she asked "Was it hot?"

Coffee
Picking

Coffee
Processing

10. PRIMARY SCHOOL

Bonnie and I attended "Nyeri European Primary School", which offered boarding facilities to children from farming communities, outlying administrative posts and Missionary stations. I liked the school, but I loved my home. During the school holidays, a great deal of my time was taken up with drawing and painting pictures, using the new easel that dad had made for me at the farm workshop. With their wonderful smooth bark and sturdy forked branches, guava trees were perfect for climbing. When the fruits were ripe and juicy, Linda and I would spend hours perched in a guava tree eating the delicious fruit until we reached bursting point. The following day was spent rushing to the loo.

At the beginning of term, I would meet with other pupils at the country railway station to take the steam train back to school. Of course, I was homesick at boarding school. But as none of my fellow-students were City-dwellers, all hailing from outlying areas, we understood each other. There was little inter-action between boys and girls, and the boys referred to us by our surnames, even Tor who, in the holidays, had become my greatest buddy. We were made to sit "boy-girl-boy-girl" in the dining-room. Occasionally, I was delighted to find myself seated next to Tor, and we could whisper happily about home.

For some obscure reason, "writing lines" was a favourite punishment meted out by teachers; such a waste of time and of no benefit to the students whatsoever. I once rushed back to the dorm having forgotten something I had to take to class. Unfortunately, Fatty Donaldson appeared at the door. I ducked under the bed, but too late. "Brown!" she bellowed, "You will write one-hundred lines, 'I shall not, on any occasion, go with boots on, into the dormitory!'" I ingenuously taped two pens together, enabling me to write two lines at a time. Fatty obviously didn't check what I had written!

It was compulsory to kneel by our beds to pray, every night. Each night I ended my prayers in the same way, "Please God, look after Mummy, Daddy, Linda and all our pets - which I would name, one by one - and please, God, stop people being cruel to animals. Amen".

At the age of eleven, I was envied for having an assignment behind the boiler-house, one night after dinner, with a thirteen-year-old boy called Alan. I stretched up to peck his cheek, then turned and fled back to the girls' dorm, quite breathless and proud of myself, while the girls gathered around to ask for the details. The next time, Alan grabbed me before I could run away, and kissed me on my lips. Wow, this time I really did have something to report! I often saw Alan after leaving school; he was always chatty and friendly. He became a successful businessman. A few decades after our behind-the-boiler-house meetings, I was horrified to learn that Alan committed suicide. Many years later, having suffered from severe depression myself, I do understand, but I was never told the reasons for what Alan did. He shot himself. Oh dear Lord, he shot himself. I attended his Memorial Service, which was incredibly sad. Poor Alan.

Why did he do it, God? Why did you allow it?

11. REARING ITS UGLY HEAD

School holidays were idyllic, spent painting pictures, or riding around the farms on bicycles with my special friend Tor. Tor and I found what must have been an old Voortrekkers' grave-yard; it was very well-hidden beneath thick bushes and undergrowth. I don't believe we ever told anybody about it, it was our secret. Although there were names and dates of birth, ranging from young babies up to elderly people, no reasons for the deaths were depicted on the grave-stones. We wondered whether the bodies had been carried until they reached a suitable burial spot, which would be doubtful before the days of refrigerated transport; it was more likely they were struck down by a sudden vicious illness and had halted their great trek until those who survived were able to carry on.

A nice Polish family, the Trzebinskis, moved onto a neighbouring farm. They were full of praise for the British, who had helped them during the war. Dad spent a lot of time with the father, Vasik, teaching him the ins-and-outs of growing coffee. Meanwhile the mother, Jane, became a close friend of our mother. There were two sons, Sbish and Atos. Sbish was a fantastic dancer: he and his girlfriend Errol would entertain us for hours dancing the *"Cha cha".* Atos often joined Tor and I on our cycling adventures.

I had my first discussion about *"sex"* with a member of the opposite sex when, addressing me by my surname the way we did at school, Atos asked me very seriously, "Brown, how do you do 'it', you know, how do you rape?"

I replied "I suppose one night you ask your wife if she wants children and, if she agrees, you go to bed and put your thingy into hers".

Atos said "It sounds awful. Apparently you girls have this wet, gurgling hole!" The way he described it, made us sound like sinks with dirty water swirling down plugholes. Looking at today's children, it is hard to believe how naive I was at sixteen....seventeen....and even at eighteen! We were never taught about reproduction at school. My mother certainly never discussed it with me. The only fact of life she imparted to me, which came as a tremendous shock, was that babies came, not from toyshops, but from their mummies' bottoms. Mum did not elaborate on this astounding piece of information, and I was far too embarrassed to question her.

12. OUR AUNT AND UNCLE

Being brought up in Colonial East Africa, we were used to either the unaccented "Queen's English" spoken by the settlers, or the rough, clipped "Jaapie" twang of the Afrikaners. Toned down with the gentler accent of the indigenous Kenyans, this strange combination made up what was, and still is, known as the "Kenya Accent". On *"home leave"* in UK, Uncle Bert had met and married Barbara, an attractive young lady from Norfolk. Auntie Barbara had the strangest accent! Thinking that any weird English accent was "Cockney", I referred to her as "my Cockney Aunt". I later learned that this was quite insulting because our Aunt in fact had, not only a Norfolk accent, but a *high class* Norfolk accent!

Auntie Barbara had us in stitches whenever she spotted a giraffe; she would shout out in her funny accent, "Oh look! A kangaroo! A kangaroo!" One year we purposely bought her a Birthday Card with a picture of a kangaroo on the front. "Oh you can't fool me anymore" she chuckled, "I know that's a giraffe!"

Auntie Barbara and Uncle Bert lived in a quaint wooden double-storied house on the Kinangop, surrounded by thousands of pansies. On the occasional weekend, we would make the long journey to visit them on the farm quite high up on the Rift Valley escarpment, where the mornings were chilly, and we would gather huge black mushrooms for breakfast. Parts of the route were "high risk" areas, with posters nailed to trees depicting a human ear and the words "Shh! Somebody may be listening!" These, of course were the days of the Mau Mau uprising.

Our Aunt and Uncle later moved to Makuyu, near Thika. I often stayed with them and they were frequently out partying at the local Sports Club. It was beautiful, a typical country club where, at the age of sixteen, I was to become tipsy for the first time. My Aunt introduced me to Sweet Martinis. After three of these, I tried to walk in a straight line to the ladies' loo. I looked up at the sound of laughter, only to realise I was being observed staggering in a decidedly criss-cross fashion across the bar-room. I giggled non-stop all the way home, and found I was unable to lie on the pillow without aeroplanes whizzing around my head. Apparently my Aunt sat up all night with a chamber pot on her lap!

Approximately forty years after this event, my son was driving me from Nanyuki to Nairobi. As we were passing through the area where my Aunt and Uncle used to live, I asked Andrew to turn into the drive of the Sports Club, the golf course of which is still used by local Kenyan farmers. I wandered through the building, which had paint peeling off the walls, pointing out to Andrew exactly where I had sat and drank the Martinis so long ago – a different life-time – a different country. I re-traced my steps along a crumbling cement floor, through a door hanging off its hinges, to the washrooms. There was a small broken mirror hanging squiff above a long bare counter, which took my mind back to the days when the counter was decorated with lacy material and laid out with pots of talcum powder, beneath a wall-to-wall mirror. Where there used to be dainty toilet seat covers, there were now no toilet seats at all, and the cisterns were broken. The place stank of overflowing sewers.

The dilapidated state of repair was to be expected in the Kenya of today and did not bother me as much as it should; what did, was when I came across a dusty old framed photograph of a tennis team dating back to the

1950's, on which I was able to recognise my late Uncle Bert.

13. MAU MAU

At the farm, we had the luxury of a noisy generator supplying electricity to the house and factory. Dad ingeniously connected the generator switch to the toilet window-lever by means of a long steel wire, meaning the "gennie" could be turned off at bed-time simply by pulling the lever. This was an important safety precaution because, in these days of the "M-M" or "Emergency" as the Mau Mau was referred to, one was careful not to venture outside at night, not knowing who might be lurking in the bushes with pangas (sharp, curved knives) and home-made guns.

In their normal fashion, my parents rarely discussed the "Emergency" in front of me. I simply accepted that the Mau Mau existed; it was an evil fact. I knew they were terrorists with Rasta-type dreadlocks who butchered mainly their own people. I knew the murderers originated from the Kikuyu tribe and it was supposedly a fight between two Kikuyu factions.

I loathed them for their senseless maiming and killing of defenceless animals. I heard they would send crude "signs" to Mzungus (white people) who employed workers from the conflicting camp. A school friend told me that a relative, I think it was his Grandmother, had been walking around the house early in the morning searching for her pet cat which, for some reason, had not slept on her bed that night. She came face-to-face with her beloved tabby hanging from a flower-covered archway in the garden, pink tongue poking out of her gentle mouth; strung up by a noose round her delicate little neck. I saw newspaper articles with photographs of cattle standing in fields with their legs hacked off at the joints; those innocent, docile beasts just standing there, *on four raw stumps*, helpless. Jesus, what indescribable horror!

At the beginning and end of the school term, we would travel by steam train, always accompanied by armed guards. Occasionally, as the train was chugging up a steep incline, bursts of blue smoke would suddenly appear next to the tracks, whereupon a number of guards would jump off the train and disappear into the bushes, guns at the ready. Apparently the engine driver would throw smoke-bombs out when there were signs of terrorist activity ahead. As the train continued on its way, we would be concerned about the guards left behind; I well remember wondering, in my young mind, how they would return from the bush, back to safety. At half-term we would travel to and from school on a bus, accompanied by two parents toting guns. I was always happy when dad was one of the guards on the bus. In wet weather, the bus would slither and slide in the mud. On "Pole-pole" ("slowly"- pronounced Poly-poly) Hill, we would alight and follow the bus on foot, supervised by our armed escorts, delightedly carrying our shoes and socks while our bare feet squelched deliciously in the thick red mud.

The School was well-guarded. There were occasions when Mau Mau terrorists were fighting in the vicinity of the school compound. As shots rang out in the middle of the night, we were ordered to lie under our beds. Lenore, in the next bed to me, would often be lying under the blankets on top of her bed reading a book by the light of a pen-torch held between her teeth, with her fingers in her ears, totally oblivious of what was going on around her. We would hiss at her to no avail until finally I would get up and poke her. Then she would lie under the bed, torch in mouth, fingers in ears, continuing to read her book!

My parents always carried guns, and slept with guns under their pillows. By this time we had plenty of pets at the coffee farm, including a dozen or so dogs of varying sizes and mixtures. Our dogs always slept inside the house. Whenever the dogs barked at night, I would see dad walking quietly towards the door, one hand shielding the gun held in his other hand. I made a habit of checking in cupboards and under my bed before climbing into it, every night. Bessy slept near my door. Nevertheless, any time I woke in the night, I would lie still, barely breathing, trying to discern what had woken me, then plucking up courage to check under the bed before putting a foot out; craning my neck to peer around the door before venturing to the loo. It was a strange existence, I suppose, but it was simply a way of life.

I frequently accompanied my father on trout-fishing expeditions into the Kikuyu "Reserves", where he always carried a gun and had to remain vigilant. But the potentially serious danger of the situation was not going to deter him from his trout-fishing! Dad always said the Kikuyu tribe were fortunate in having the most fertile parts of the country. Certainly the areas we passed through on fishing ventures were very lush and hilly, covered in colourful indigenous flowering trees and bushes. We drove over dangerously rickety make-shift bridges across fast-flowing rivers, often skidding on wet red-murram roads.

Just when the frightening period of the Mau Mau tribal-fighting was petering out, we had our only experience of an "ambush". Mother and I had been given a lift to Makuyu Sports Club, which was about twenty miles from home, to take part in a tennis tournament. My father brought Linda along to meet up with us, have a couple of drinks, then drive back home. It was dark when we left the clubhouse but it was full moon. Dad took a shortcut home via a back road. The road was very twisty and dusty, the red earth flying up around the windows; "buck" (gazelles) ran across the road a couple of times.

Suddenly a shape loomed up on the road ahead. As we approached, we saw it was a tree across the road. I immediately sensed danger and had a peculiar feeling in my stomach, as dad applied brakes and stopped the car. Everything was eerily still and silent, with red dust floating around in the beams of our headlights. Dad said "It looks as if the rain has knocked down a tree!" as he began to open the car door. Mum grabbed his arm, "No Andy, it's been cut!" She leaned over and switched off the car lights as a gunshot rang out. Dad began reversing the car at great speed down the track, made possible thanks to the full moon! We heard further explosions, and saw outlines of running figures, but nobody caught up with us.

The gunshot woke Linda, who had been fast asleep across my lap. "What was that" she asked, frightened.

"We hit a buck", mum lied.

"Oh no! Is it all right?" asked Linda.

"Yes, it's fine" mum told her. Linda lay down again.

Then dad drove home the long way round, by the main road.

When there was terrorist activity on a neighbouring farm, everybody would be alerted by a series of short rings on the telephone. Mum or dad would lift the receiver and arrangements were quickly made as to where the women and children would be dropped off, while the men sped off to whichever farm was being invaded by intruders who had taken the barbaric "Mau Mau Oath".

Throughout the "Emergency", we never had a problem with security at our home though, oddly, mother often noticed vegetables and chickens went missing.

When mum went out on her rounds in the trusty Ford Prefect, delivering home-made pickles and jams to neighbouring farms, Linda was sometimes left in the care of our trusty pishi, Kibui. It later transpired that dear old Kibui was a Mau Mau "Oath Administrator"! When the house was empty, he would hold meetings and cook up meals for the terrorists, who would appear from nowhere to sit around our kitchen. My parents, in retrospect, agreed that it had been worth losing a few cabbages and chickens for the sake of our safety!

Although thirty-two "Settlers" were killed during the eight years of the Mau Mau uprising, it was mainly Kikuyus that were horrendously butchered, and by the *thousands*. All we who lived through this scary time are bewildered that this period of horrific killings of Kikuyus by other Kikuyus became referred to as the "Struggle for Independence". Contrary to normal African customs, they brutally assaulted their own elderly folk, women and children, in indescribably gruesome ways, because they happened to be from the "opposing side". "Fight for Freedom"? Huh?

14. COAST HOLIDAYS

In spite of having to find sh 1,000 per term for my school fees, my folks were able to save up to buy a brand new Volkswagen Beetle. We loved this little car, which we named "Thumbelina". In August, we took off in Thumbelina at 4 o'clock in the morning, for our first holiday on the Kenya coast. We dropped our pisho off at the railway station where he took the overnight steam train to Mombasa. We thoroughly enjoyed the dusty road journey, in spite of breathing in noxious choo-smelling fumes as our parents chain-smoked for the duration of the journey. For some unfathomable reason, Linda and I always squeezed into the tiny luggage compartment behind the back seat. Here we sat facing each other while I taught my little sister silly songs and poems:-

"Tra-la-la, three monkeys up a tree.

One fell down and broke his

Dicky was a bulldog, lying in the grass.

Along came a bumblebee which stung him on his

Ars-k no questions, tell no lies,

I saw a Policeman doing up his

Flies are a nuisance, bees are worse.

And that is the end of my little verse".......

Our journey by road took eight hours, not including a stop at Pop Pearson's house for his popular, Full English Breakfast; not including one stop to watch a rhino at the side of the road and another to allow a herd of elephants to cross in front of us. Not including, either, a two-hour stop while we waited, in a queue of vehicles, for a flash-flood to recede. Water was rushing at great speed along one of the thirty-seven "drifts" which the road crossed. Instead of wasting time whilst waiting for the water to subside, dad joined a group of stranded white Kenyan holidaymakers who took off into the bush to shoot guinea-fowl for the pot. When the torrent abated sufficiently for cars to cross, rescue had to be made of a bus blocking the drift at an angle, with water pouring straight in through the windows on one side and out through the other. All passengers were safe.

On a trip to Mombasa, Alan Judge, a farming friend from Makuyu, came hurtling around a bend in his VW Beetle, slamming on brakes as he pulled up behind a large elephant standing in the middle of the road. In slow motion, the elephant sat down on the bonnet, crushing it flat as a pancake!

Mombasa itself was a hot, clean, whitewashed city, teaming with friendly, smiling people. Driving across the island of Mombasa was like taking part in an obstacle race; nobody was in a hurry. Cyclists zig-zagged across the road in front of vehicles, calling out greetings to one another and wobbling precariously as they turned to wave to friends, smiling apologetically at vehicle drivers. There were dozens of happy people wearing little white hats and long white gowns: selling carvings, fruit, coconuts, and all sorts of interesting dishes giving off aromas of cloves, cinnamon and other warm spices. Our upcountry pishi tut-tutted loudly and covered his eyes in shame, at the sight of topless Giriama ladies!

We rented a large cottage on a brilliant white, palm-fringed beach, exactly one hundred and ten feet from the high tide mark; by Law, this was the closest to the ocean *that* one was permitted to build. The very basic cottage was constructed of mud and wattle. The base of the outside walls measured up to four feet wide, to give support to the roof, which was thatched with "makuti", (coconut palm fronds). There was nothing in the roughly-made window frames to give protection against the elements, only thin strips of wood in criss-cross patterns. There was an outside flush toilet, and a shower with cold running sea-water. In the mornings we would discover that large mushroom-like fungi had grown out of the walls overnight! In typical Colonial-style, the kitchen was a separate building outside the back door, with an old wood-stove, a kerosene refrigerator and a wire-netting food safe.

We loved this little car, which we named "Thumbelina"

Linda & I on ♥ Tiwi Beach ♥

The Mau Mau fighting seemed another world away. We felt very secure. We never locked a door...didn't even bother to close the doors of the house at night. For two heavenly weeks, we swam in the sea and walked on the beach. We lived on fresh fish, prawns, crabs, mangoes, pawpaws, huge mangrove mushrooms, coconuts, and the occasional crayfish.

The coastal tribes were wonderfully friendly people, totally laid-back. They would work until they had earned sufficient to meet their immediate expenses, then simply didn't show up again until they needed more money. They had their fresh fish, cassavas and coconuts; what more did they need? It was often said that a Coast Man would sit for days sleeping against a palm tree, waiting for a coconut to fall down! The main religion on the coast was Islam. In those halcyon days I just knew Muslims to be gentle, kind, easy-going people.

In later years, the situation on the coastal strip changed so very much. Our doors were no longer left open at night and windows were burglar-proofed with ugly iron bars. The friendly coastal people were incited to violence, with frequent eruptions of so-called "ethnic-cleansing", where a small proportion of coastal people terrorised the workers from upcountry, forcing them back to their home areas. This was all reportedly politically instigated by Mr Moi's followers, sending those from upcountry areas back home to cast their votes, which he badly needed.

15. RELIGION AND ALL THAT

I often told myself I should learn more about the Koran. For instance, due to various out-of-world experiences not written here, I do understand why Muslims revere cats because I know cats have special insight; having said that, however, if they are so revered, I do not understand why a badly torn and suffering cat will be left to die in agony in a gutter. And why hate dogs? Dogs also have perception beyond human understanding.

There was a businessman whom I came to know well whilst living on Tiwi Beach, and whom I respected greatly. One "Holy Day", as arranged, Ali brought his family to spend the day on *"our"* beach. When Ali wore his Western-type clothes, our little Spaniel knew him well and Ali would make a great fuss of him. On this particular day however, Jimmy barked tentatively upon seeing an apparent stranger step out of his car wearing a little hat and long flowing robes. Almost embarrassed upon catching Ali's familiar scent, Jimmy ceased barking; until, that is, Ali confounded us by leaping around like a person possessed, pumping his legs frantically up and down beneath his robes. This action, of course, really set Jimmy off. Barking delightedly at this great new game, he ran after my friend all the way back to his vehicle.

Ali was waving his arms around and yelling to his children to stay in the car. There they sat hunched up, windows wound up tight, little frightened eyes popping out in sheer terror. I was thoroughly bewildered. I laughingly called out "Ali, for Goodness' sake what's the matter? You know Jimmy well, he wouldn't hurt a fly!" From the safety of his car, my friend tried to garble something about dogs' saliva being unsavoury – I cannot recall the details. To this day, I remember how upset I was when Ali drove swiftly away with his family, not spending the day on our beach after all our arrangements. I did not even get to meet his wife and children.

But there is much I cannot comprehend about the way the Christian religion is conducted in Kenya, either. Many wananchi pay up to ten per cent of their wages to their chosen Church; if they fail to pay, a Church Collector calls on them: fearing everlasting hell and damnation, they pay up. Apart from our Politicians whose corruption is global knowledge, the main people making vast amounts of money in this country today are Church Preachers: as evidenced by the humungous Churches going up everywhere - they are on a par with our extraordinarily corrupt Police Officials.

I fully understand our poor suffering world is in a continual conflict of Good against Evil. God against Satan. Mungu against Shaitani. Healers against Magangas (witch-doctors). I also accept that Good usually prevails, but all too often Bad is getting in the way, trying to balance things out in its favour. Good then fights back. It is a never-ending battle, inflicting horrendous killings and hostilities.....if *only* it didn't have to be done so savagely.

Dear God, why does it have to be carried out so savagely?

16. OUR STRICT FATHER

Looking back on our childhood days, I realise we were quite fortunate to have the parents we had. Although I was never as close to my mum as I would have wished, I was very close to dad; in Linda's case it was the reverse! Our upbringing was fairly normal for kids brought up in isolated places in the 1950's and 1960's. Sometimes dad had strange ways of showing how much he loved us; but I know he did.

Never once did I hear my parents argue. They never even disagreed about anything in our presence. Our father ran the household with a rod of iron; my sister and I simply did as instructed and I guess mum did the same. Sometimes I struggled to do what dad expected of me, such as finishing all the food on my plate! I let him down when it came to under-boiled eggs. He would sit over me, saying sarcastically "I never met *anyone* but Wendy, who could find bad bits in an egg!" To me, this was most odd, because under-cooked eggs were full of bad, snotty, slimy bits.

I will never forget the time dad and I had gone to the bottom of the garden to inspect some hippo prints. We did not take Linda, as she had not been around. As we walked back up the lawn, Linda's angry little face appeared at an upstairs window. Spluttering with fury, she shouted out the very worst words in her vocabulary "You...you...you...*GREEDY OLD THINGS!*" We doubled up with laughter. I realised afterwards we shouldn't have laughed, really. This was a very serious matter to Linda.

Just imagine, she was born and raised in the bush; brought up by a strict disciplinarian of a father whose continual sarcasm never failed to hurt her. With a mother who, in spite of loving her daughter above anything, would under no circumstances criticise her husband. Whether it was for the sake of peace, or because mum was so much under his thumb she had lost much of her oomph, I never fathomed out. What a horrible fate for the bouncy redhead, with such enthusiasm for life, who would have become a Commissioned Officer in the Women's Air Force, had she not infuriatingly fallen pregnant.

Religion had no place in our home and I was careful not to let dad catch me kneeling by my bed. Dad had set ideas and often described his strict Scottish upbringing when the only day off was Sunday, but that day was spent being dragged along to three Kirk Services. He told me religion was "superstition" and "superstition destroys lives". He contended the Bible was partly an ingenious story put together by clever people, and partly a history book. As far as he was concerned, most of the Bible's "miracles" were simply explained in Emmanuel Velikovsky's "Worlds in Collision". (Actually, the fact that so many "miracles" could be explained in this book, made me more inclined to believe in the Bible!) I accept what dad meant was there was no way we could all have literally come from Adam and Eve; but another of his quirks was he adamantly refused to accept Darwin's theory that man originated from apes. He had absolutely no time for monkeys and baboons. *"Apes our ancestors? No blooming way!"*

He referred to himself as an "atheist".

Mum explained to me that, although dad did not attend Church, he lived a more "Christian" life than most people you would meet. He was honest to the point of absurdity: he once walked back the whole length of Government Road in Nairobi, to return a few cents' change he had erroneously been overpaid by an Indian shopkeeper. I tried hard to live up to my father's standards. I never thought to question his actions; he was always "right". I never heard my dad use a swear word. Even "shut up" was forbidden in our house. Kids at school used to swear, which meant lots of "shurrups" and a few "bloodies". At school, naturally, I did the same.

During one holiday, I was to spend the night at my friend Liz's house, some miles away. Her mother collected me, together with mum and Linda. Dad was coming to fetch them in the evening. My mother, who was engrossed in a game of Scrabble with Liz's mum, expressed astonishment upon hearing Liz call out "shurrup" to me. Liz's mother laughed, saying that they used the word a lot. I confessed to mum I, too, used the forbidden word at school: a long discussion ensued on the subject, interspersed with much laughter. Dad arrived and, when I heard him ask, "Where's Wendy?" I popped my head gingerly round the corner and, as per plan, said "Shut up, dad!" Oh wow, did the whatsit hit the fan! My mother started to make a half-hearted attempt to explain what had brought about my appalling act of rebellion. My father silenced her with one of his chilling looks. In a deathly hush, he pointed to the door. I had to pack my bag, and that was the end of my night out. On the journey home, Linda kept giving me sympathetic sideways glances while mother uttered not a word.

As briefly mentioned, dad always made sure my hair was chopped off just when it was beginning to look half-way decent, and he made me feel guilty for allowing it to get into such a mess – he used to refer to it as "uncontrolled". Like an unpruned coffee tree, I guess. On the first day of each half-term or end-of-term holiday, throughout my eight years of boarding-school, dad would glare at me in his very own, intimidating way, making motions of clipping scissors with his fingers. It was exactly the same a day after returning from College in the UK, when I was seventeen. I always resented having to wear my hair so short. My sister was allowed to have long hair. I never understood why my mother didn't defend me. She had perfected a habit of pretending not to notice: a dreamy expression would flit across her eyes, while her bottom lip protruded, enabling her to blow cigarette smoke straight up into the air, as she closed her eyes into tiny little slits against the incredible puff of smoke.

Looking down now, dad will see that my hair is even more uncontrolled and unmanageable. But he won't mind.

***

Veterinarians were few and far between out in the middle of the bush. Most farmers would shoot suffering pets and bury them in the garden. Finn Aagaard had an awesome bull terrier who insisted on fighting with a huge male baboon that continued to maraud the vegetable patch. Three times, the bull terrier staggered into Finn's house with half of his scalp hanging over one eye. Finn would stitch the scalp back together with fishing line and a sacking needle. The nearly dead dog would lie on his blanket until the wound was sufficiently healed, then he was straight off after the baboon again!

Wherever we lived, we had a house full of dogs and cats, often taking over animals left behind by friends who were proceeding on holiday. Thus our menagerie included spaniels, poodles, bull-terriers, many Heinz varieties, and a dachshund named "Liggly" because Linda used to tickle its tummy saying "Tickle Liggle Liggly!" We also had a multitude of cats, including special Frankie, a tabby christened "Frankenstein" by Peter Davey. But the pets would come and go; the only one who remained constant was my Bessy. I would return for the holidays to discover a bull terrier was no longer there, or "Liggly" had gone and even Frankie disappeared. For some reason I rarely questioned where they had vanished to because, when I did, mother would mumble something incoherent whilst blowing cigarette smoke straight up to the ceiling.

One time I came home from school in my early teens, to find little Linda red-eyed, unhappy and silent as I went around as usual, searching for each and every pet, but was unable to find our Sealpoint Siamese cat "Susong", who had been pregnant when I left for school. Eventually, stoically holding back tears, Linda described how dad, fed-up with "all the blinking kittens" had tied the kittens in a sack together with their mother and drowned them in the water tank that we used as a swimming-pool.

It was at the beginning of a holiday in my sixteenth year, that I managed to clamber out of the car without being pounced upon by my beloved Bessy. Mother explained she had been growing old, and was developing "a growth".

So dad had shot her.

"Bessy didn't feel anything" mum explained. "I had given her a plate of food. She was eating and knew nothing about it!" Looking back, with vets being few, far away and far between, I guess Bessy suffered as little as she would have done at a vet's surgery.

All the same, dad's animals loved him, probably in the same way that I did – with more than a little trepidation, and absolute obedience! We had a goose named Samantha after the goose in "Friendly Persuasions". As soon as dad came home from work and sat down with his black-and-tan, Samantha would waddle into the house and put her head on his lap to have her neck scratched. Dad had a smoker's cough and often, when he coughed during the night, Samantha would answer him with loud honking! When it became too much, dad would go marching out in his dressing-gown, tuck Samantha under his arm, and walk all the way down the farm track to deposit her in the dam!

One of my favourite memories of dad, was his wonderful singing voice. He sang frequently, in the happier days. I still feel the tears starting when I recall him serenading mum with "Bless Your Beautiful Hide", "The Girl that I Marry", or "I'll Take You Home again, Kathleen". Every Hogmanay he would stand, with mug of beer in his hand, and sing in a beautiful tenor "Jer-ooo-salem! Jer-ooo-salem! Lift up your hearts and sing...." As I write this, remembering, I have a lump in my throat and I miss my dad terribly.

Although I felt very close to my father, I have never met anybody else who was able to look directly into your eyes in the way he could, impelling you to meet his unwavering stare without flinching; "chilling" is the only way I can describe it. I was to learn later that Mike's eyes could be chilling, stone-cold in fact, whereas dad had feeling in his eyes, often great warmth, particularly in the days before my mother left him.

Not so Mike, whose eyes, completely devoid of feeling, were like pieces of shiny grey steel.

17. THE STUPID WORD

Our kitchen toto, Kasili, originally taken on at dad's first coffee-managing job, moved with us from one farm to another. He was only a few years older than me and, naturally, always called Linda and I by our Christian names. Gradually, mum trained him to cook and carry out all the household chores and he became elevated to the position of pishi-cum-houseboy.

When we were in our early teens, Liz and her mother were spending the day with us. Her mother overheard Kasili referring to my friend as "Liz". Her beautiful violet eyes opened very wide as she looked up from the Scrabble board and asked mum, aghast, "Did you hear that? He called her *Liz*!" At home, all their staff called Liz and her little brother "Memsaab" and "Bwana"; Liz's brother was only eight years old at the time, but that is Colonials for you!

I suppose it can be difficult to draw the line between being an "employee" and a "friend", especially when you have grown up with the same family and worked for them over a long period of time. One evening I needed a sharp kitchen knife in a hurry. I rushed into the kitchen and, unable to find the knife in the drawer, asked Kasili "Where's the knife?"

Kasili handed me a soupspoon, "You mean this?"

"No, no! The knife, I need it quickly please!"

With a grin, he handed me a fork. Then a teaspoon.

Exasperated, I said "Kasili, don't be stupid! I want the kitchen knife!"

He gave me the knife.

At dinner time, I noticed that Kasili was laying the table with a particularly grim expression on his face. Having entirely forgotten the little episode of earlier, I

74

waited until he had returned to the kitchen before commenting to my parents "Something's wrong with Kasili? He's really pouty and miserable!"

When he brought the soup to the table, slopping it over the edge of the tureen as he set the tray on the table, mother asked him what his problem was. In Swahili he replied "Wendy called me *stupid!*" He slammed the door as he returned to the kitchen.

"Did you call him stupid?" mum asked.

"Not exactly, I told him not to be stupid!" I explained why, pointing out he was in fact being very stupid. Which he was. Mother told me I had better go and apologise to him. I did so, though not understanding why I should.

This was the first time I had come across this absolute paranoia that some Kenyans have about the word "stupid". Perhaps the translation of the word in Swahili, "pumbavu" has a much worse connotation? I cannot say. But I am sure most of the people who have settled in this country have become very cagey about using the word; I believe some have even been brought before the Courts for using it!

Incidentally, after working with us for over eight years, Kasili was eventually sacked for driving the little Company pick-up truck around the estate at great speed, quite drunk, with a dozen passengers in the back.

***

It was a full thirty-six years later that I stupidly repeated this sin but, because it comes under the same "heading" I must add it here! Paul, the upcountry Chef in our restaurant at the coast, had allowed boiling water from the crab sufaria (saucepan) to overflow across the kitchen floor and through the door. Being a "Born-Again Christian", instead of concentrating on cooking, Paul had taken to reading passages from the Bible to the kitchen staff – all of one but whom were Muslims. Helping to clean up the mess, I pointed out to him that, quite apart from the fact that the other kitchen workers would rather hear passages from the Koran than the Bible, there was a time for religious meetings and a time for working. A heated discussion ensued, during which my employee was extremely rude, and I uttered the fateful words "Don't be stupid, I am not saying you shouldn't read the Bible, just that there is a time and a place for everything....." That did it! *"You call me stupid?"* he yelled. All the inane things he had said and done suddenly became totally irrelevant, as my employee chased me out of my kitchen wielding a meat cleaver.

The last I ever saw of Paul, he was disappearing down the driveway in great leaps and bounds, throwing his arms up in the air and shouting to the Heavens.

18. HIGH SCHOOL

Back to 1958. After leaving Nyeri Primary School, I boarded at the Kenya European Girls' High School, where I was not happy at all, and my schoolwork suffered as a result. Our dormitory matron was a miserable old lady with gigantic bunions; we could see her shadow as she took her shoes off and crept along the corridor, sliding with her back against the wall, hoping to catch us talking after "lights-out". She took an instant dislike to me when my parents dropped me off in "Thumbelina". Her husband had been in a German concentration camp during the war. "Unforgiveable! How could your parents buy a German car after all that the Nazis did to us in the War?" I wonder how she felt about the German Ambassador's lovely daughter, Dorothea, who was also in our House. In fact, Dorothea was allowed to go home every time she had her monthly period, which was most unfair.

Was the word "Vegetarian" even in the Dictionary in those days? As applied to humans, I mean. I never heard the word mentioned at school. I recall a dinner-time at the KEGHS when the menu was "liver". I did eat liver at home, though not enthusiastically; but at home it was tender and edible. Liver at school was greyish, thick, lumpy and full of white strings and circles that looked like ulcers. I vividly remember Mary Sharpe gagging at the dinner table. A member of staff told her she had to eat it. She said "I am really sorry, I just can't!" The rest of us left the dining-room, with poor Mary sitting crying over the disgusting slab of ulcerated liver on her plate.

The Headmistress prided herself on her Prefects who, she said, could "run the School by themselves". Dad said the Prefects were like an "Army". He referred to them as "Little Hitlers". (Wow, is that double-standards from

77

somebody who had a Volkswagen Beetle, ha ha!) What bullies the Prefects were, they set their own rules and meted out punishments ad lib.

I was so petrified of the Algebra teacher I would often suffer from a runny tummy prior to her lessons. A dour Scottish lady, she would pick on me to stand up in front of the class to give a solution to an Algebra equation. If I hesitated, she would say to the class "Look at her! She's like a bally coo leaning over the fence chewing the cud!" That aside, she must have been a brilliant teacher, because Algebra was my favourite subject. When it came to school-leaving exams "KCPE", I attained ninety-six per cent in Algebra and all credit is due to this teacher. Perhaps that is why I have won prizes for Cryptic Crosswords since, and also why I spend hours working out Sudokus, Solvit puzzles, etc.!

19. THE BEACH

After our first outstanding beach holiday, we went to the coast every August and usually at Christmas-time. We would normally drive down through Tanganyika, crossing at the Namanga border, passing through Moshi and Arusha, then travelling back into Kenya via a lovely drive along the coast road from Tanga. In Tanga we would spend a night or two with friends from the Groundnut Scheme, my "doctor" puddle-swimming friend Anne and her parents. There were no hassles at the borders in those days; we would stop to take photos next to a sign welcoming us to Tanganyika. At the end of our holiday, we would travel back upcountry by the direct three hundred mile Mombasa-Nairobi road.

Coast Holidays, we would usually drive down through Tanganyika

The Likoni Ferry. Beautiful baobab trees on Mombasa Island

We holidayed in various types of accommodation, on different beaches north and south of Mombasa, before finally deciding upon our favourite spot. This is where we were to spend our vacations, year after year, in "self-service" rented accommodation on the beautiful secluded beach of Tiwi, south of Mombasa. Further along the beach was a campsite, frequented by Kenyan holiday-makers and the occasional European traveller. With each progressive year, as the number of "overlanders" increased, so the class of campers on the site deteriorated. "Overlanders" was (and still is) the name given to budget-travellers from Europe, Australia and New Zealand who spend months at a time travelling around Africa in huge trucks.

My friends and I were instructed by our parents to keep away from the campers, many of whom apparently smoked "evil cigarettes" and were "stoned out of their brains" most of the time, according to the adults in our households. Bonnie and I noticed the glazed, dreamy expressions of some of these campers, who would leer at us and make suggestive comments as we passed them on the beach. We would furtively watch camping couples playing in the sea, openly fondling each other and kissing with wide-open mouths. Our parents would call us away, embarrassed by the disgraceful behaviour of these totally uninhibited people. It did bother us that our local fishermen and fruit-sellers were witness to such abandoned behaviour by white people!

20. THE LUNATIC EXPRESS

Occasionally, we would travel overnight to or from the coast on the so-called "Lunatic Express", not on the hard wooden slatted benches in the Third Class compartments where our pishi would travel, but in First Class. The First Class compartments were of varnished wood, with bunk beds, each with its own reading light. There was a wash-basin, clean hand towels and a dispenser of drinking water with a supply of new plastic tumblers. The WC's were spotlessly clean, with endless supplies of toilet paper. While we were in the Dining Car, polite stewards wearing smart khaki uniforms and red fezzes on their heads made up the bunks with comfortable mattresses, soft pillows, and clean bedding.

The Dining Car was lined on one side by tables for two, while the tables across the passageway sat four. It was very romantic, with little red-shaded lamps on each table. The silver cutlery was engraved with "EAR&H", (for East African Railways & Harbours) as in Roger Whittaker's song. A silver wine caddy stood in the centre of each table, with quarter bottles of Red, White and Rose Wine. We were each handed an embossed menu, with a choice of starters, main course and dessert, followed by cheese & biscuits, then coffee or tea. The train left Nairobi at 7 p.m., arriving in Mombasa at 8 a.m. the following morning. It was very exciting; I never met one single person who did not love this journey, which I must have undertaken at least twenty times in my life: with family, or sometimes as a school group, later as member of a hockey team.

Sadly, the standards dropped gradually but surely over the years. My last journey on the Lunatic Express was in the eighties. The reading lights over the bunks did not work. In some compartments, no lights worked at all, while others flashed on and off ceaselessly, all night long. The wash-basin was still there, with not a trickle of water, there was no towel and of course no drinking water. The stinking WC's were virtually unusable, with no toilet paper. A disgruntled steward made up my bunk with damp, torn sheets and no mattress. In the Dining Car there were no red-shaded table lamps, no silver cutlery, and no wine caddies on the tables. A rather intoxicated waiter shoved a scruffy, fly-spattered menu in front of my face and there were only two unappetising choices. When I returned to my compartment, my sunglasses had disappeared from the cupboard. The proper door-lock no longer functioned, and a small sliding bolt had been nailed to the door at an awkward angle. I was woken a few times during the night by somebody knocking on the door of my compartment; I did not open the door and was worried a hard shove might easily break the bolt.

21. CRUISING TO BRITAIN 1961

Nineteen sixty-one. Finally my days at the miserable school were over. Dad's home leave was due and we took the steam train to Mombasa. We sailed from Mombasa on the "B.I. Kampala" via the Suez Canal, taking three weeks to reach Southampton Docks.

The cruise from the Port of Mombasa was exciting. On the voyage, I had a white Rhodesian "boyfriend" called Dave. Dave, at eighteen, was two years my senior. Ordinarily, Dave was not the type of boy I would choose to go around with. I assumed he must be typically Rhodesian, being almost unbearably egotistical, much more so than the classic Colonial "KayCee" aka "Kenya Cowboy". He had the most horrendous laugh, a continuous high-pitched gasping sound that made me feel extremely uncomfortable. But it was holiday-time! We held hands while walking on the deck, or the streets of Marseilles, Barcelona and Gibraltar.

Cruising to Britain

It was a magical holiday, which took place in between two very different stages in my life.

As we slowly cruised along the Suez Canal, "Gilly-Gilly men" climbed to the very top of thin, precariously swinging masts, handing out cheap packages of tacky items for sale, calling out "Mrs MacKenzie, Mrs Simpson, buy...very sheep today...". Dave bought me a heart-shaped packet containing seven pairs of panties, in seven different colours, hand-stitched with cheeky quotes, one for each day of the week. A peanut seller managed to leap from a mast as it curved in an arc towards the deck. He continually pestered us "Mrs McKenzie...buy peanuts...very sheep!" I kept telling him to go away. He would not. Finally, to get rid of him, I purchased a huge brown paper bag of unshelled peanuts which I proceeded to eat one after the other until the bag was empty. I spent the night visiting "the heads" and throwing up. When I eventually managed to stagger up on deck the following morning, I was immediately met with "Mrs MacKenzie...buy peanuts..." Groaning, I put my hand over my mouth and disappeared.

I still cannot eat peanuts, since that day, five decades ago!

Gibraltar

Of course Dave drank beer, the consumption of copious amounts of this brew being a compulsory past-time amongst all Colonial males, and Woe Betide any poofter refusing to join the elite *B*eer-guzzling Brotherhood. With bottles perched in crooks of arms, it was essential for groups of these macho men to shun female company and stand around bars until the early hours, singing with tremendous sincerity and emotion, crude versions of "The Quartermaster's Stores", or "She'll be coming round the Mountain".

At the end of each passionate rendition, another round of beers would be ordered to the unmelodious notes of a little ditty, chanted with great depth of feeling by every bleary-eyed male around the bar:-

"That was a *horrible* rhyme!

Sing us another one, just like the other one!

Sing us another one, *do-oo*!"

This would be the cue for an upstanding purple-nosed servant of Her Majesty's Colonies to take centre stage and, with tears in eyes and hand placed on puffed-out chest, sing in a throbbing off-key bass "Who killed Cock Robin?" whilst pointing accusingly at a culprit, who would reply, "I...". The seemingly never-ending ballad would eventually finish in a l-o-n-g drawn-out note, harmonised in a variety of fluctuating octaves that would put Welsh choirs to shame.

One evening when Dave was downing his seventh or eighth pint and screeching out his insufferable laugh, I bravely ordered a Martini, being very knowledgeable about this particular drink. But instead of the anticipated sweet brown liquid with a maraschino cherry, I was served the most frightful solution I had ever tasted apart from Quinine. It was colourless and had a salty olive in it! My introduction to Gin and Vermouth.

Dave kissed me! Not with open mouths or anything like that, but it was a very grown-up thing to do, all the same! One night, returning to our separate cabins after walking on the deck holding hands, we were turning a corner, laughing, when Dave said "Oh look out, there's your old man!" My father, his face like thunder, had been walking around the ship looking for me, *wearing his pyjamas!* He grabbed my arm in a vice-like grip and hauled me downstairs to our cabin, giving me a lecture about "acting cheap....like a tart". When I left the cabin to visit the loo later, I came across a few of Dave's beer-guzzling buddies, who taunted me, "Did Papa come looking for you in his pyjamas, then?"

Marseilles was incredible, with trams hurtling along at great speed. We walked along the quayside, flanked on the landward side by a never-ending row of souvenir shops and cafe-cum-bars which stayed open all night, with drunks in lumpy chairs engrossed in noisy televised operas; and on the other side by a continuous row of houseboats parked side by side. There was life on every houseboat, usually in the form of a drunken party with the occasional reveller falling into the water. We watched a couple screaming at each other in the throes of a domestic row, kitchen utensils flying through the air. Often, large, beaming ladies wearing headscarves and floral dresses were hanging out washing on lines stretching from the quayside to hooks on the roofs of the boats. We loved this untidy, happy and carefree city.

Although beautiful, Barcelona struck me a harsh, angry city! Whilst attempting to explore a beautiful Church, Dave and I were shoved roughly out through the door by an extremely angry Spanish gentleman. We never discovered what the man's problem was: whether we should have remained silent, whether we were supposed to have been barefoot or, as someone later suggested, I should have worn something on my head. The Spaniard was waving his arms around madly, without any explanation at all!

In a tourist market, mum bought me a little black bull ornament, with spears sticking out of its back, which I was holding in my hand when I walked into another stall. This stall-owner was convinced I had stolen the bull from him. As the only Spanish words I knew were "Buenos Noches", I could not explain it had been purchased from another stall. After a shouting match in which nobody got anywhere, I made a hasty retreat, minus ornament. We then spent a fascinating half-hour watching balloon-cheeked glass-blowers sitting cross-legged on the floor, making perfect bottles of all shapes and sizes.

The following day, Dave announced he had purchased two tickets to a bullfight. "Who's going with you?" I asked.

"You are, don't be silly!"

"ME! A BULLFIGHT! Forget it!"

Needless to say, I ended up going along to the bullring, which was reputed to hold one hundred thousand people. We were ushered up seven flights of stairs and squeezed ourselves into the first available space. There were no seats: one had to sit on bare concrete, amongst the feet of those in the row behind. A band struck up a lively tune, while a man in gaily-coloured clothing rode into the arena on a beautiful white horse. As the horse began its dance routine, we were interrupted by a group of people wanting to pass; we stood up to allow them to go by. This was greeted by screams, shouts and yells from behind. A calm American voice drawled, "I guess they're asking you to sit down, ma'am".

"I know!" I squeaked, "But these people have to pass somehow!" I then plonked myself down thankfully, as the music stopped and the white horse was ridden out of the ring. A young black bull charged into the ring like a tormented demon; his mood was aggravated by men hiding behind wooden partitions around the walls of the arena, who kept darting out to wave orange cloaks in front of the poor beast. There was silence all around. Soon a "Picador" rode into the ring astride an armoured horse, covered in a thick padded material, with blinkers over its eyes. The rider carried a spear. He rode the horse around the edge of the arena. The enraged bull charged directly at the horse; every time it was attacked, the poor horse was lifted up and driven into the arena wall. The rider delightedly jabbed the spear again and again into the bull's hump, causing blood to trickle down its back. Having sufficiently maddened the wretched bull, horse and rider left the ring.

A Matador strutted in. He was handed two pointed sticks. Holding the sticks straight out in front of himself, he sprinted confidently towards the bull. He leapt at the beast with great gusto, driving the pointed devices deep into its back. The bleeding, tormented animal was snorting and stamping furiously on the ground. Apparently, the object of this horrendous display was for the Matador to place six of these cruel weapons into the hump on the bull's back, so that all six stayed in. This man managed five and the crowd seemed OK with that. The despicable excuse for a human-being was then given a red cloak and a spear. He waved the cloak around, while the bull charged at it, exactly as they do in cartoons and picture-books, with the crowds yelling "Ole!" and all that goes with it. At last, the Matador lifted his spear and lunged at the bull. The lunge was misdirected and the beast did not go down as it was supposed to do. The Matador had another attempt, this time jabbing the spear into the bull's spine. The animal gave a terrible bellow of pain. Moaning loudly, it sank to the ground, groaning and gasping in helpless agony, its hind legs paralysed. As the struggling animal attempted in vain to rise, I turned to look at Dave with tears pouring shamelessly down my face. Dave looked very glum. The American's voice drawled from behind "Aw Shucks, not very nice, is it?"

Was I really sitting here, witnessing this barbarism? This was unreal, as if I was experiencing the very worst nightmare. A large well-built Frenchman beside Dave moaned and collapsed, and had to be carried out. It was easy to spot the foreigners amongst the spectators; they either had hands over their faces or, like me, were crying. Eventually a man ran into the arena with a sharp knife and blessedly cut the suffering creature's throat.

Having witnessed sufficient brutality and slaughter for one lifetime, I motioned to Dave that we should go, and I began to stand. Noisy objections from behind convinced me to sit down again. With the entrance of the next bull, the music became exceptionally loud. A divine-looking Matador sailed in, bowing to the "Oles" of the swooning crowd. A young Spaniard flew down from somewhere behind, to squeeze into the space that had been occupied by the unfortunate Frenchman. Clutching the rail in front, his eyes feverishly bright, the young man moaned "Aaaaaaaah! Antonio!" He turned to us with a maniacal expression, as if to say "Isn't he *wonderful*?" The Matador lounged nonchalantly on the edge of the arena, flicking his cloak at the bull's nose. As the bull bellowed, Antonio strolled casually into the centre of the ring. The bull tore after him and ripped a chunk out of his cloak. "Antonio! Antonio!" roared the crowd, as the Matador leaned over backwards, in the way that only Spanish men can, placing his hand on the bull's neck as it encircled him. The nut-head beside us let out a gurgle and it seemed for a moment that he would leap into the arena. Antonio killed the bull at the first attempt. I let out an involuntary cry as the beast sank to the ground; this so flabbergasted the young fanatic, that he turned to gaze at me in total disbelief and bewilderment, his jaw dropping loosely towards his chest.

We took the chance to make a quick exit. Vowing to ship a few Cape Buffaloes from Africa to the Spanish bullrings, we walked down the flights of stairs and through blood-filled stalls out onto the road. We hailed a taxi. After explaining our destination by drawing on the back of Dave's cigarette packet, a ship sailing on waves, we discovered we were right out of pesetas! The rude taxi-driver nodded "No" to both Kenyan and Rhodesian money; nor would he try to understand we would pay him in pesetas at the dock. Now we had a problemo. Just as he was about to drive off huffily, a familiar American voice drawled behind us "Can I be of help?" It was the American from the bullring. He gave us money for the taxi fare, declining our "Mickey Mouse money" in exchange. We waved back at our rescuer until the taxi turned a corner, our new-found friend passing out of our sight and out of our lives.

We left Barcelona and set sail for Gibraltar, an altogether friendlier place; the views were amazing and the tail-less monkeys were wild and free!

22. BEAUTIFUL BRITAIN!

We were met at the docks by Aunts, Uncles, Great Aunts and Great Uncles, and Cousins, some of whom had driven many miles across this wonderful green Island, to be there when our ship arrived - only to drive back again after a delicious plastic-wrapped snack and refreshing "cuppa" at a mind-boggling fast-food restaurant on the outskirts of London. What a wonderful greeting; how warm and friendly they all were! Uncle Ray delivered a smart red-and-grey Ford Consul that dad had hired for the duration of our holiday. In this elegant vehicle, we were to clock up more mileage across England and Scotland, than most of the Island's inhabitants would do in a life-time!

We stayed in London, whose history over-awed me. All those streets and buildings with names straight off the "Monopoly Board". We had relatives there, some of whom had real Cockney accents! With our cousins in Kingston, we spent many glorious hours exploring nearby Richmond Park, where our cousins knew the locations of pheasants' nests, which they kept secret and left well alone. They were bewildered by my excitement upon coming across herds of wild deer. "But you live in AFRICA!" It was difficult to explain the thrill derived from spotting wild game right in the centre of an enormous "First World" City.

On the way up North we spent a few days with dad's brother, who had been Chief of Police in Bradford. We sang "On Ilkley Moor ba tat" while driving on the moors in our two-wheel drive Consul, feeling quite at home while laughing at signs stating "Four-wheel Drive vehicles only beyond this point". We saw cities surrounded by slag-heaps. We visited the home of the famous Bronte sisters in Haworth; I so envied my cousins for being surrounded by so much history. And yet another incredible accent! My cousin Mavis's accent was quite different to any I had heard to date; her pronunciation of her own name sounded more like "Meh? – vis" than "May – vis". Dad and I were very careful to avoid each other's eyes when Mavis announced at the tea-table, "U'm saw glud eye-yuvunt pkt oop that orfl Yawksha ukzunt! (This is Yorkshire for "I'm so glad I haven't picked up that awful Yorkshire accent).

Well, maybe I could speak better English than my relatives brought up in England. But, in spite of suffering eight years of boarding school in East Africa, I was years behind the worldly-wise Mavis, who kindly invited me to join her at a dance that evening. She said she would lend me "something to wear". I so, so wanted to – but I simply did not dare. Mavis went to "get ready". She left the room as a spotty, jeans-clad kid, with long stringy hair. She returned looking absolutely stunning, in a minute black skirt, tight top, high-heels; wearing glossy silver-white lipstick, jet black mascara and thick black eye-liner. Her back-combed and lacquered hair was piled up high on top of her head. Oh Boy, was I relieved I had declined her invitation; there was *no way* this backward, country bumpkin could have matched that! For a start, I had never worn any make-up whatsoever in my life, and I would never have had the confidence to dress up as she did, though I yearned to.

Added to the shame of having a boy's haircut, I was SO skinny. The next day, Mavis took me to a heated indoor swimming-pool in Bradford. A young man struck up a conversation with me, in the strange dialect that they have. I didn't understand and asked him to repeat what he said. He pointed at a pool-cleaning pole with a net on it that was lying beside the pool, and said "Is that your partner?" Oh, what mortification.

(When I returned to Kenya and started earning my own money, I bought disgusting "weight-on" diets, one after the other. They were an orange powder that had to be mixed with warm water; the packets showed pictures of voluptuous ladies. They didn't help skinny me.)

In the south of Scotland, we stayed with a selection of dad's relatives. What a beautiful part of the world.

My parents decided they would leave me behind in England to attend college. In reply to mother's query, I told her I really wanted to attend Art College. Apparently Art College would be too expensive and the course would take too long, therefore my parents decreed I should take an Administration/Book-keeping/Secretarial Course and, after that, when I was earning money I could enlist in an Art College. I was upset about this. In private rebellion, I threw away my drawing books. It was nearly five decades later that I started to sketch again. I sat a series of entry examinations for the "Great Yarmouth College of Further Education", which was only a twenty minute walk from my youngest Aunt's house. College was free, and mum and her young sister, Sylvia, agreed my parents would pay for my keep. My parents and little sister drove to London, from where they boarded the "B. I. Uganda" back to East Africa.

I did enjoy the College, and three periods a week at night-school. I became very close to a sweet, gentle girl called Judy, who lived a few yards down the street from my Aunt. Judy would call at my Aunt's gate and together we would walk to college, singing one Cliff Richard song after another along the way.

I loved living with my young Aunt and Uncle. Only being a few years older than me, Sylvia was more like a big sister than an Aunt. They were wonderful to me and it was like a "home away from home". I had a comfortable room, with a streetlight right outside my upstairs bedroom window, by which I was able to read in bed at night, thus saving on electricity. It took a few months before I stopped checking under the bed and inside cupboards for intruders, before retiring for the night. If I happened to wake in the night, I would lie very still, listening for strange sounds, then I would laugh to myself in relief "You're in England now, silly! No Mau Mau here!" before dropping off to sleep again. "Syl" as I called her, and Ray, had one dear little daughter and their second daughter was born while I was living there. I loved my young cousins and treated them more like nieces.

I learned so much from my eighteen months in the UK. Having been brought up in Colonial East Africa, I was in for many eye-openers. I recall watching on television "Ban the Bomb" demonstrators sitting in Trafalgar Square. Not even considering the reason for their demonstrations, I shot up out of my chair in shock, pointing at the telly and shouting "Look at all those *white* people *sitting on the pavement!*"

"Why shouldn't they?" Sylvia asked. "What's so special about them?" Stuttering and spluttering, I tried to explain the white people simply did not do things like that; we had standards to uphold!

On another occasion, Sylvia and I, wearing shorts, were crossing the marine parade in Yarmouth on our way to the tennis courts. A bus driver leaned out of the cab window to whistle at me. Absolutely gob-smacked, I blurted out "Did you *hear* that? That *bus driver* actually *whistled* at me! How *dare* he?" My Aunt laughingly replied, "I'd be so lucky!"

During the holidays, I would meet up with relatives from all over the Island. Scottish cousins came to stay with us; I travelled around on buses and trains to stay with various relatives in England. One holiday I took the fast train to Scotland. My cousins and I walked for miles and drove for miles. We visited hidden lochs; we tracked pheasants; we drove to far-away beaches. We climbed local hills that the Scots called mountains. We crossed fields and were chased by huge black bulls, and walked through woods full of bluebells. We visited old churches, castles and graveyards, and explored areas I knew of from poetry and songs: "Maxwelton Braes are Bonnie....." It was a heavenly country.

I spent many happy weekends with my maternal Grandparents, "Nanny and Pop", in Hopton-on-Sea. Pop spent most of his time tending his picturesque garden in front of the house and his vegetable patch at the back. Nanny always seemed to be doing housework. At one time she was found to be anaemic and was advised by her doctor to "drink a bottle of Guinness a day" to boost her blood. Every morning, a bottle of Guinness, a glass and a bottle-opener would be placed on the kitchen table. Dear Nanny, who had hitherto never sampled alcohol, would stop washing dishes or doing the laundry at 11 a.m. daily, when she would sit down and open the bottle of Guinness. She would drink it as if it was a foul medicine, her lovely face screwed up at the awful taste. When finished, she would leap up and sing away happily, giggling as she danced through the rest of the laborious housework!

It was terribly exciting when the first snow fell. It was night-time and I rushed out of the door and down the path to the gate, in my nylon nightdress! On the way to college, Judy and I would be ambushed by boys throwing snowballs...surprising how they could hurt!

23. HOME TO KENYA!

Then back to Kenya, to live in an old Colonial-style house on yet another farm, "Anglo-French Sisal Estate" in Thika District. Although predominantly growing sisal, the farm also had one thousand acres of coffee, that dad managed. Linda was studying at Thika Primary School. I took a temporary job in the local District Commissioner's offices, earning five shillings per hour typing voters' rolls. Then I was successful in applying for the position of secretary to the District Commissioner at that time, Noel Hardy. Noel was followed by Johnny Johnson, who left Kenya at Independence and later returned as British High Commissioner.

Very nervous, I took my driving test under the eagle eye of a ferocious-looking English Driving Instructor. To my surprise, at the end of the test, his miserable expression turned to a big wide smile as he told me that I had passed! Having driven around farms for nearly ten years, I could finally drive on public roads! In those days, the standard of driving in Kenya was generally excellent and the rules of the road were strictly adhered to.

I have a clear recollection of the time I was driving past the doctor's surgery in Thika on my way to work, when I noticed an outstandingly good-looking African gentleman, speaking in a very relaxed manner to an European lady, right there beside the main road! She must obviously be a visitor from abroad, to act in such a brazen manner. I craned my neck to watch them as I turned the corner, and there they still were, talking to each other and laughing as if it were a normal thing to do, in full view of everybody!

Wow, times were definitely changing.

In fact, times were changing so rapidly, that there was an article in the daily press suggesting that African men should now be referred to as "Mister". Yet another article stated that, henceforth, "Houseboys" must be referred to as "House Servants". Having been brought up in the old Colonial system, it sounded really strange, and there were jokes, e.g.: "My House *Servant* is called *Mister* Kasili. Ha-ha-ha!" Colonials, a one-off breed.

It was not long before I had saved up one hundred pounds, which I excitedly spent on a second-hand Morris Minor "convertible" at Shah Motors in Nairobi. The vehicle broke down as soon as I reached Thika Road; apparently the fan "went into the radiator". I had it towed back to Shah Motors, who promised to fix and re-sell it. They eventually gave me back forty pounds! I borrowed mum and dad's VW Beetle until I had saved up three hundred pounds, which I spent on a brand new, absolutely beautiful, yellow Toyota 700. The Yellow Peril was my Pride and Joy.

One day, a good-looking black gentleman walked into my office. I immediately recognised him as the person I had spotted talking to the Mzungu lady outside the doctor's surgery. He wanted to check whether "Johnny" had put his name on the voters' roll, as he "didn't trust the old rogue!" I realised who he had to be, but asked all the same "What is your name, please?" "Mungai" he said. "Dr?" I asked. "Yes, that's me!" Dr Njoroge Mungai's name was of course on the voters' roll. We talked for some time, before he went into my boss's office. Much laughter emanated from Johnny's office. Had I led a shielded life, or what? This was the very first European-educated, truly sophisticated, African, that I had held a conversation with! He was absolutely charming. Once back home that evening, I told my mother about him, "Mum, I tell you, he even has a sense of humour like ours!" Mum liked this.

"Humph!" from behind dad's newspaper.

24. MZUNGU FRIENDS

My social life was brightening up. With groups of male and female friends from surrounding farmsteads, I would watch films at Thika's "Vedesh Cinema" and at the Drive-In cinemas. We would attend dances at Thika Sports Club.

For some reason, our male friends always appeared to earn far more money than we mere girls; they would wine and dine us, and supply the transport. Then they would expect "payment". "What the heck d-ya mean '*No*', I've spent a bloody fortune this evening!" One Italian Romeo was extremely miffed at my refusal. He commented "White-a girls no good anways!"

"Jeepers! You mean you sleep with *black* girls?" I had never met a white man who slept with black girls – at least, that I knew of.

"Sure I do" stated Romeo. "They enjoya the sexa. They not ow you say 'freejeed' like-a the English!"

"You're saying *black girls enjoy sex*?" Astounded!

"Where you bin, Baby?" Laughing. "You all-a made-a the same-a!"

One special friend I had was Mervyn. Mervyn's family were Afrikaners: loud, rough-and-tough, hard-drinking and hearty. Their forebears had travelled overland in ox-wagons. Mervyn's mother could "play the spoons" brilliantly, for hours on end, which I found absolutely fascinating. Their parties were always quite rough affairs, ending up with games of "Bok-Bok" where the person at the head of the line hung on for dear life to a verandah post, or edge of a bar, with the rest of the team clinging onto the back, or hips, or legs, of the man in front. The sturdiest men bent over in the middle of the line as they had to bear the brunt of the onslaught from the opposite team. The object of the opposing side was to jump onto the backs of Team 1, sending the lightest men first as they had to land up as far forward as they could, leaving as much room as possible for the team-mates leaping on behind them. As far as I could fathom out, the only rules were that Team 1 had to remain standing and the other side had to get as many people astride the bent-over backs as possible, without any parts of their bodies touching the ground.

All games of Bok-Bok ended up in a total muddle of arms and legs all twisted up like one of those children's toy balls made out of rubber tubes. Rarely did I witness a game of Bok-Bok that did not end up with at least one broken or badly-sprained limb, black eye, broken nose or missing tooth. Not to be seen as poofters, it was compulsory for all team members – alive, half-alive, or nearly dead – to roll around the floor guffawing with laughter to show what fun they were having.

Mervyn did not indulge in trivial conversation. His very special quality was his affinity with animals. I once saw him swipe his gardener across the face after discovering a trap at the bottom of the garden full of little weaver birds that the gardener was trapping for supper. We would often drive around the bush at night, virtually weaving between giraffe legs, until he spotted an antelope. He would caution me to keep silent as he stopped the car, slid out and gently walked right up to the impala, dik-dik, or gazelle, whereupon he would stretch out his hand and touch the wild animal's face. Beautiful.

I have no details but, as I heard it, Mervyn was murdered outside a bar in Cape Town some years ago. Having known him in the bush, alongside wild animals, I can only imagine how out-of-place he must have felt in a town as civilised as Cape Town. My poor rafiki.

Look after him please, God.

My farm friends and I would attend parties in Nairobi City, at one of which I was to meet my first real boyfriend Roy, with whom I "went out" for over a year. In his car, a Consul named "Connie", Roy took me to his folks' luxurious house in a high-class suburb of Nairobi. I was enthralled with the guest bedroom and its en suite bathroom. The bathroom was fitted with a beautiful imported shower-stall, bath, loo, washbasin and footbath, all in duck-egg blue. When I returned to the drawing-room, I commented on the blue footbath. Later, Roy managed to draw me aside to explain that it was not a footbath, but a "bidet". After much searching in the dictionary for "beeday", "bi-day" etc., I eventually found what I was looking for. "Ohmigod! Low oval basin for washing the genital area!"

Roy and I climbed Mount Kilimanjaro with a group of his sister's intrepid school-friends, from the "Boma". Our guide was Diwant Singh, who had been guide to Ernest Hemingway. We used the Outward Bound route which was always considered to be the best trail, via Tanzania but starting in Loitokitok on the Kenya-Tanzania border. This route took "three days up", giving time to acclimatise, and "two days down". My boss, Johnny Johnson, was delighted to give me time off to climb the mountain; he was an avid mountain-climber, together with a well-known co-mountaineer friend whose name escapes me. One morning when taking dictation in Johnny's office, there was a sound at one of the windows. We looked up to see a leg appearing over the window-sill, followed by the body of his mountaineer friend! Johnny looked up unsurprised, and said "Oh hello, how are you? Be with you in a moment!" Hilarious.

I was nearly nineteen when I lost my virginity. It happened in Roy's car "Connie", at the Thika Road

Drive-In Cinema. I yelped "Ouch!" Roy leapt up in fright and had difficulty extricating his leg from the spokes of the steering wheel. Heaven knows how he got into that position but I did not elicit the assistance of a cafeteria waiter, who was watching Roy's antics with great interest through the car windscreen.

25. MOVE TO THE SHITTY CITY

Kenya became more relaxed racially, as the inevitability of Independence sunk in. These days, all schools were becoming healthily mixed: black, white and brown. Quite happy and secure in my job, I was becoming used to meeting men and women from all races and creeds. I would greet black and brown acquaintances *on the street* and, depending who was watching, I would even stop and talk to them. The freedom! It was wonderful and I loved this new Kenya. Mwangi, an African author and friend of my boss, frequently visited the office and I would be called in to join in the discussion. I would bring in a tray of tea and biscuits, and we would chatter and laugh together.

Johnny Johnston   Njorege Mungai

Just before Independence, Dr Mungai asked me to come and work for him in the City, where he would be a Minister in Kenya's first Independent Parliament. My white boss encouraged me. He said "Go for it! This is the new Kenya! This man is going to go far, and you will be there from the beginning!" Johnny said he would be leaving Kenya and that, if he returned, he would be under a different flag. My future employer met my folks and apprised them of his offer to me. My mother seemed delighted. My father did not. Anyway, I moved to the City.

My parents found me accommodation in "Mary's Hall", a ladies' guesthouse which was sterile and not very friendly. A "Seventh-Day Adventurist" aptly named Miss Grey, would join me at the breakfast table. She appeared to have convinced herself I was a suitable candidate for conversion. However, no matter how hard she tried, it frustrated her that she was unable to stop me from eating bacon, in spite of typing out passages for me to read, entitled "The Vision of the Unclean Beasts", which were supposed to explain why we should not eat pork, one of the best meats in the world.

At this time, I was still going out with Roy. One Sunday morning I returned from a party, just as the ancient early risers were sitting down to breakfast. As I crept past the dining-hall in my evening-dress, a dozen blue-grey permed heads swivelled around to follow my movements, the old dears looking disapprovingly down their noses and "tut-tutting" with raised eyebrows. One of them was Miss Grey. She never again joined me for breakfast; eating pig flesh *and* staying out all night, I was obviously a lost cause.

Furthermore, I drank alcohol! I was found to be anaemic and, reminiscent of Nanny a couple of years previously, I was advised to drink Guinness daily. Initially I would sit with a glass of Guinness in one hand and a banana in the other: swig of Guinness, bite of banana, swig of Guinness... Eventually Guinness became my drink of choice, preferably mixed with Babycham to make a cheaper version of "Black Velvet".

There was another young girl at Mary's Hall: Jan, a pretty little thing with blonde hair, enormous blue eyes and bright pink cheeks. We became good friends. Jan's fiancé Ian, in vivid contrast to Jan, was an exceptionally tall rugby player with dark curly hair! She confided in me when she became pregnant. Her parents took her to Tanganyika where an "ex-Gestapo butcher" performed abortions for fifty pounds. Jan and Ian were married about six months later. Meanwhile, Roy left the country.

I became Personal Assistant to the Minister, and I loved my work. My boss met many of my friends and they all liked him. He was charming, a gentleman, and never failed to treat me with the utmost respect. I would travel with him to various institutions outside the City, where he would deliver lectures and speeches. One weekend at home on the farm, my father told me he was distressed that many of his friends were not happy I was working for a black man. Dad was upset when one of the farmers had told him accusingly, "I saw your daughter being driven around in a carload of Africans".

How was I supposed to reply? I was living two separate lives, one being my social life with my Mzungu friends, and the other my work-life which included "social-cum-business" with my African boss and acquaintances. The difference was, that my Mzungu friends only mixed with other Mzungus, whereas my boss's socialising included equal numbers of people from all races, many of whom were work-connected and hailed from Europe and America, and who were generally of a much higher class and social standing than I would ever have met otherwise.

One person who shared "both my lives" with me, was a vivacious young lady from America whose father was Dean of an American University giving scholarships to Kenya students. Meg, a few years older than me, had come to Kenya with her American husband, who was frightful. He enjoyed shocking people and embarrassing Meg, such as the time they happened to be at a rather "proper" dinner party and he was heard to comment very loudly "Yes, it was a hidden secret; you know, rather like Tampax!" He had an affair with an Afro-Kenyan lady broadcaster, though quite what she saw in him I could not fathom out. She had a miscarriage, and he put the foetus in a bottle and brought it round to show Meg, who had moved in with her Afro-Kenyan University Professor boyfriend. I spent much time with Meg; many weekends we would drive off to distant parts of the country in my little Toyota. I loved showing off my beautiful country to this kind human-being, who was to become a close friend.

Another good friend was a chirpy little nurse from Annan. She came straight from that little village in the South of Scotland to work at Kikuyu Hospital on the outskirts of Nairobi. She was upset by the huge number of wife-beating cases, the diseases and unnecessary deaths. But, most of all, Sheila was horrified by the misnamed "female circumcision". I saw my friend in tears after a circumcised mother had been brought to the hospital, refusing to let go of her dead baby that had finally exited from her body after huge struggle, leaving the mother jaggedly ripped and torn, and bleeding copiously. Sheila told me that the scarred skin was sometimes stretched so tight the women had trouble peeing, let alone giving birth.

I had never heard of female circumcision, although I knew male circumcision entailed snipping off a piece of loose unnecessary skin that covered the end of the willy. I asked Sheila how on earth it was possible to "circumcise" women, who don't have a disposable piece of skin in that region. She explained the process entailed the *chopping off of the clitoris!* Considering what "circumcision" entails when applied to men, surely it is quite the wrong word for the cruel and brutal act performed on women? Men who advocate this barbaric procedure should be made to suffer similarly by having the most sensitive part of their willies chopped off with blunt knives.

26. NON-MZUNGU FRIENDS

I had a fantastic job. I earned a good salary. I enjoyed arranging cocktail parties for the Minister, either at his rather grand Government residence, or at top hotels. Mungai was fond of my mother, and would invite her to parties at his residence; I recall mum chatting happily to Mzee Kenyatta at one of these official gatherings. At one such party, I was offered the job of Personal Assistant to a gentleman from the US, whose name I have forgotten but he had a grand title. I declined the offer, because I was quite happy where I was! Can you imagine my job description on my Business Card, "Personal Assistant to the Executive Secretary to the Lieutenant Governor of California"!

After these occasions, I was always delivered home by official transport, with the exception of the time one party ended at the New Avenue Hotel, when I was given a lift in a private car *sans* chauffeur. I was very happy and quite tipsy. Instead of delivering me straight home, this special Afro-Kenyan gentleman diverted and we ended up at his home. He put music on the record-player, and pulled me up to dance with him. He sang along to one of Harry Belafonte's songs, changing the words to "I met a little girl from Thika Town", making me laugh. Oh dear, I had never danced with an African! This was the sort of thing that happened to other people, not me! If I closed my eyes, he felt just like one of us!

And so it turned out that the second man I slept with, was *a black man*. Meg was annoyed, because she felt he had "taken advantage" of me. Had he really? The answer would have been "No" had he been exactly the same, but "White". Then I missed my next period.

I told him that I needed fifty pounds (at that time, one thousand Kenya shillings) in cash, on Saturday. He said we should have a "brown baby" and then get married and have more. I pointed out to him there was no way I could have even a white baby whilst unmarried, let alone a brown baby, Heaven Forbid! On Saturday morning he gave me an envelope containing one thousand shillings. I thanked him; he was not a Happy Chappie. Meg was waiting downstairs in my car. We set off for the Tanganyika border.

Under different circumstances, it would have been a great weekend. The drive could have been fun. Meg was fascinated with the Maasai morans; they were waving us down, all adorned with elaborate bead necklaces, their long hair plaited and thick with red mud. "Shouldn't we give him a lift?" I explained that he would stay in the car as far as we would agree to take him, only to "hitch" back in the direction he had come from! "Besides", I told her, "they really smell quite strong!" which was quite true, they did have a strong smell in those days, reputedly due to their diet of blood and milk.

Upon arrival at our destination, we popped into a small hotel for a snack, and I looked up a "Safari-operator" friend's address in the local directory. We found Rusty's house quite easily. We had to sit for a few hours, making polite conversation, until his visiting clients left. I did not contribute much to the conversation while Meg quizzed my friend about the German doctor who, according to my friend, had an excellent reputation. Rusty gave us directions. It was now nearly eight o'clock at night. We knocked on the door of the doctor's establishment; it was opened by a large frau in a head-scarf, who spoke no English. Meg was able to converse with her, and insisted we had to see the doctor. After much

110

gesticulating and pointing at watches, we were shown into the doctor's immaculate, sterile study.

"Yes, Ladies. Vat is your problem?" he enquired.

"I'm pregnant!" I blurted out.

"Yes? So. Congratulations!"

"She must have an abortion!" said my down-to-earth friend.

"Then vy haf you come here? I cannot help you!"

I had not expected resistance! "Uh....." I stammered. Without Meg, I would probably have walked out.

No-nonsense Meg butted in, "Cut the bullshit, doctor! Let's get on with it!"

"Who told you I vill do dis ting?"

"I heard from a friend who visited you a few months ago".

"Oh really? Vell, come back tomorrow, and vee vill discuss!" He drew back his chair and started to rise.

"Wait a minute!" Meg stretched out an arm and clutched his wrist. "We mean NOW!"

"It vill cost fifty pounds".

I put the money on the desk.

Then it was all "action stations" as my dad would have put it. Their efficiency was incredible. The doctor and his large assistant were extremely professional and, now all was agreed, they turned out to be very cordial. In no time, they were wearing white gowns, scarves, masks and gloves. Meg wiggled her fingers "Bye" as they wheeled me into a spotless, well-equipped operating room, with blinding overhead lights.

"Just count to ten slowly, as you go to sleep".

"What if I don't go to sleep?" Panic!

"Oh yes!" he laughed, "You will go to...."

When I awoke, birds were singing in the garden, and Meg was sitting by my side. She told me I had been rubbing my tummy and repeating over and over "Has it really gone? Has it really gone?"

The large now-smiling frau brought us croissants and a pot of coffee. She waved us off, as we left the tidy establishment at seven o'clock in the morning, before their first Sunday morning clients started turning up at the surgery.

Meg drove back, which was extremely precarious! A jackal ran across the road and I automatically looked around for its mate. Of course Meg didn't, and had to swerve dangerously, narrowly missing the second animal as it tore across the road in hot pursuit of its partner. I told her to keep her eyes on the road and not on the Maasai warriors in all their finery, their clothing consisting of nothing but thin red cloths which blew in the wind, showing glimpses of lean bodies and long, muscled legs. In spite of everything, she returned me safely to the "Hall", where she stayed for an early dinner, before leaving me to "crash out" for the night.

On Monday morning, I was in the office before eight o'clock, and the job continued as normal.

27. MEETING INTERESTING PEOPLE

I recall the morning Dr Mungai was unusually late to work when I heard the "Red Telephone" ringing in his office. I dashed through to his office, lifted the receiver, and answered "Minister's office, Good Morning!"

A deep voice barked "Where is he?"

"Bloody cheek" I thought to myself, before saying indignantly "I *beg* your pardon?"

"Where is he? Where's Mungai?"

"And may I ask who wants to know?" I queried in a stern voice.

He said his name, but I could not get it. "Would you repeat it?"

"OK, have you got a pen and paper?"

"Yes!"

"Write it down." He proceeded: "K...pause...E...pause...N..." when he reached "Y...." my knees went wobbly.

"Yes, Mr President" I whispered as I sat down with a thump, "I'll pass on your message!"

Mungai appeared shortly afterwards. I told him "The President wants you to call him".

"Aw Gee!" looking at his watch. "And I'm late!"

A few minutes later, guffaws of laughter erupted from the Minister's office. Shortly afterwards, he put his head around the door, "Miss Brown", he chuckled, "could you please spell the President's name for me?"

Mungai's daughter was studying in the States. I can still see him replacing the receiver after talking to her on the telephone, wiping his eyes with a handkerchief; "Silly girl!" he sniffed, "What's she crying for?" Mungai had studied in the States himself; he attended Stanford University. He told me the amusing story of when he was called into television studios and unsuspectingly introduced as Guest on the "This is Your Life" Programme. He said "Gee, they brought in friends and family from all over the place!" What really got to him, was when a voice came from the wings "MunGAI, MunGAI" - I can still hear him as he copied her voice - and in walked his old mother, all the way from Kenya!

I did meet some interesting people in this job. I was invited to Parliament Buildings to attend a function in honour of Dr Banda, President of Malawi. I heard Mungai's throaty laugh as I lined up in my very smart mini-skirt to shake Banda's hand. I had worn it on purpose; after all, this was the fashion at the time, even if mini-skirts were banned in Malawi.

Dr Kaunda, President of Zambia, was due to visit Kenya. My boss knew I was interested in meeting him. Kaunda was very well guarded and the reception in his honour was to be held at State House. I would not be invited. Mungai told me to go to a side-door at a given time. I drove to State House and was immediately allowed through the gate as my name was in "the Book". I was met at the side-door by a good-looking Mzungu gentleman who was in charge of Security; he was expecting me. He led me to a little office at the top of a flight of stairs. I had only been waiting a few minutes before Kaunda walked in. He sat down and chatted happily as if he had all the time in the world. Before leaving, I asked for his signature and he wrote "To Miss Brown – let us all keep smiling as we try to serve mankind – the best of luck". He laughed when I pointed out that the term was actually "The best of British luck!" I later went out for some time with the charming Mzungu who was in charge of security.

I spent one "official" lunch-time seated next to Jaramogi Oginga Odinga. It was quite hilarious, because he spent an hour trying to convince me of the virtues of socialism; he insisted that I should join the Civil Servants' Trade Union forthwith. I understand he had carried on his "further studies" in China.

A special person who became a friend, was Tom Mboya. A great man, with a wonderful sense of humour. I recall a day in Parliament when a certain MP stood up to respond to a statement from Mboya. The MP stuttered in broken English "Would the Ho-Ho-Ho-rable Minister please clarify...." whereupon Tom jumped to his feet "On point of order, Mr Speaker", he announced "I am not a horrible Minister!" This brought the House down!

The last time I ever spoke with Tom Mboya, was unexpectedly en route to spending a weekend with the family in Thika. As I was approaching the Blue Posts Hotel, a car that had been following me started to overtake, and drove alongside me. Tom was in the passenger seat; he rolled down the window and pointed to the Hotel, mouthing the words "Blue Posts". I gave the thumbs-up "OK!" We had a couple of drinks at the Blue Posts, before proceeding on our different routes. Not long after that, *Tom was murdered* on my sister's Birthday. I was in the line at Parliament Buildings, to sign the Condolence Book. I can still see the face of the obnoxious person at the door as he hissed at me, actually *spitting* as he told me, with contorted features, that I should not be there: "This book is for *dignitaries* to sign". Simply being a friend, I was not good enough to sign The Book, so I left. Did those dignitaries care as much as I did? So long Tom, True Statesman, rafiki. What a tragic, tragic waste.

28. A RESPECTABLE BOSS

I was to discover that my father had been busy looking for a more "dignified" job for me. Mum telephoned to say an interview had been arranged with somebody that I shall call Mr Browne, a highly-respected Mzungu gentleman, who was Chief Executive Officer of a body representing a section of mainly white farmers throughout the country. I was offered the position of Secretary. I accepted. Now I had a respectable job, meaning poor old dad was no longer ashamed to tell people where his daughter was employed. Phew!

Mr Browne was a rather pompous, married man, with four children and an extremely irritating habit of smoothing then twirling the ends of his long moustache with licked fingers. He was well-read, a great story-teller, with a morbid sense of humour. There was no evening work attached to this position, and I was free from four-thirty most evenings. When I was not with my Colonial Mzungu friends, I frequently met up with Meg and her boyfriend, also Sheila my nurse-friend, who was soon to return home to Scotland.

Mwangi, my author friend from three years previously, had recently had a new book published. One day, out of the blue, he walked into my office to bring a copy of his publication to Paul Gitata, our Public Relations Officer. I introduced Mwangi to Mr Browne, and they hit it off from the start. Mr Browne invited Mwangi back for further discussions on books and the world in general.

One day, Mr Browne had a visit from a farmer, with the intention of discussing an apparent security leak involving one of the Trade Union outfits. As Mr Browne related to me afterwards, the farmer had quizzed my employer as to how on earth he could be concerned about security leaks, when he had *me* working in his office. "That girl in your office: she consorts with undesirables!" My very indignant reaction to the term "consorts with undesirables" convinced Mr Browne that, just because I had African friends – such as Mwangi – it did not mean I was passing on Company secrets! In fact, he insisted I accompany him to a farmers' meeting at Thika Sports Club, with the intention of "showing face", and letting the white farmers know he was not ashamed of me. Very staunch in his support of me, Mr Browne introduced me to the congregation of White Farmers. My dad was at the meeting. I took the Minutes and all went off without a hitch.

He must indeed have felt sympathy for me because, on the way back to Nairobi, my respectable boss reached along the back of the seat and quite unexpectedly put his arm around my shoulders and drew me towards him. I sat rock still, thinking "Oh my God, no! Oh my God, no!" This man had supported me and I did not want to make an enemy of him. When he pulled me closer, I admonished him, "Mr Browne! You're happily married! What would your wife say?" He told me that his wife had accused him of sleeping with me "anyway", which made me feel absolutely awful! I could not understand why he found it necessary to mention it to me.

In fact, I wondered about many of the things he found "necessary" to mention to me. Such as the time he had been called out to shoot a puppy because two young African children had hammered nails into its eyes. When describing the horror story to me, he mimicked the puppy, opening and closing his mouth soundlessly and feebly flapping his arms. What was the point in telling me this shocking tale, which still creeps back into my mind, fifty years down the line.

In spite of all his idiosyncrasies, I became quite fond of this person, and had tremendous respect for his intellect. He had a great influence on my life. I have no idea where he is now, but would like to meet up with him again, now that I am much older though no wiser! Mr Browne, whom I never, ever called by his Christian name, was very good to me in so many ways. He insisted, quite rightly, that I should get out of the accommodation I was in, to share a house with others of my age; I should go swimming during my lunch-hour and return to the office "with my hair dripping wet". He pointed out an advertisement in the East African Standard, seeking single girls to share a house.

At lunchtime he drove me to the address, 69 Bernard Road, himself. We were met at the door by an attractive girl called Audrey, with long honey-coloured hair that she could sit on, and an open, friendly face. She gave us a tour of the house, and showed me what was to become "my room" for the next couple of very happy years. This was a really good move. I joined Parklands Sports Club; I did go swimming every lunchtime and returned to the office with my hair dripping wet, and I played hockey or tennis almost every evening.

29. COLONIAL MISFIT

We had a great social life. We had parties at the house, which was known by the local Colonial males as "The Virgins' Retreat"! Being a group of single girls, we were frequently invited *en masse* to various parties. We did have some problems of course, such as the night we were woken up because some prankster had called the Fire Department to report a fire at our house, meaning we had to apologetically turn away three very angry fire-engine drivers. Once we were threatened with fines for having City Council bus-stops lying in the garden on a Sunday morning!

I had not been at Bernard Road for very long, when I was invited to the 21st Birthday Party of a very pleasant Mzungu girlfriend. As always, it was an all-white party. Many of the guests were "Japies", Afrikaner-type whites, and I was extremely uncomfortable with the racist jokes being bandied around at the party. Fancy, this type of conversation was still going on in our Independent country! After dinner, we all left for a night-club. Mwangi, whom I had not seen for a couple of months, brought his wife over to greet me in the car-park. One of our group murmured in my ear in a guttural accent "Christ! I didn't know you were a nigger-lover!" I was surrounded by the racist party-goers, all waiting for my reaction. I did not dare to acknowledge my friend. I did one of the singularly most awful things I have ever done in the whole of my life: I pretended not to know Mwangi. He backed away, hurt.

I'm so sorry, Mwangi. How I prayed for the day when this particular, die-hard type of Afrikaner would leave our country forever. To this day, I turn hot and sweaty with shame, whenever I recall this incident, when

I dropped my friend dead. What a different Kenya it was when, a few years later, I bumped into Mwangi again and sat next to him at a bar, chatting freely. He was big enough to have understood; he had forgiven me. What an extra-special guy.

I went out for a while with a young man who hailed from Seychelles. Reg was such a nice guy but the relationship was just too difficult to sustain. We used to meet up for a couple of drinks in small hotels in the Parklands or South C areas of Nairobi.

One night we went to watch a movie at the Thika Road Drive-in; a carload of white Kenyans was in the entrance queue behind us. They followed us closely until we stopped and set up the speaker on the driver's window, then they swerved in an arc and drove towards the front passenger door, where I was sitting. They stopped a few feet from my door, at a ninety-degree angle to us, shining the headlights directly onto us. We could hear their derisive laughter and chants while they sat for what seemed like an eternity, lighting us up in their headlights. I sat with my hand shielding my eyes from the glare; I plainly recall Reg's face in the bright headlights, as he sat with wide eyes, staring straight at the lights, not moving or talking.

My parents threw a wonderful Cheese and Wine Party at Bernard Road, for my twenty-first Birthday. All the guests were Mzungus. Mum and dad spent the night at the Grosvenor Hotel and left the Party after midnight. I have a treasured photograph of my father at this Party, his arm flung nonchalantly around my shoulders, and both of us laughing. This was the day I decided to grow my hair longer.

My Twenty-First

"his arm flung nonchalantly
around my shoulders"

With Mum & Dad

30. GETTING TO KNOW MY HUSBAND-TO-BE

My boyfriend at the time, Chris, was a Safari Operator. Some years previously, he had returned *"home"* to UK to live. When I asked why he had come back to Kenya, Chris explained he had been travelling on a bus in London, when he spotted a Travel Agency with a poster depicting a thorn tree in the sunset. That was it: he hopped off the bus, went into the Travel Agency and booked his ticket back to Kenya!

I still loved showing off my little Toyota 700. Chris let me drive us in my car to the coast for a brief holiday at Tiwi. Chris used to joke that, flat-out downhill with a tail-wind, it reached sixty-miles-per-hour! Two months after my 21st Birthday, Chris wanted to show me Lake Magadi. I really wanted to see that area of Kenya, and asked again if we could go in my speedy Toyota! It was a great day, driving across the soda lake before heading off to the Ewaso Ngiro River for a swim. I discovered a few days later that the soda had caused the engine of my poor little car to very nearly cease up. I drove the juddering shuddering car to a petrol station on Sadler Street that was managed by a good friend, Derek Gates. He promised to have my car thoroughly cleaned up in a nearby workshop "of good repute".

At lunchtime the following day I was on my way to Parklands swimming-pool, when my recently "cleaned-up" car broke down. From a service station I telephoned Derek in frustration, and he promised to send a mechanic immediately. Within a short time, a huge Daimler-Benz turned up. With top shirt button undone and loosely-knotted tie nonchalantly tucked into his shirt above the third button, a Mzungu man leapt out of the limousine and enquired, "Got a problem?"

"Cheeky bugger", I thought. "It's OK, thanks" I replied, elbow on roof of car with chin in hand, totally fed-up. "The garage is sending a mechanic".

"That's me!"

John Stanley.

While fixing whatever was wrong with my car, John noticed the radio was not working. He asked me to bring the car to his workshop sometime and he would repair the radio. This I did, and he found something else needed fixing; and so it went on. He was partner in Kenya's Jaguar Agency, "Campbell, Schwartzel & Walker". One of his partners was his cousin, and the other was later to become known as the photographer who visited Diane Fossey in "Gorillas in the Mist". At the time I met John, he told me the amazing lady who could be seen speeding around the streets of Nairobi on a Harley-Davidson motorbike with drop handlebars, hair flying in the wind and bottom in the air, was the wife of his photographer-partner!

John was twelve years my senior, polite and charming. He invited me out. John had a Kiwi accent: he told me he had been married twice, the second time in Kenya, and his wife had wanted to go "home" to New Zealand. Whilst in New Zealand, he had changed his name by Deed Poll from Schwartzel to Stanley. He said that he had separated from his wife and had a girlfriend called Shirley with whom he travelled from "top to bottom of both the North and South Islands" of New Zealand. He returned to Kenya, leaving behind his girlfriend, his wife and his three-year-old daughter. He carried in his wallet, a photo of the dear little, smiling, blond haired-girl.

After a month or so of dating John every now and then, he asked me not to go out with anybody else but him. I looked at him in utter disbelief! This was madness! I was twenty-one years old, sharing a house with five other girls, and having the time of my life! However, I agreed to "try it" for a while. I was worried sick in case another "boyfriend" should turn up when John was around; he was very possessive and would be quite rude to them. Mother was most upset. She thought I should have loads of boyfriends, and should not be serious about any of them for at least another ten years or so!

I was offered a really high-salaried position with the United Nations in Brazzaville. I went so far as to take an advanced French Course with *Alliance Francaise*, to brush up on my Schoolgirl French. Both John and Mr Browne pointed out that Brazzaville was just across the river from the site where the public hangings took place in Kinshasa; they said it would be madness for me to go. My folks, who visited Nairobi about once a month, on their "monthly shopping expedition", made a special trip to Nairobi with the sole aim of persuading me to go to Brazzaville, so serious were they about ending my relationship with John. The next morning I drove to work with the intention of telling Mr Browne that I would shortly be departing for the jungles of Deepest Africa.

He greeted me with the question, "Have you made up your mind?"

"Yes" I replied, confidently.

"All right. Now you can read my views on the subject". He handed me a letter listing all the reasons why I would be crazy to go to Brazzaville. The result was that I did not go. Purely because of Mr Browne's letter.

After "trying it" for over six months, John and I were still an "item". Though I admit to being terribly upset to discover quite by accident that, after all this time, he was still in constant touch with Shirley, the girlfriend he left behind in New Zealand.

John had really special relatives in Kenya, and he spent his time living variously between cousins and sisters. I came to know his parents well and liked them a lot; his mother enlarged upon her comment that he was a "bad boy" by telling me that he had not informed them of his first marriage – they learned of it when a Petition for a Divorce arrived in the post! They were living in UK at the time and "young girls were always knocking on the door and asking for John": his mother guessed it must have been one of these girls he had secretly married!

John's two sisters were just the best; they were as different as chalk and cheese! Oddly, both were married to Aircraft Engineers, one from Switzerland and the other from Australia. I became close to the younger sister, June. She was a gentle soul, with an adorable daughter, Karen, who was often left in my care and whom I almost looked upon as my own child. Apart from his cousin Peter, who was a partner in the Jaguar Agency, John had one other cousin in Nairobi. She was a warm, friendly lady, married to a wonderful Policeman who was a dog-trainer from South Africa. Both cousins eventually moved to South Africa with their families. John's cousin Peter was married to Jackie, a super lady, sister of Alan Root who we used to visit with his wife Joan, at their home in Naivasha. I remember visiting Alan in hospital when he lost a finger with compliments of a fang, when he was milking a puff-adder. I am proud to say I am related to Alan Root, because I was once married to his sister's husband's cousin...

At John's insistence, I had left the Virgin's Retreat and rented a flat on Riverside Drive. We held great parties

125

there, being on the top floor with a vast balcony. We installed a ladder from the balcony to the flat-topped roof; luckily no revellers fell off! The roof was wonderful for nude sun-bathing as there was no way anybody could see me! That is, until the day my rally-driver rafiki Gerry Davies, phoned me "Were you by any chance sun-bathing on the roof today?"

"Yes I was" I replied, puzzled. "Why?"

Gerry laughed "I just received a call from a pilot friend.....!"

My sister Linda, meanwhile, was boarding at the no-longer-European girls' secondary school that I had hated so much. She was very unhappy and I could not bear to see her that way. I would visit her, park the car around a hidden corner; Linda would jump in and hide under the dashboard while I drove her out through the school gates for a few hours of freedom and fun. Luckily we were never caught, in those days it would have been a real sin and she would most likely have been expelled. Linda did become much happier after I introduced her to my ex-Minister-Boss's daughter, who became her best friend. I am delighted this lady remains, to this day, one of Linda's closest friends.

I booked Linda into Delamere Girls Day School, a ten-minute walk from the flat. I did not tell my parents until it was a *faite accompli*. I loved having Linda living with me. After leaving school, she took a Secretarial Course then continued to live with me while she worked in the City. We were very close telepathically; one morning whilst slicing through a frozen packet of butter with a carving knife (of course!) the knife cut straight through the butter and my finger, stopping at the bone. Linda came rushing through to the kitchen calling out "What have you done?" I hadn't uttered a sound as I looked down, horrified, at my exposed bone. I rushed down to Gerry's flat, where she burnt a piece of cotton wool and applied it to my finger. I had a few stitches...I still have that scar.

Of course, living in a flat, we were not able to have a pet dog. On a cold Saturday evening, John arrived with a tiny object wriggling in his pocket. He pulled out a completely black, very fluffy, teeny-weeny kitten. She easily fitted on the palm of my hand. My kitten purred and settled into a tiny ball on the *pouffe* in front of the electric fire. "Isn't she a little Tuppence?" laughed John. We named her "Tuppy" for short.

Wearing a little red collar, Tuppy would sit on my shoulder in Supermarket aisles, looking down her nose at remarks of "Good Heavens! Look at that CAT!" She would come to the Drive-In cinema with us. She would come to the farm at Thika for weekends. We never went to the coast without Tuppy, whether we were travelling by road or by steam-train. She loved the beach.

"Tuppence" in her
favourite position
←

And swinging on a
weekend visit to the
coffee farm ———>

Tuppy at the Outspan
Hotel, on a weekend
at Nyeri

Tuppy on the lunatic Express, en route to the
Coast

My parents remained adamantly against my association with John. He was "too-much-older" than me; too worldly-wise – meaning he had been married previously. Heaven forbid that they should ever find out that he was *still married*, or that he had been *married twice*. Mum said they were worried I might "drift into a marriage relationship" with him. I should remain a virgin until married.

Unfortunately John suffered from the Jekyll and Hyde complex. He could be extremely nasty when he drank spirits, and yet he could drink beer all night and remain pleasant. He should have stuck to beer, like any Wild Colonial Boy. Every Friday evening, I would check with John whether he would be turning up for lunch the following day, Saturday being a half-day. He would always confirm he would come for lunch "straight after work". He probably meant it at the time. Silly me, I always believed that "this week would be different". I always had a meal ready for one O'clock. He never, ever, made it before three O'clock, when he would, without fail, arrive drunk from "a workshop drink" with his "Kalasingha" (Sikh) friends. Invariably, Saturday afternoons ended up in a terrible row, with John bounding down the fire-escape, leaping into his car, and driving out in clouds of dust. On one such occasion I threw his Spaghetti Bolognese out of the kitchen window, narrowly missing his head as he opened the car door.

I threw it together with the saucepan.

He glared up at me with bloodshot eyes, slurring, "Well, that'sh IT!" Quite what "it" was, I never found out because, as per normal, he arrived on Sunday morning, fresh and breezy as if nothing had happened. He would be so nice on Sundays that I dared not spoil the atmosphere by referring to the previous day's episode!

One Saturday John and I, together with my friend Anne-Marie who was visiting from France, were invited to a birthday celebration for Kugi, John's extra-special Kalasingha friend, at the "Brilliant Hotel", which was renowned for its yummy curries. There were a dozen of us. The waiter took our orders for drinks and we sat around the table drinking and chatting, anticipating the extra-special curry that was being wheeled to our table on a large trolley. A young Mzungu man stood at the counter drinking a beer while waiting for his "take-away" curry. Two casually dressed African gentlemen walked into the restaurant, glancing around before striding over to the bar and ordering beers.

The barman looked most uneasy. He recognised them as plain-clothes policemen. Unbeknown to us, the restaurant licence only permitted the sale of alcohol until two o'clock in the afternoon. It was now a few minutes past two. If he were to serve them, they could arrest them.

"Sorry, but I cannot!" he stammered, in a dilemma.

"Then why are all these people drinking?" roared one of the respected upholders of the Law. The two cops rushed to our table and overturned the food trolley, sending dishes of curry, rice and chapattis slithering and smashing across the floor. They collected the bottles of beer, Guinness and Chivas Regal Royal Salute from our table, carefully decanting the remnants from glasses and half-empty bottles so they could carry away full bottles without missing a drop. They ordered everybody from the restaurant to proceed downstairs to the prison van that was conveniently waiting outside in the car-park.

The poor chap waiting for his "take-away" was herded into the van to the open-mouthed astonishment of his wife and two little kids who were sitting patiently in his car waiting for their take-away lunch.

131

At Eastleigh Police Station we were ordered to remove our shoes and put them into a large revoltingly smelly trunk that was brimming with filthy shoes. John and the other men were thrown into a cell already containing at least a dozen male petty criminals, whilst Anne-Marie and I shared a cell with two prostitutes, who told us they had been locked up the night before, for refusing to give free services to the Officer on patrol.

Billy, cousin of the Birthday Boy, had avoided arrest having been in the gents' loo when we were all driven away. He now stood on a bank outside the tiny cell windows, laughing like a hyena. I climbed onto Anne-Marie's shoulders and yelled my lawyer-friend's name to him through the rusty bars. By this time, Billy was doubled over in fits of laughter. However, when I managed to convey to him that we would be in for the weekend if my lawyer did not turn up before six o'clock, he took off. My lawyer "Mac" Makhecha arrived at five minutes to six. We were all released on bond and instructed to attend Court at eight o'clock on Monday morning. It escaped the notice of the police that everyone in the men's cell plus the two prostitutes left with us!

The restaurateur invited us all back for a free curry dinner. John and I were supposed to be spending the night out at the farm at Thika, but it was already too late for that. From the restaurant, I called home. My sister answered the phone.

"Please tell mum and dad we're really sorry we can't make it". I explained "We were arrested and have spent the afternoon in the prison cell!"

Linda's concerned response? "But you *have* to come. Mummy's cooked roast pork!"

In Court on Monday we were fined a token five shillings each for the offence of "consuming alcohol after hours". However the barman was let off Scot-free because, as Mac put it "My Lud, it would appear that the Police have drunk all the evidence!" Thoroughly enjoying himself, Mac did not charge us for his services.

On Tuesday morning, I was inundated with phone-calls from delighted friends, who had read all about our imprisonment in the local Press.

Life continued. I took up an administrative position with the United Nations. I was happy in my eight years working for the UN, particularly so when I was transferred to a section of the World Health Organisation that was situated in wooden offices in Nairobi's industrial area. The whole team was very friendly. The overall boss, Gunnar, was from Sweden: certainly one of the most exceptional people I have been lucky enough to know; together with his wife Brenda, they are still good friends. Gunnar's team of experts was comprised of two from UK, who are my children's Godfathers, one a true gentleman from Afghanistan; one an absolute character from New Zealand: Bruce, who found it impossible to act "serious" and always had the rest of us in stitches.

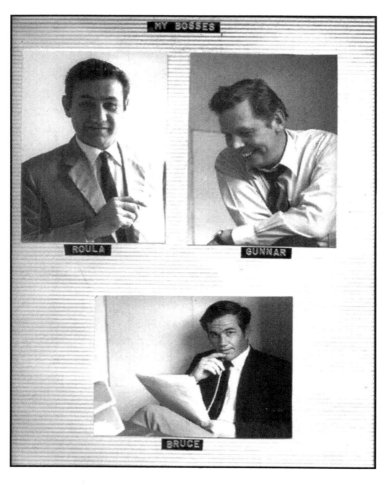

MY BOSSES

ROULA

GUNNAR

BRUCE

Brenda and Gunnar, also Bruce, frequently played tennis at the Impala Club. I have never witnessed another person who could play tennis the way this Kiwi person did! Bruce was absolutely infuriating to play against. He never hit a ball hard. Every single shot was precisely calculated. Without appearing to move – in fact his movements always appeared rather awkward, due to serious back problems – he would reach a ball landing at any far corner of the court. He would return shots coming at him like bullets, somehow either returning them so they soared in slow motion up towards the heavens to land far behind his opponent, or by landing gentle drop-shots that skimmed the net by millimetres. If his panting opponent was lucky enough to reach the ball and then stupidly wait for it to bounce, the blinking ball would spin off at a crazy angle, impossible to return. What a talent!

My family, together with John, still spent our annual holidays, all together, at the beach. John would sleep under a mosquito net on the verandah, while I shared a room with Linda. In 1968, a plot on our favourite beach, Tiwi, came up for sale, for the grand price of three thousand pounds. Mum and dad borrowed one thousand pounds from Standard Bank, another thousand from close friends and, amazingly, I was able to come up with the balance! Now we had our own "place at the coast"!

Looking at the Ocean →

Next to the Ocean

Halfway to the Ocean

Beach Holidays

After having John around for over two years, my parents were beginning to accept him, meaning they wanted us to start thinking about marriage. There was no way I could co-habit with a man I was not married to. I contacted a lawyer, who instigated proceedings for John to divorce his second wife. Nearly another year later, I was making plans for my Wedding. My parents had only just managed to repay the bank and their friends, for the money borrowed to purchase the coast property. Having insisted that John and I should marry, they now found themselves in a dilemma because they could not afford the expense of a Wedding! Eventually, they spent fifteen pounds on a beautiful, three-tiered Wedding cake, made by Bunty Owen.

I wanted an "Autumn-coloured" Wedding. I wore ivory silk. My Bridesmaids were dressed in copper satin and the flower-girl, John's adorable little niece Karen, wore gold. Her posy of flowers was quite large and, when she misplaced the posy after putting it down on a chair, she ran around in a panic asking everyone "Where are my trees? Where are my trees?" All flower arrangements followed the same colour theme: copper chrysanthemums, with a variety of other blooms in creams and rust-colours. I so enjoyed the planning and arranging. It wasn't until I was halfway down the aisle on dad's arm that I asked myself "Wendy! What the *hell* are you doing here?"

We held the Reception at the Golf Range.

A beautiful, three-tiered Wedding cake

31. GETTING TO KNOW MY HUSBAND

After a further two years in the little flat on Riverside, we decided we should purchase a house. In those days, Mortgages from South African Mutual were very easy to come by and, with John and I both working, repayments were simple. After work and in the evenings, I would go house-hunting. I found a dear little house on Hatheru Road, Bernard Estate, not far from the Virgin's Retreat. Over the next six years, we were to expand the house to twice its original size. I suggested to mum and dad they apply for a mortgage to purchase a house right next to ours that was up for sale, with little guesthouse attached. They did. Linda moved into the guesthouse.

I was always a tennis fanatic and, now being a member of the Impala Club which was not far from our home, played tennis a minimum of two times a week. Outside work, when I was not playing tennis, I was busy making our home beautiful. We had three telephones, a red one to match the red-green-black decor of the living-room; a dark blue telephone to blend in with the curtains in the dining-room; and a yellow telephone on an extending arm, to match the yellow-orange-white curtains in the master bedroom. The en-suite bathroom to the master bedroom had pink, red and white curtains: and pink toilet paper! There was always blue toilet-paper in the guest loo which had blue and white curtains.

Marriage suited me fine, although the person I was married to was sometimes a bit of a problem. A discerning lady described "nagging" as something the male gender always blamed on women whereas, in fact, men "nag by their actions"! For instance, John chain-smoked. He would wake each morning with a coughing fit; this was the signal to reach for his cigarettes. His trembling fingers would drag a cigarette out of the packet while he tried in vain to stifle the rasping sounds which would keep bursting through his closed lips in splats and splutters. In his haste to strike a match, it was normal procedure to drop the matchbox, spewing its contents across the floor. Then the cigarette would fall from his mouth as he was hit by a further paroxysm of coughing. Swearing and blasting, my naked husband would crawl around the floor until he managed to light a cigarette, invariably setting light to the filtered end, to the accompaniment of more unrepeatable language. As soon as the killer weed was glowing to his satisfaction, John would lean back blissfully whilst drawing an incredibly l-o-n-g injection of smoke into his poor abused lungs. His eyes would be closed in sheer ecstasy, while he filled the bedroom with the stench of long-drop loos.

Then, all of a sudden, I would nearly drop the cups of tea I was carrying in, as a wracking cough started up from the depths of his chest. With a look akin to terror in his eyes, his arms would shoot straight out in front, with hands clenching and unclenching as if groping for air. He would spit the offending article out of his mouth as he choked and wheezed with his body doubled over in agony. As his face turned puce and his scarlet eyes poked out of their sockets, it would sometimes be such an age before he was able to draw a breath that many a time I thought he would choke to death. This performance would be repeated a number of times until he settled down to a more manageable level of wheezing and coughing.

After so many years, I had given up expecting my husband to come home in time for lunch on Saturdays. I simply kept his food in the oven until he staggered in, poured himself another drink to prove to me he wasn't

140

already drunk, put the telly on, and plonked himself down in an armchair.

Many was the time I would wake in the night and there was no sign of John. I would go through to the lounge, switch on lights, to find him sitting in an armchair with a tumbler of whisky beside him and a rifle across his lap. He would slur that he had "heard a sound outside". Sometimes on a moonlit night, I would find him peeping out of a window from behind a curtain, his rifle perched on the sill, presumably hoping an intruder would come into the garden.

I did love John quite a lot, as one would love an older brother, and I did look after him as well as I could. A big plus for John was that he was very popular with men, as well as with women. I must have inherited my intolerance from my father, who didn't have any infuriating traits. I didn't think I had annoying habits until my mother commented about forty years ago that I made loud noises when crunching celery; since then, I have avoided eating celery in company.

At this time, I planned a trip to Paraa Safari Lodge in Uganda, to celebrate Linda's twenty-first birthday. Together with Brenda and Gunnar, John and I chartered a small Cessna Aircraft for the trip, which was piloted by our friend David Robinson. We had a wonderful few days travelling by boat up the river to the foot of the incredible Murchison Falls, a waterfall on the White Nile River, where the Nile forces its way through a seven metre wide gap in the rocks, before crashing down forty-three metres. John was initially brought up in Entebbe: he told us his dad had built the first bridge over the Falls when he was the Chief Government Architect in Uganda. The river was teeming with crocodiles and hippos. Along the river banks we spotted elephants drinking and mud-sliding, crocs and hippos basking and a variety of antelopes including the Uganda Kob. At the Lodge itself, I took photographs of the staff chasing elephants away from the dustbins! Linda thoroughly enjoyed her birthday.

To make a marriage perfect, every couple had to have children. I wanted a baby before I turned thirty and, in fact, I decided that 10 March would be the right date to have a baby, because that would fit in precisely with my tennis schedule, and the maternity leave would coincide with my annual leave, giving me a few months off work at the right time. I stopped taking The Pill on 1 July, carefully working out exactly nine months from that date.

Meanwhile, Linda had bravely decided she would sell her car and buy a ticket on an ocean liner to South Africa. This, she did. And it is quite likely one of the most sensible things my sister has ever done.

32. PROBLEM WITH MOTHER

As did all of their family and friends, I truly believed my parents' marriage was The Perfect Marriage; *one that proved marriage was made to last until Death Did Them Part*. Dad loved my mother, who fitted in precisely with his strict rules and ideals. My mother never complained about her lot in life. I thought she loved my father.

I *knew* she did, once.

Sure, my father never helped with the housework; but men weren't supposed to, were they? He couldn't cook; but they weren't supposed to do that, either, were they? However, as I already said, nobody made a better cup of tea than my dad. Over a period of many years, Linda and I used to sing out from our beds in the mornings, a very tuneful "Daddeee, we love tea-eee. Can we have a cup-of-tea-eee, pleeeze, daddeee?"

My sister was in South Africa, dad was on the farm, and I suppose I was too busy being pregnant to grasp what mother was up to. After Linda left for distant places, mum decided that the cottages on the beach plot required renovation. I realised she was spending more and more time at the Coast, leaving dad alone on the farm.

When mother was on one of her "Coast trips", I bumped into a family acquaintance at Kasuku's Mini-Market, Valley Arcade. She looked at me sideways and made the snide comment "I saw your mother dancing at Mombasa Club last week. She was having a *whale* of a time with some fellow!" This remark upset me tremendously. My mother did not have the implied "whale of a time", without my father, anywhere!

Dad was totally bewildered at mum's frequent absences. In my naivety, I was convinced her temporary insanity was due to the fact that she was going through the menopause which was simply the lack of certain hormones and over-supply of others. I explained this to dad as well as I could, although finding it extremely awkward, as we had never, ever, had such a private and personal discussion. I expressed the hope I might be able to convince her to see a doctor about regulating her input and output of hormones, after which she would be back to normal again: hopefully before my sister was to return home to Kenya. Writing to Linda, I never mentioned the Problem With Mother.

My mother began talking to me in a way she had never done before. It was as if she had dropped back to my age. I was no longer her daughter, but her confidante. There were very few girlfriends I would have such discussions with, let alone my *mother!* She told me she was having an affair with a man a couple of years my junior; she described how this was "so good for one's ego!" In my mind, recognising it was all due to a hormonal imbalance, I swallowed, took many deep breaths, and decided to go along with it until she recovered and regained her sanity. I once ventured to say "Well, I suppose it's good you have found someone who appreciates you!" This was a totally asinine comment to make, because mum took it to mean her philandering was absolutely fine with me, yippee.

Mother visited us in Nairobi. When I insisted she visit her home and her husband, mother asked me to accompany her to the farm. After dad retired that night, mum and I stayed up late, talking. I suggested she make an appointment with our family doctor, to sort out her hormones, pronto. She insisted she was "absolutely normal". Thus ensued what was to become the first of many, many arguments.

"If dad is so unbearable, why did you stick it out with him for so many years?"

"I only stayed with him for the sake of you girls!"

"What a dreadful thing to put on our shoulders!" I exploded. "If you wanted to leave dad, you should have done it years ago, when he was young and fit enough to find somebody else. Now what will he do?"

33. MY CHEATING HUSBAND

All the same, I was very grateful mum was there for the birth of my beautiful little girl. The doctor arrived late, terribly apologetic for not having arrived in time for the birth: actually this was just fine because nobody missed him. After a completely painless labour due to my undeviating adherence to Irna Wright's "Natural Childbirth", the midwife gave me a tiny cut, and Jeni shot out with such speed and determination I was sure she had missed the bed entirely and would hit the opposite wall. Luckily the midwife caught her! My daughter came into the world in the manner in which she was to continue. She has never lost her drive and indomitability since the moment of birth; she is irrepressible.

Jeni arrived on 15 March, therefore I was only five days' out with my planning. Although Linda was aware my baby was not supposedly due until the following week, she somehow "knew" I was in labour, as evidenced by the letter she wrote to mum and dad at the very time I was taken to hospital.

John must have been very pleased with the birth of his little daughter. On 16 March he celebrated her birth in great style at Impala Sports Club. In hospital, I was busy writing letters to friends and family world-wide, telling them about the birth of our adorable baby, and how happy we were. When John visited me in hospital two evenings after Jeni's birth, I noticed he was somewhat distracted. He continually walked to the mirror and proceeded to smooth his hair and moustache, turning this way and that to check on his appearance. This was most unusual behaviour for John. When I jokingly questioned whom he was meeting, he became quite unpleasant and left immediately. I did not see him the following day.

Luckily mum was there to drive Jeni and I home from the hospital. All the way home, I was looking out through the rear window, telling mum "Careful, there's somebody overtaking!" Or "Look out, this fellow's driving really fast!" Mum just smiled at my concern for my perfect little baby. "Yes Dear, I can see him!" Mum stayed a couple of days with us, before taking off for the Coast again; it was good she was there because John was suddenly working long hours and coming home late. When our daughter was two weeks' old, I decided the time had come to talk. He was startled to see me sitting waiting in the lounge when he walked through the door that night. When he had poured a drink and sat down, I enquired directly "Who is she?"

"Who?"

"The woman you're seeing."

"I don't know what you're talking about!"

Realising I was not going to let it rest, he finally admitted her name was Lynda. Lynda Laika. She was American, working for an Aid Project in Kenya. He had met her at Impala Club, at the celebration party for his daughter's birth. He was really upset and confused. He needed my help, because he loved both of us and he had to choose between her and me!

I tried to bring him back to the Real World by reminding him "This Lynda is a complete newcomer on the scene; you barely know her! You already *have* me, and we have a beautiful little daughter!"

"Yes" with a long sigh and confused shake of his head. "But Lynda has just been through an awful marriage, to a dreadful German guy!"

"Oh poor Lynda!" said I. "You have to be joking!"

John moved into the spare room. Oh heck! Now what was I to do? This was the kind of situation one reads

148

about in novels. I went over the pros and cons. John said he loved "both of us"; I had just mailed letters to everybody on earth, informing them about the birth of our daughter, and telling them how happy we both were. Must I now write to them saying "Actually, I got it wrong; John wasn't happy after all. He has left me!" I couldn't do that.

I decided to hang in there. This was not an easy decision. The only soul I mentioned John's affair to, was Gunnar, my extra-special boss. With my husband sleeping in the spare room, I found I spent a lot of time crying. When visitors came to congratulate me on the birth of our baby, I would feel the tears starting each time I left the room, even to go to the loo.

John had told me the general area where Lynda lived. One evening, I drove around until I saw where his car was parked, outside a block of flats at "Adam's Arcade", then I drove back home. Shortly afterwards, John's work took him away to Kisumu for a few days. I drove to the dreaded apartments and went around knocking on each door until I found Lynda. She was nice-looking, with long dark hair and a wistful smile. I persuaded her to accompany me to our house for a "chat". I took her to our perfect home with the colour-coordinated telephones and matching toilet paper, and introduced her to our beautiful baby. I poured each of us a drink and we sat down in our matching armchairs with the toning cushions.

I enquired, "What exactly are your intentions with John?"

"I want to marry him!"

"Aaah!" Pause. "He's already married."

"Yes...." she sighed forlornly. She had an annoying habit of leaving sentences hanging in the air. She sighed again. After a while I drove her back to her flat. "Please ask him to call me when he gets back."

John returned from Kisumu that evening. As he walked through the door, he noticed the extra used glass on the shelf. "Who was here?" Obviously he had come directly home, otherwise he would have known.

"Lynda" I replied.

"Ooooof!" He collapsed into a chair. "What happened?"

"She wants you to call her."

John obviously did not call Lynda, because she phoned me a couple of days later, very upset, asking me why she had neither seen nor heard from him. I reminded her, very politely, that it was his wife she was speaking to! I did not inform her he had moved back into our bedroom, but I did tell her I was making an effort to sort our marriage out. A couple of weeks later, I received a really nice letter from Lynda, written as she was about to fly back to the States. She apologised for all the upset she had caused and said "John would be crazy" to think of leaving me. If only John had not disposed of her letter, I would scan and print it here! Sure, John had moved back into our bedroom. I stayed with him through the birth of our adorable son twenty-eight months later, and for a further three years after that. But I never, ever, trusted him again.

Eighteen years later on a visit to England, together with my children Jeni and Andrew, plus a person I shall call Hans, I was delighted to meet up with John's extra-special first daughter.

Yet a further thirty years down the line, we were to learn John had done much the same to his second wife upon the birth of his first beautiful little daughter, as he did to me. Knowing what I now do about the man I married, I often wonder just how many siblings my children may have, dotted around the globe!

It appears John had suddenly and silently left New Zealand. His wife had called at the office of the Company he worked for, only to be told he had flown back to Kenya, without repaying any of the money he owed her. Neither his wife nor daughter ever heard from him again. Disgusting. Thanks to Facebook, Jeni, Andrew and I are still in constant touch with John's first lovely daughter and, also, with his equally-lovely ex-wife; she is amazing and I shall never be able to understand how he could have "dumped" the two of them in such a despicable manner. If only I had known the truth about John, from the beginning. I have to say, the very first time I met his parents, his mother immediately warned me that "John is a very bad boy!" At that time, I was astonished his mother could speak of her son in that way!

34. MOTHER'S INSANITY PERSISTS

It transpired mum had successfully applied for the position of managing a private Club at Nyali, on the North Coast. She took off for the salty blue ocean, white beaches, and the hot sun and excitement of the Coast. After twenty-nine years of marriage, she simply upp-ed and off-ed. Just like that.

In dad's car.

Mum left her "important" files for me to deal with, dad never having written a letter nor dealt with any correspondence in his life. That is, unless you include the telegram he sent to mum enquiring who I was, when I was born.

At the time Mum took off, dad was in Nairobi Hospital, recovering from a spinal operation. He had a trapped nerve, requiring the removal of a portion of bone from his hip to be inserted between two vertebrae at the top of his spine. This was performed through a hole in the front of his neck, below his Adam 's Apple. When dad was discharged, I took him back to our house on Hatheru Road for a couple of weeks' recuperation. Then I took him back to Thika, as he had to return to work. The big Colonial-style house seemed empty and lonely.

Having a brand new grand-daughter helped my father tremendously to cope with his distressing situation. Luckily dad had the use of the Company pick-up and, after so many years spent avoiding "The City", he drove to Nairobi to spend every weekend with us. Mum went back to the farm briefly, to collect the remainder of the items she wanted to keep. Immediately following her visit, my father arrived to spend a long *"Public Holiday weekend"* with us. Dad had been so good, taking me at my word that mum was merely going through a period of adjustment due to the menopause. Now, my ultra-strict, stiff-upper-lipped father suddenly broke down and wept. His body shaking, hands covering his face, he sobbed, "Your Mother mentioned the word *divorce*. I dinna understand."

I had nightmares....I recall John shaking me awake while I was shouting out to my mother.

I did visit mum at her little cottage at Nyali. She was happy working at the Club, had made a whole new circle of friends, and a special "man-friend", whom I also met. She had lost a lot of weight, shedding a few years at the same time. She had a new life of partying and boozing. No longer the somewhat motherly person who had brought us up, I hardly recognised this lady who had taken to wearing eye-shadow, bright lipstick and tight, short skirts.

When Jeni was six weeks old, my sister returned from South Africa. Linda was surprised to be met at Mombasa Docks by this slim, carefully made-up, elegantly dressed, bubbling lady, who was her mother! I was playing tennis at Impala Club when mum drove Linda up to Nairobi. Linda met her new niece, who smiled up at her from the carry-cot she was being pushed around in. At the first opportunity, my sister asked "What's with mum?" I explained I had originally hoped it was all due to the normal change of hormones, but expressed my fears it now appeared to be much more serious. My transformed, well-adjusted young sister did not appear to be unduly surprised at our mother having gone totally off her rocker. In fact, Linda completely confounded me by taking it all in her stride, whereas I, the Experienced Elder Sister, had reached the stage of calling out to my mother in my dreams, often shouting at her when we met.

With Linda's return, life progressed more normally. Dad struggled on alone at the farm, mum lived it up at the coast, and I was managing to keep my marriage together without telling anybody about my husband's affair. I realised what I really needed, was to keep myself occupied one hundred per cent of the time. It was time to find a dog! A Spaniel, naturally. I ended up purchasing two adorable black-and-white Cocker Spaniel puppies: one named Bessy, of course, and her sister Sally.

"I ended up purchasing two adorable black & white Spaniel puppies"

How I miss those Spaniel days

35. MY DAUGHTER

Linda was wonderful with Jeni. She would often ask "Are you gorgeous?" to which my little girl would reply "Me not Gawjush. Me Cheni!" Dad made a tremendous fuss of his grand-daughter. Whenever I told her off, she would stick her little nose in the air and threaten "I gowin' a tell my Dandad!"

Jeni was toddling by the time the Company my father was working for was sold, and he moved to manage a farm near Ruiru, necessitating my spending a few days packing up for him, and sorting out all the things he and mum had accumulated over three decades. Eventually, I had "had enough" and, when it came to my old toys, I found myself throwing out teddy bears and so many things. How often have I regretted this, since? Jeni thoroughly enjoyed the clearing out of my old toy-box. She managed to save one Teddy Bear and my toy dog "Fido". I still have Fido; aged nearly seventy, he looks rather moth-eaten! We had the equally-precious Teddy Bear for a further four years, until Jeni drew a huge willy on him with an indelible pen, so Teddy was disposed of.

I realised Jeni needed a little brother to play with. I would call him Andrew, after my dad. I wanted at least two years between them, and stopped The Pill accordingly.

On one weekend visit to dad on the farm at Ruiru, we were reclining in comfortable lumpy armchairs waiting for the cook to announce curry was served, when I noticed Jeni flat on her tummy, reaching under a sofa. With a contented sigh, she pulled out an interesting dust-covered item, which she immediately put to her mouth, biting off a lump. I stood up and walked over to my daughter, who began munching furiously on the delicious morsel, the remainder held tightly in her little hand behind her back.

"What is it Jeni? Show it to me, please!"

"No no no no no! *Mine!* Cheni's!"

I prized her fingers open and removed an intriguing lump of what looked like seed-cake, which I showed to dad. He turned pale; it is interesting that he didn't say "That is rat poison!" Instead, he stammered "Oh God no, that's the stuff they put down for the rats!"

I clasped my wriggling daughter tightly under one arm, holding her little mouth open with the other hand, while Linda attempted to pour salty water down her throat. Jeni swallowed some of the water, but most of it must have gone into her ears and down our arms.

On the way to Gertrude's Garden Children's Hospital, I had to keep shaking Jeni awake. Upon arrival at the Hospital, we rushed through the wards and offices, searching for a doctor. The only adults in evidence were in the kitchen, preparing food. "Where can we find a doctor?" my sister and I shrieked in unison. The cook who was stirring the soup looked across at the lady buttering bread, and they both shrugged their shoulders as if to say "A doctor? Here? Are you mad?"

We got back into the car and drove straight to Nairobi Hospital, where the staff were marvellous. With my unborn son kicking inside my tummy, I had to leave the theatre to pace up and down the corridor, having witnessed my sister laying half across Jeni to hold her still as a tube was pushed down her throat. My little girl's panicked cries floated out of the tunnel at the top of the tube.

Jeni came out of it fine, and we had missed out on a yummy Sunday curry lunch.

36. INTRODUCTION TO THE MONSTER

On one of our visits to the coast, when I was quite large with my son in my tummy, my sister introduced me to a man called Mike. He was incredibly good-looking, and quite obviously knew it. When Linda introduced us, I noticed his eyes were the colour of steel. I was to meet this Mike person again, three years down the line. And two-and-a-half years after that, the man I shall call Hans, whose own blue eyes were soft and warm, was to describe Mike's eyes as "the eyes of a Wolf". Lovely, gentle Hans, whose own blue eyes were soft and warm.

Actually, to be quite correct, what Hans said was "Mike az dee ice off a Volff!"

37. MARRIED LIFE CONTINUES

Tuppy, the dogs, Jeni, the ayah, John and I would often travel down to the coast plot for a few days. Sometimes, dad would accompany us. Whilst there, our Independent Mother would call on us. Mother had found a steady boyfriend, who acted like a gentleman, seemed to be very fond of mum, and she was absolutely besotted with him. Initially, Linda and I approved of him. A couple of years later, this man was to treat mum very shabbily indeed; it was quite dreadful to witness mum's grief after he suddenly, viciously, dumped her.

Whilst holidaying on the beach at Tiwi, I often drove the twenty-five kilometres to visit mum at the Club where she worked, taking Jeni, and Linda if she happened to be with us. It was good fun visiting her, provided we forgot she was our mother, because she had turned into a flirtatious party-going person, always out having a good time: probably making up for the past three decades of domination by our father. One morning, after we had partied out with mum and her boyfriend, I complained to Linda about my hangover. She suggested I try one of the pills she had discovered in South Africa that "really helped". It really did! I found these tablets were easily available in Nairobi, and would take one or two each time I had had a particularly boozy, or late, night. I once asked my Chemist friend at City Pharmacy what these pills were. He replied in his musical Asian accent, "They're m'ft'mins". "Wow!" thought I, "For multi-vitamins they sure work quickly!"

To begin with, I only occasionally took one of these tablets in a day. But their effect was so amazing that I began to take my multi-vitamins more and more regularly until, seven years later, I was taking two or three every day. They kept me really fit. I reached the stage where I had difficulty sleeping, but a nightly sleeping-pill soon took care of that.

The round table in our dining-room sat eight people and, every Thursday night, I invited six friends to dinner. Thursday was a good day because it was nearly, but not quite, the weekend. I could not fathom out why Linda would prefer to sit around on unmatching cushions on the floor of her little guesthouse, chatting to friends while eating spaghetti and drinking cheap plonk, rather than dress up and come to our place for Beef Wellington or Stroganoff with Ratatouille on a Thursday Night!

Almost every Friday and Saturday, John and I were invited out to some party or other. Linda would comment that there must be something lacking in my life, to make me so obsessed with my perfect colour-schemes and "correct" social life. However, I managed to convince myself that we were very happy.

38. TONY THE SCHOOL TEACHER

Whilst delivering a friend's child to Braeburn School, I met a very handsome, tall, blond, young schoolteacher-cum-games master, called Tony. I told my sister about him, hoping she would show interest. When I next met Tony, I invited him to the drive-in cinema with us. Almost from that day forth, he and Linda became an item. They certainly suited one another! They both preferred to sit around on cushions, laughing and talking, rather than dressing smartly and going out for a formal meal. In fact, there was nothing they despised more than "formality". On the spur of the moment, they would decide to pack a tent and a couple of pans on the carriers of their motorbikes and take off for Lake Naivasha, or some such place, for the weekend; or they would put their motorbikes and tents on the train and whizz off down to the coast.

These were such happy, carefree days for Linda, and we were delighted for her. She had a very responsible job, as Personal Assistant to a business tycoon in the City centre; there was sufficient formality there for her! Then she would return on her beloved Honda 250 motorbike to the haven of her comfortable little home and her gorgeous, caring boyfriend.

I recall one Thursday night when Linda and Tony did condescend to "make up the eight" around our dining-table. At around one o'clock in the morning, when everybody was chatting in the lounge, there was a shuffling sound emanating from the door through to the bedrooms. Everyone stopped talking and turned towards the sound, just as the door burst open with a whoosh and in pedalled Jeni on her tricycle! As cool as a cucumber, she cycled around the room greeting all the guests! It was hilarious; as I write this, I am smiling to myself at the memory. Tony's infectious laughter still echoes in my ears.

39. MY SON

Twenty-eight months after Jeni, Andrew was born. Labour started at home just after 10 p.m. and Andrew was lying in my arms in Nairobi Hospital, at 11.30 p.m. Compared to Jeni, Andrew was a big baby, weighing eight and a half pounds. And compared to the time it takes to get to Nairobi Hospital today, he would certainly have been born in the car.

My son came out screaming, only to shut up as soon as I held him. He was like a bleeper gadget that goes off when you are moving away; each time he was taken away, he bawled, always to become silent as soon as he was handed back to me.

Andrew was one of those gorgeous, curly-headed, ever-smiling babies that everybody wanted to pick up and cuddle. He was a little angel to bring up. He and his sister adored each other. Jeni would "help" to bath him, feed him, and change him: always, of course, meaning that the process took three times as long as it should have.

40. MY SPANIELS

At different stages, I took over two highly-pedigreed male Spaniels, Perry and Dougal. Perry was positively hyper, while Dougal was the calmest and laziest dog that ever existed. Jeni, Tuppy, Bessy, Sally, Perry and Dougal all got along famously. If Jeni refused to sleep, I would simply put her in a basket with the dogs, and she would drop off immediately. I began entering the dogs in shows and they all won prizes in various events. Perry was by far the most "classically" beautiful.

The entire day before the Dog Show would be taken up with "plucking" and "stripping" all four dogs. Three of the dogs enjoyed this treatment, but Perry had to be muzzled! Then all four would be bathed, be let out for a run around the garden, often becoming thoroughly muddy, meaning another bath. Sally's white patches always managed to look slightly "mucky" for some reason, so I used to add a drop of blue Quink Ink to the "final" rinse. I eventually got the blue ink down to a fine art, after the first experience which left Sally's coat a unique contrast of brilliant blue and black!

On a particularly hot day at a Dog Show, I decided to change into shorts bringing an official complaint from an elderly lady on the Committee. Unfortunately our events were not due to take place until mid-afternoon. As the day wore on, becoming hotter and hotter, three of the dogs fell asleep in their stalls, while Perry became increasingly neurotic.

At last our turn came. Bessy and Sally were entered in the "Brace", and won first prize. When Dougal's turn came, he was so sleepy I had to carry him to the line and hold him up until he wobbled into ring, where after he proceeded to flop down with a huge sigh, every time we stood still. He did not win a prize! Perry, on the other hand, leapt to the ringside like a spring lamb; he looked absolutely beautiful, and I overheard comments about how he was obviously the Number One Spaniel in the country.

That all changed when he bit the Judge, and was disqualified.

Linda with "Tony the Schoolteacher"

Bessy & Sally were entered in the Brace and won First Prize

Spaniels on Holiday!

41. MARIANNA

Apart from having sufficient friends among the tennis crowd, the hockey gang, the office set and the doggy-owners, over the years I would befriend what my mother referred to as "waifs and strays". These would range from young children, to elderly people. Although many of them did require care and attention in one form or another, many became friends. Dad, in his typical manner, would refer to them as "hangers-on" or, worse, "parasites".

One such person was Marianna, the only daughter in an "out-of-the-ordinary" (to put it mildly) family with whom I unwittingly became closely involved: the Knights. This family was comprised of a brilliant but totally bizarre father, an opinionated mother that John described as a "Socialist"; a gentle, confused elder son; a pleasant but mixed-up younger son; and, in between, a wonderfully normal but unsurprisingly insecure daughter. Of course, many geniuses are accepted as being somewhat eccentric: well, in actual fact, Charles Knight was a genius; he was renowned for his accounting skills and his clients included many of Kenya's elite. But Oh Dear!

I do know that, over a ten-year period, my children and I were able to give Marianna the normal family home she would otherwise have utterly missed out on. I vividly recall the one and only time John and I were invited to the Knights' house for dinner. The meal was roast lamb. Our host expertly cut off a few slices of meat; then, to our astonishment, proceeded to pile them all onto his own plate, before helping himself to vegetables. He then sat down and dug into his meal with great gusto! Caitlin, his wife, asked John if he would mind slicing up some meat for the rest of us, which he did. It was quite delicious. As we began to eat, Charles, having added a few extra slices to his plate, stood up and rushed the remainder of the joint out to the kitchen, telling us there would be "no seconds"!

The next time I called at their house was with Andrew's Godmother, Pam, who was visiting from Switzerland. Marianna happened not to be at our home at the time, and I wanted her to meet Pam. We walked in, to find Charles sitting in front of the telly, watching a cricket match. He was wearing full cricket gear, including gloves, knee-pads, and cap pulled down over his forehead, excitedly thumping his bat on the floor and bawling at the players on the screen. Pam turned to me, her eyes opened wide in disbelief, trying not to laugh. Without turning his head, he answered in response to my question, "She's not here!" We left; Pam with hand over mouth smothering giggles.

Marianna lived much of the time with us. She helped me to bath and feed Jeni and Andrew; she sang to them and read stories to them. Marianna had a way of encouraging Jeni to eat her food when I could not; she would play "aeroplanes" with spoonfuls of food: "Here comes Concorde!" zooming the spoonful of food straight down into Jeni's mouth. Jeni, aged three, was helped up the steps to the top diving-board at Impala Club swimming-pool. Marianna, treading water, called out from below, "Jump, Jeni!" whereupon Jeni leaped off the high board with complete confidence, to be retrieved and swung around by a laughing Marianna.

One early morning I was woken by a strange sound in the back yard. John was snoring soundly. I crept down the corridor and peered through a window, to see Marianna in fits of giggles, waving her arms around and hissing "Stop it! Stop it!" while half a dozen teenagers were playing football with our dustbin. I learned a lot about bringing up teenagers from having Marianna "in the family"!

Wherever we went, Marianna was generally with us. To the coast, to game-parks, to Lake Naivasha. Naivasha was a favourite weekend get-away. Driving out of Nairobi, through green thickly forested areas, to eventually reach a warning sign, "You are now approaching the Escarpment. Engage low gear". And then quite suddenly the whole world was spread out beneath you. The steep twisting climb down to the floor of the Rift Valley was quite hair-raising, with no guard rails for protection. There were a number of lay-bys where we would stop to take in the breath-taking scenery. In those days, vendors would sell punnets of delicious black mushrooms collected from the surrounding ranches; it is many years since I saw a black mushroom; whatever happened to them all? Nowadays we can only find those tasteless little round pink so-called mushrooms, to which I add mushroom ketchup to give flavour when cooking!

42. TONY THE SCHOOL TEACHER

During one school holiday I was taking Jeni, Andrew and Marianna to Nairobi Game-Park. Seeing Tony's motorbike parked as we were passing Linda's little house, I tooted the horn and asked if he wanted to join us. He did. When we dropped him off a few hours later, we were met by a very upset Linda. I couldn't understand what her problem was, and thought she was huffing because we had spent a lovely afternoon in the park, while she had had to work: which would have been understandable. But in fact it was worse than that.

Linda later explained that Tony had been suffering from black-outs while teaching at school. Seeing his bike parked, she thought he must have gone off on one of his habitual walk-abouts. After a couple of hours had passed with no sign of him, she really began to worry. I felt very bad, and wished I had known of the problem earlier.

43. GETTING TO KNOW MY CHILDREN'S FATHER

Much of our socialising was at Impala Club, where I still played tennis two or three times a week. We used the swimming-pool at weekends. We watched movies and attended discos there. Most of us had our children sleeping in the backs of our cars in the Club car-park when we went out at night. John and I had a Peugeot 404 station-wagon, meaning a mattress fitted perfectly in the back. I was recently discussing the very different security situation in today's Kenya with Andrew Nightingale. He had me in stitches when he related a tale of the time families from outlying farms had met at an upcountry Club; while the adults were partying, the children decided to swop cars. When the adults eventually came out, they got into their cars and drove to their homesteads, many kilometres in different directions. Upon reaching the particular destination of the car he was in, Andrew was woken by the shocked voices of parents asking "Where's Jimmy?" To which he replied, "Oh! I'm not sure which car he is in!" Ha ha ha! Just imagine the chaos that followed!

John was proud of his children, and had no problem with them provided he wasn't expected to take any part in their upbringing. Terrified of dropping them, he didn't dare to pick either of his children up until they were a few months' old. Jeni picked up her little brother and carried him, long before John did! John would spoil the children, giving into their demands for the sake of peace and quiet. A few times when the ayah happened to be off duty and I had no option but to leave them in John's "care", I would return to find that they would not eat their supper, only to discover that John had given them a tin of drinking chocolate, or a jar of jam, with teaspoons.

It was on a hot, sunny, Sunday that we were sitting around the swimming-pool. The pool was absolutely *packed* with people. Jeni was sitting on the grass with John and I; baby Andrew was sleeping in the carry-cot. I asked John to keep an eye on them while I went to the Ladies' loo. When I came back a few minutes later, there was no sign of Jeni; her armbands were on the grass nearby. "Where's Jeni?" I asked. John looked around in surprise. "Dunno, she was here just now!" he replied, still sitting, drinking his beer.

I walked to the edge of the pool nearest to where we were sitting, at the shallow end, where it was possible for adults to stand. Kids were floating in tyres, teenagers were playing with a beach-ball; adults were fooling around. In a gap between the mass of bodies, I located my little girl, sitting, in her striped swimsuit, on the *bottom* of the pool, her eyes and mouth open, hair floating behind her, arms outstretched in front of her. (To this day, I still have nightmares of this vision!) I jumped into the pool, swam across to where I had seen her, and picked her up. I can still remember the shock and horror on the faces of the people around; shock that they had not even noticed she was there. John came over and took her out of my arms as I climbed out of the pool. A friend with knowledge of First Aid, pumped a little water out of her. I wrapped her in a towel and sat hugging her until she stopped shivering. Later, for both our sakes, I put the armbands on her and took her back into the pool to play.

One evening at home, I was sewing in the small room off the bedroom, when I heard Jeni screaming. I tore through to the living-room, to see Jeni holding a candle with the burning wax dripping onto her arm. As I rushed over to take the candle from her, the flame was already singeing her hair. John turned away from the football match on telly with a bemused look on his face, as he took in his daughter's frizzled hair and burnt arm.

"Whatever were you thinking of?" I shrieked.

"She asked me to light the candle!" he answered, stating the obvious; as if I'd gone bonkers and couldn't see.

One Saturday night I threw a party to celebrate John's forty-fifth Birthday. Of course he knew about the party well in advance. All the invited guests had been partying for a couple of hours before John drove in. It turned out he had already been celebrating with his Kalasingha rafikis. He staggered through the door and slumped into a chair, saying not a word. Immediately taking in his condition, I tried to humour him. In an attempt to avoid embarrassment in front of the guests, I told him we were ready to bring the cake through. He replied that he "Don wan any blurry cake. Jus' wanna blurry drink!"

I went through to the kitchen store to get the cake. Discovering I had tears running down my cheeks, I pulled the door closed behind me. The door was quietly opened by my dad, who simply said "Dinna fret, we can see what's going on. We know what you put up with. You're not alone." I just said "Thanks, dad" as he went out of the kitchen. After that, life felt so much better. Dad knew! He understood! Things weren't so bad after all. I could cope.

I had what I wanted. A beautiful house, two perfect children, a special cat and my Spaniels. John was regularly away on business, more often than not in Kisumu. One morning, I popped in on a neighbour for a coffee and chat. She introduced me to her guest, an attractive nurse who was working with an Aid

Organisation in Kisumu. In a conversation with my neighbour, I heard the girl say "Keep my suitcase here; John will be bringing it up on his next visit to Kisumu." It was only because of my host's obvious embarrassment that it dawned on me that the "John" being referred to, was my husband.

44. MARIANNA'S MOTHER

On a stormy night, I received a phone-call from a very nervous Marianna. She was calling from the Thorntree Restaurant in the City centre. She asked hesitatingly if I would mind if she stayed the night with us, because her mother had failed to pick her up. Naturally I drove into town to collect her, and brought her to our home. As she was in quite a state, now more certain than ever that her mother didn't give two hoots about her, I gave her an Ativan with a cup of hot chocolate before she went to bed. I attempted to defend her mother, in spite of inwardly seething. I decided to leave her to sleep in the next morning, before judging whether or not she was in fit condition to attend school. I had to keep Jeni out of Marianna's room, because Jeni loved to jump into bed with her in the mornings.

Mid-morning, Caitlin arrived at our house. Thinking she must have realised that her missing daughter would somehow turn up at our house, I poured a couple of cups of coffee and sat down to hear what she had to say. Caitlin talked about her problems with her husband, but not a word was uttered about her daughter. She finished her coffee, rose from the chair, and walked out to her car. As she opened the car-door, I asked "Don't you want to know about Marianna?"

"What about her?" she snapped.

"Don't you even want to know how she is?"

"WHAT!" she shrieked, "You mean she's *here*?"

"You forgot to pick her up yesterday, remember?"

"I couldn't. I had to attend a meeting!" Explanation enough!

"Didn't you wonder where she was last night?" I pressed.

Ignoring me, Catilin spluttered, "The *stupid* girl. How DARE she! She's late for school!"

I explained I would deliver her to school later. Caitlin went totally ape-shit. She shoved me aside, rushed through to Marianna's room, flung the door open and shook her daughter awake, all the while berating her and telling her how stupid she was.

To this day, I regret I mentioned Marianna's name, at all.

45. TONY THE SCHOOL TEACHER

Mother often came up from the coast to spend a few days with us. On one of mum's visits, I was sitting in the bedroom brushing my hair when she walked in and told me Tony had to fly to UK for "more tests". Not having talked to Linda, I didn't understand what mum was talking about. Mum said Tony had been diagnosed as having a brain tumour.

I went completely cold all over. "Mum! What are you saying? Not a *brain tumour?* It can't be! People *die* of brain tumours!"

"Yes" mum nodded, "I know."

Oh no oh no oh no oh no. Please God, no. Not Tony. Oh, Linda!

Tony flew to the UK a few days later.

46. A LITTER OF SPANIELS

I recall an incident at school in Urambo in 1952, when two dogs had become "stuck" to each other; teachers poured buckets of water over them until they were forced apart, both bleeding. The bitch was owned by the family of one of the pupils, who was obviously terribly distressed: none of us had a clue about what was going on. Don't you think it is an example of where Nature went terribly wrong, when you see a stray dog and bitch in a "tie", where other dogs are busy tearing the male to pieces while he is unable to extract himself? Where we live, the shrieks of bitches being torn apart internally, and the howls of dogs "on the job" being chewed to death by a pack, are not an uncommon occurrence. I have a couple of moronic male acquaintances who are not concerned when their dogs tour the district with local packs following bitches on heat; these acquaintances say brainlessly "Why should I have Buster's balls knackered. Let him have his oats!" Imbecilic selfish assholes.

My Bessy was a very gentle-natured lady, of high breeding. She was mated with Perry. Having witnessed plentiful roaming packs of dogs, I thought that "sex" came naturally to the canine species. *No way!* Dear Bessy, at doggy-eighteen, was as ignorant about sex as I had been at human-eighteen! An experienced dog-mater was brought in. On 25 August 1978, Bessy and I gave birth to six Spaniel puppies! The previous night, she couldn't sleep properly; nor could I. She was very restless; so was I. If I happened to drop off to sleep, Bessy whined and patted my arm with her paw, most offended. Eventually we both sat in the basket with rumbling tummies, commiserating over innumerable saucers/cups of tea.

At twenty past five in the morning, Bessy gave a little yelp. There was what appeared to be a small polythene bag protruding from her nether regions. I gently eased it out and helped Bessy to burst the bag over the little head so the puppy could breathe. I cut the cord with sterilised scissors then tied cotton around the cord. I placed the shiny black and brilliant white object in the basket, where it instantly latched onto a teat. Bessy looked lovingly at this tiny pink-nosed cross between a domino and a sausage, and glanced up at me as if to say "Aren't we clever?" She didn't appear to feel the other pups being born! She lay back happily feeding, quite content to leave the rest of the procedure to me. Puppy number seven was stillborn. I removed it quickly and never told Bessy about it; but she became agitated and left the basket for the first time, to search for her missing baby.

Bessy would go for walks, meals, etc., if I was with the pups. I was allowed to do the same when she was in attendance. John built a wall to close off a large area of the verandah, for the puppies. Gradually, we left the pups more and more to themselves. The funniest times were when the family – both adult dog and human members – were sitting in the lounge, and high-pitched squeaks would erupt from the kennel on the verandah, whereupon Bessy would cock an eye at me as if to say "Is it your turn, or is it mine?" If I got up, Bessy would relax again and close her eyes.

Oh how I miss those Spaniel days! Talk about 101 Dalmatians! I would arrive home and walk through the door, to see black and white bundles of fluff hanging from curtains, climbing onto chairs, chewing carpets and shoes. I would shout "BASKET!" then all the dogs would rush for the large basket and leap in, whereupon the basket would go sliding along the polished floor with puppies hanging over the sides at all angles, until they bumped into the wall at the far end of the living-room. What a hilarious site, with Bessy sitting upright in a careering basketful of puppies, looking as if butter wouldn't melt in her mouth, the expression on her face saying "What, me?" before crashing into the far wall.

I registered my kennel under the name "Jendrew" after Jeni and Andrew. Each puppy was given a "Nursery Rhyme" name. We kept one pup, "Jimmy": registered name "Jiminy Cricket of Jendrew."

Where's mum ?

She's having a break
from puppy-minding

47. MARIANNA'S FAMILY

Marianna's younger brother, Bobby, was very fortunate in that he was obviously loved by his mother. The time came when Caitlin, perfectly justifiably, decided to leave her weird husband. She asked me to collect Bobby from school daily, and to get there before his father had a chance to "kidnap" him; I thought she was severely over-exaggerating the situation, but agreed to assist. Apart from being of the opinion Bobby should not be entrusted to his father's care (for reasons I shall not go into, here) I also felt that Caitlin would be a more grounded person when out of the clutches of her eccentric, dominating, husband.

I duly collected Bobby every day; until the day I arrived at the school just in time to witness the poor young boy being literally dragged off at arm's length by his father. I called out "I've come to collect Bobby!"

"Bobby's coming with me!" The poor little fellow was looking back at me with a pleading expression on his face, while I watched, powerless. When his father had had enough of him, Bobby was returned to Caitlin. Poor boy; he was quite bright, but mixed-up, and with good cause.

Caitlin and family had a frightening experience. Late one night, a gang surrounded their isolated little cottage, throwing stones and trying to break down the door. The elder son was very cool; he bravely dispersed the would-be intruders by firing pellets through a window with an airgun, after which the family plus dogs ran for their car and drove straight to....guess where! Caitlin took over the sleeping arrangements and we managed to fit them all into our house, with Caitlin sharing what was always Marianna's room.

Things had more or less calmed down. I was sitting on our bed with the younger children, telling them a story, and Caitlin was showering at the other end of the house. All of a sudden, Caitlin came rushing through our bedroom in her undies. She dashed through our dressing room into our pink and red bathroom, calling out that she was borrowing my deodorant. With a lot on my mind, I couldn't figure out why her action had puzzled me. It was a couple of days later that I realised....it was surprise that she had even been into our private bathroom let alone that she knew where to find my deodorant. "GO" deodorant, it was called, and I only bought it because the screw-container was bright pink and matched the decor of our bathroom!

48. TONY THE SCHOOL TEACHER

Tony's diagnosis was confirmed; he had a brain tumour. The operation appeared to be a success. Linda flew to England. Initially, she stayed with relatives near London so she could travel on the underground to visit Tony, daily. When he left the hospital, she went with him to his parents' home in beautiful Somerset. When he settled into chemotherapy sessions, Linda returned to Kenya. While she was away, I temporarily sat in for her, at her job working for an amazing blind gentleman, Ray Cuthbert, the "Chairman" of International House on Mama Ngina Street. En route to work, I dropped Jeni off at a Kindergarten not far from our home. Sometimes mum would come to stay and look after the children while I was working in town, plus we had an excellent ayah.

49. MARIANNA'S MOTHER'S LOVE LIFE

Caitlin met a charming American gentleman. Chuck really did bring out the best in her; I had much more time for her now. Caitlin's husband wrote a funny letter to me, saying that everyone must be considering him to be the "Black Ogre of the Piece"; the letter was very anti-Chuck. Trying to assist Caitlin, I replied that, to my knowledge, nobody was considering him to be "The Black Ogre..." but I stressed that I really liked Chuck.

I do not remember how long Caitlin had been dating him at the time I first visited Chuck in hospital. There he lay, full of jokes and smiles as usual, with his leg bound up and suspended from the ceiling. It was very mysterious, nobody could fathom out how the problem had come about. He was found to have gangrene in his foot. A while later, it was decided that his leg must be amputated below the knee. A few nights later, Caitlin turned up at my house in a dreadful state. She told me between sobs that the doctors had now decided that Chuck's leg required amputating *above* the knee; she cried and cried. I tried to console her, saying that having the amputation above the knee was a necessary precaution against the spread of gangrene.

Chuck came out of hospital and carried on with his business much as before. Then one night he dropped down dead from a heart attack. He was only sixty-three. There was a beautiful Memorial Service, with Marianna reading lines from Kahlil Gibrain's "The Prophet". Caitlin blamed his illness and untimely death on Witchcraft. I was really surprised at this. I pooh-poohed it: I was a total cynic on the subject. I was aware that "Mgangas" (Witch-doctors) terrified most of the wananchi. I believed if a person was told by a Mganga he was going to be run over by a car, he would leap in front of the next speeding car that appeared, knowing this was the end; and so it was. But as to Mgangas having real out-of-the-world powers, enabling them to kill people from a distance by planting goats' heads in their gardens and so on, forget it! It was all superstition, as my dad always said.

Yes, I pooh-poohed it. At that time. Not anymore.

My heart bled for Caitlin.

50. TONY THE SCHOOL TEACHER

News came that Tony was sinking into a depression due to the chemotherapy, and was refusing to carry on with the treatment. Linda flew back to England, and I took over her job once again, working for Ray Cuthbert. Tony had lost all his beautiful blond hair, even his thick black eyebrows. Linda bought him a hat. Together they travelled around to visit relatives and friends. She left him in a much happier frame of mind, vowing he would return to Kenya as soon as possible. They were in constant communication.

One morning while Linda was away, Ray came to work and when settled in his office, he ushered me over and cupped his hands around my ear. "Keep this under your bra" he said. "Mzee passed away last night!" Being close to Kenyatta, he would obviously be one of the first to be told. I gasped; I was devastated. Of course, we discussed the question of who would "take over": would it be my ex-boss Mungai, or perhaps Kibaki, or even the Attorney General, Njonjo? Any would be acceptable.

Daniel Arap Moi had been given the post of Vice President as a clever political move: being from a minority tribe, he would cause no trouble. So now, being V.P., he would obviously take over "temporarily", while Jomo's successor was established. Well, twenty-four years down the line, Moi was still there, contrary to everybody's expectations. We heard that he taught the Police about corruption; when they asked for higher wages he asked why the Government should pay salary increases when they had the whole country out there, go get it .... giving them the green light ...and so so so much more.

51. MY INCORRIGIBLE CHILDREN

My children were a constant source of delight and amusement. Cheeky little Jeni always up to mischief, Andrew with his angelic smile! If I was a bit down in the dumps, my children would start their game of pulling funny faces. The more I laughed and said "Stop it!" the more they carried on.

I was in Mansion Pharmacy, ordering more of my special multivitamins, with Andrew tugging at my skirt to come and look at a "scary" poster on the door, which Jeni was staring at in fascination. It was an advert for a worm medicine, depicting a body with all intestines visible, indicating the passage of this particular brand of medicine in the human body. Jeni declared loudly enough for all the customers to hear, "Look mummy, that man's eaten an *awful* lot of superghetti!"

In many ways, my children had a marvellous childhood. I was forever going out of my way to travel through game-parks en route to and from the coast. Jeni and Andrew became quite blasé about wild animals "Oh, not another zebra!" I remember when they had been playing Lego on the back seat of the car, not unduly bothered about the animals in the park, only to shout excitedly "Oh look, goats, how sweet!" as we left the park and had to stop for a herdsman to usher his livestock across the road.

Andrew was developing a very dry sense of humour. He would come out with something extraordinarily funny but, if it was missed, would never follow it up. Jeni, on the other hand, was prone to exaggeration and would come out with a fantastic story that she would repeat in case anybody had missed it!

Whilst driving into Nairobi, Jeni was showing off her reading skills by spelling out one neon sign after the other:

"Sony!" she shouted.

Then "Strikes!"

"Back!" came a quiet little voice from the back. When it registered with me I turned, laughing, to see a cheeky satisfied smile on Andrew's face.

When Linda was visiting Tony in England and I was filling in for her, mum would bring the children to have lunch at Marino's Restaurant in International House. The restaurant was owned and run by Marino Lavarini and his sister, my friend Eddie. When Marino Lavarini "retired" (ha-ha – as if!) after he sold "Lavarini's" it was not long before he opened a new restaurant in his Christian name! It was at this restaurant, when I was sitting with one of the boss's clients at lunchtime that my children came rushing in ahead of mum, having diverted to the Gents' loo on the way. They proudly placed handfuls of mothballs in the middle of the table, "Look what we found, mummy!" It was at this restaurant that Jeni, after eating a piece of my pork and realising she needed to throw up, lent over my open handbag and vomited the contents of her stomach into it, rather than shaming me by spewing up over the clean floor of the restaurant.

52. MY NON-MARRIAGE

The Jaguar workshop closed down. After a couple of jobs, the first a very good one as an Insurance Assessor with Bill Blakeman (Bill paid for our wonderful honeymoon to stay with John's parents in Durban); the next, working for the AA of Kenya. Poor John gradually reached the stage of lying in bed late in the mornings, not wanting to get up. Looking back, I really wish I had been more worldly-wise and much more understanding; as it was, I simply did not know how to cope. Of course he lost this job. Luckily, I kept working throughout. When my contract with the UN came to an end, and all my wonderful bosses left Kenya, I made good money by taking in work at home. This kept up our mortgage payments on the house. It also meant I had time to travel to the coast with the children over half-terms, holidays and long weekends, sometimes with John but often not. I was building a new cottage on our family plot at Tiwi. Just as mum had before me, I was using the work at the coast as an excuse to get away from my unhappy marriage. And just like my mother, I did not let on how disastrous my nine-year-old marriage was.

But mother had kept silent for nearly *thirty* years! Mother was adamant she had remained with dad only for our sakes. Hell's Teeth! If she had left him years earlier, they could both have found new partners and lived happily ever after. From personal experience, I am now of the opinion that, in general, marriage is for old people who need companionship or young couples who do not want children. I did not want to emulate my mother's mistake, waiting too long before ending a non-working partnership, but I did not know how to go about disentangling myself.

I had noticed with sorrow that Marianna, for some reason, appeared to have cut off contact with us. Although Jeni and Andrew continually enquired about her, I knew the poor girl had plenty of her own family problems to deal with, without being brought into the fragments of yet another broken marriage. I was still fond of John in a protective sort of way. When overseeing the building of the house at the coast, I would telephone him every evening from the office of the next-door Twiga Lodge. On one occasion, I was confounded when a child answered my call.

I said "Oh sorry, wrong number!" and dialled again. The same young voice answered, so I asked who was speaking.

"This is Bobby!"

"Oh hello Bobby; whatever are *you* doing there? Can I speak to John?"

"He and mum have gone out to dinner".

"Oh! Please tell him that I called".

Was that how Caitlin knew where to find my pink deodorant in our pink and red bathroom?

53. ENTER THE MONSTER

It was over a half-term holiday, on one of my many visits to the coast to supervise the building, that I wandered across to the Twiga Lodge for a well-earned injection of alcohol. I had never done this before, on my own, at night. Sitting up ramrod straight at the corner of the bar, was an incredible-looking guy. There was a stirring in my memory when he flashed perfectly even, brilliant white teeth at me, from a mouth that was moulded into the shape of a smile; a smile that did not reach his eyes. Steel-grey eyes that bore unnervingly into mine. Two grey blocks of ice. The eyes of a wolf.

Mike.

He would not let me pay for my drink. Or the next. Or the next. We talked for hours. Crazily I found myself telling him about my disastrous marriage. He was so charming, so understanding! Having found a new man friend, I stayed at the coast for longer than intended.

Mike worked as a vehicle mechanic in South Sudan. Throughout the first year of knowing Mike, I was to meet up with him in Nairobi en route to one place or another; in between contracts he would camp on the Kenya coast, which he loved – if indeed he was capable of loving anything. From the very outset, he insisted I should leave John. I agreed I should, but never imagined I would be able to go through with it. When he was away, Mike would phone me frequently, always asking if I had filed for a divorce yet. Every time he returned to Kenya, Mike became more emphatic and aggressive about it, until I did eventually tell John our marriage was over.

John was sitting in the lounge, he put his hands over his face. He said "Ever since Lynda, I knew this would happen!" I felt so rotten. I can remember putting my hand out to him, nearly touching his shoulder: it was terribly difficult to restrain myself but I knew, if I did so, I would never be able to leave him. Further, I doubt whether I would have had the courage to part from John had I not seen my mother extricate herself from what, as she described it, had been a miserable marriage. And I dreaded Mike's anger. I did not see that Mike was already beginning to rule my life. I went to see a lawyer about a divorce. John moved out of the house to stay with relatives. With John away, Linda frequently forwent the comfort of the cushions in her friendly little guesthouse next-door, to spend evenings keeping me company in the colour-coordinated lounge of my perfect house. When Mike called again, I was able to confirm I was consulting a lawyer, and John had moved out. Mike sounded thrilled, which made me feel very relieved.

One evening when Jeni and Andrew were safely tucked up in their beds, while Linda and I were playing Scrabble in the lounge, we heard a car speeding down the driveway straight into the locked gate. It was John, after a few drinks. He continually reversed before driving with speed into the gate, eventually smashing the lock. While John was trying to break through the burglar-proof bars on a corridor window, my children dashed through to my bedroom, jumped into bed and pulled the blankets up over their heads. I followed them into the bedroom, to see two pairs of big round frightened eyes staring up at me. I can still hear Jeni's accusing little voice, "Mummy, *why did you marry that man*?"

Meanwhile, Linda was trying, through the window, to talk some sense into John. Finally he calmed down and Linda unlocked the door to let him into the sitting-room, where she sat up for most of the night, trying to instil some sense into him. Concerned about John's conduct, Linda took to spending whole nights with the children and me.

My lawyer was delighted to hear about my husband's irrational behaviour; he said it suited our case perfectly.

MIKE THE MONSTER AT TIWI BEACH
MOUTH MOULDED INTO THE SHAPE OF A SMILE

BOR, SUDAN: AND DROVE AROUND THE WETLANDS, PHOTOGRAPHING BIRDS

WHERE I PLAYED TENNIS DAILY

54. MY HUSBAND & MARIANNA'S MOTHER

On a Saturday morning, I was walking with Jeni and Andrew past the Thorntree Restaurant, when the children suddenly yelled out in unison "Marianna! Marianna!" Letting go of my hands, they rushed over to where Marianna was sitting with a couple of dustbin-kicking friends. Following my children, I smiled down at Marianna and was taken aback to note an expression akin to guilt mixed with distress flutter across her eyes, almost like a shadow that was clearly there one second, then it wasn't. She was avoiding my gaze.

"We haven't seen you for ages. Are you OK?" I asked.

"No, I'm sorry," evasively. "Yes, I'm fine!"

To my children's distress, I said "Bye then" and dragged them away, puzzled.

Shortly after this incident, I was surprised to receive a call from my lawyer, to inform me John was in hospital. John – who disliked camping – had uncharacteristically been camping in a game-park and "got burned". I could not understand why John had suddenly taken to camping in game-parks, any more than I could understand how my lawyer had got to hear about it. I remembered we had an Insurance Policy somewhere and, when I dug it out, discovered it had expired the night *after* John's accident. He should be able to claim! Being concerned about him, I drove to the hospital, armed with the Insurance Policy, a bottle of Lucozade (which I always maintained was the best thing about being in hospital!) and the latest copy of one of the motoring magazines that he loved to read.

I walked into the ward, and there was Caitlin sitting on John's bed. After my initial shock, everything suddenly became crystal clear. Such as Marianna's embarrassment at the Thorntree. Such as my pink deodorant...an incident that had occurred sometime before I met up with Mike.

Of course, it didn't matter; I was now "with" Mike, after all! John deserved much better than me. He needed friends, and it was great that somebody was there for him. But the SHOCK that it was Caitlin! They both appeared ill-at-ease when I walked in. Caitlin explained they had been camping in Amboseli when the accident occurred. For some idiotic reason, John had thrown petrol onto a barbecue, somehow managing to splash petrol onto his face and hands in the process, and all had caught fire. It seemed Caitlin and Marianna had taken turns to drive the two hundred miles on horrific roads to the hospital, in the middle of the night. Marianna. My Marianna! I had never let on that there was a problem between John and I, her "adopted parents". Then, horror of all horrors, John had moved in with *her mother!* As she explained to me much later, her mother had instructed her not to get in touch with me, or to tell me "anything". Poor kid.

John was not too badly burned. I left the Insurance Policy with him. I went home and collected every single item of his belongings, plus exactly fifty per cent of our Wedding presents, and dropped them off at Caitlin's house.

Our divorce went through quickly. Caitlin became John's fourth wife and together they moved to the south of Scotland. John had loved our time in Dumfriesshire when visiting my dad's family and said at the time he would like to retire there. I was pleased for him, that his dream had come true.

55. MOVING AGAIN

At this time, when so many changes were going on, dad was admitted to hospital for a second operation, almost identical to the first. A piece of bone was chipped off the other hip and fused between yet another two vertebrae. Medically, the operation was as successful as the first, with the big exception that his vocal chords were damaged, and he lost his voice entirely for six months. Eventually he was able to talk, but he was never able to sing, ever again.

Mike said I should sell my perfect house and move to the coast plot. After all, dad - already on the beach - also wanted me to move down there. Dad already had Bessy living with him. Jimmy would be happy down there whenever I was away, as Mike told me he wanted me to "travel" with him. I put the sale of my house in the hands of an estate agent. I found a good home for both Perry and Dougal, together. Poor Sally had suddenly lost the use of her back legs and had to be put to sleep; Janet Godfrey, the Vet, said there was no alternative as the poor doggie couldn't even drag herself around.

Now...Tuppy.

Mike said the only solution was to have Tuppy "put down". I kept telling myself that many cats were put to sleep and it was often the kindest option. I tried to tell myself that my beautiful, fluffy, black cat had had a wonderful life and was, after all, nine years old... I am having trouble writing this because I cannot see the keyboard properly through my tears. I called Tuppy who came straight to me, purring; trusting me, the one who had arranged her execution. She jumped into the car and sat happily on my shoulder as I drove to the Vet's surgery. I took her into the surgery, thinking I would be able to sit stroking her while the awful deed was done, the way I had with Sally. It wasn't like that, I was told it was different with cats. I went outside and wandered around for fifteen minutes until I could stand it no longer. I opened the door to the surgery to see Tuppy sitting on the metal-topped table. One man was holding her while the Vet plunged the needle straight into her great big little heart. I screamed "NO! NO!" But she was gone.

I didn't know it was like that. I didn't know they did it like that. I thought she would be given a sedative then a gentle injection into a vein and simply fall asleep. I am choked up. I still regularly have nightmares, tormenting myself with the memory of watching them kill my adorable cat, on my instructions. Thirty-six years ago. Forgive me, Tuppy, my precious little friend. As you look down from Heaven, please please try to forgive me. If I am lucky enough to end up in Heaven after all the wrongs I have committed, we shall surely be together again.

Not long ago, I was relating this awful story to my Grandson's cat-loving Godmother. Julie told me that, contrary to what I have been feeling, Tuppy probably didn't have the faintest idea of what was happening. She trusted humans, nobody had ever hurt her, and she could just have thought they were checking her over. This has helped me a lot. Thank you so much, Julie.

I have to say that, even more recently, my fifteen-year-old dog Shenzi suffered a stroke and had to be put down; my partner Oreste was stroking him and he simply fell asleep. Just after that, my twenty-year-old cat had to be put down. As with Tuppy all those years ago, this Vet asked me to go outside and when I asked why, she explained that, with cats, it is normal that an injection has to be given into the heart, which I might find traumatic!

So, just maybe, it all makes a bit of sense now and it wasn't that horrific for my little moggies?

56. BECOMING A PUPPET

It happened over a relatively short space of time, that I no longer had a mind of my own and gradually could only do what Mike told me to. Having, largely due to pressure from him, left my husband; put my perfect house up for sale; taken my children out of school; given two of my dogs away; had my beloved cat murdered, I found myself floundering aimlessly when he was away. Gradually, this obsessively private, powerfully dominating man, introduced me to a way of approaching life, of living life, which was completely foreign to me. For instance, he drummed into me and managed to convince me, that it was natural for a man to live with three or more women, all of whom would love him utterly and live together in complete harmony. Any man who said he could settle forever with one woman, was a liar, because no such man had ever been born. He would point out "Look at animals: a herd of Impala for instance, one male and how many females..."

A woman, on the other hand, must be totally and unconditionally faithful to her man. On this point, there could be absolutely no discussion and no deviation whatsoever. Step by step, I was becoming exactly what he must have spent years looking for. At first, I thought he must love me. I tried to do everything right by him, naively thinking if I was good enough, it would prevent him from chatting up other women. Stupid, imbecilic me. As there was no way I could ever tell a soul about the way Mike was beginning to dominate me, I began to find great solace in writing daily to my Diary, in the form of poetry. I would write bravely, fantasising about what I would say to Mike. It was only when I began to record the events in my life that I dug up my old Diaries again, after more than sixteen years spent gathering dust on a shelf. And the memories came flooding back, as if it was only last month. I have pages and pages of poetry I wrote to Mike but which, of course, he never knew about.

He had a dreadful hang-up about what I might have done prior to meeting him. He wanted to wipe out all my past.

"No no Mike, NO!"
Do not go on so
About what I might have done
All those years ago.
You say it's not right
For me to gripe or moan
About what you'll do tonight
When you go out alone
There is no logic;
In fact it's quite sick."

Mike went to England for a few weeks. I was at Tiwi, looking after the cottages we rented out. The day after he returned, I drove up to Nairobi, as he instructed. In Nairobi, we stayed at my house, as the sale was not yet through. My red telephone rang; I answered and a woman's voice asked for Mike. I heard him making plans to meet her at the Hilton Hotel that evening. He told me she was one of the British Airways hostesses on the flight over; he had spent the previous night with her at the Hilton Hotel, where the crew was staying.

"So you're meeting her again", I stated the obvious.

"Yes, and you are coming too!" he said cordially.

The attractive Oriental stewardess was obviously surprised to discover that Mike had a "woman". While Mike was ordering drinks, I took the opportunity to explain we had been together for a few months, and I knew he had been with her the previous night. She was very embarrassed; she was a decent person. While we sat at the bar, she invited one of the pilots to join us. I could see that this made Mike angry. Although he was friendly to the hostess and outwardly polite to the pilot, he completely ignored me. When it became obvious the pilot wasn't going anywhere, Mike said we would leave. He drove my car erratically, silently fuming beside me.

Breaking the silence, I queried "What have I done wrong?" This so enraged him that he pulled into the bus stop at Lavington Green Shopping Centre and started striking my face, first with his palm, then back of his hand, palm, backhand, palm, backhand. I cried out "Stop!" which maddened him even more; he balled his hand into a fist and hit me harder. My nose was bleeding and I could taste blood in my mouth from a split in my top lip. Both my eyes were throbbing. He pulled out onto the road again. I was unable to contain a sob, whereupon he yelled "Stop snivelling!" and smashed me across the face as he was driving. I tried not to whimper.

When we reached home, I walked back to shut the gate as he unlocked the door of my house. At the gate I paused, debating whether to risk running up the drive to Linda's house; I could shout to her to open the door and let me in. But I realised Linda might not wake immediately and, once awake, she would have to unlock the padlock, burglar-grilles, door, by which time Mike would easily have caught up with me and God knows what he would do. While I hesitated, deliberating, I heard Mike calling to me, coaxing me to come back to the house. I locked the gate and walked back to the house. Mike was standing in the doorway, leaning with one hand on the frame. As I reached the door, he brought his hand down and I automatically cringed and drew back in fear.

"Oh, don't be frightened of me" he cajoled in a soft, compassionate voice. "I won't hurt you!" He caressed my face gently. He bathed my wounds, all the time sympathising and cooing "Poor Baby!"

"How dare he? How DARE he? I'm Wendy, I'm ME!
And who is he? Just what is HE?
He is a sadistic, supercilious prig.
He is a beastly, cruel, calculating PIG!
Should I tell him so? No I wouldn't dare try.
It would be a sure way of inviting another black eye.
I'll just take his abuse, and keep my mouth shut
Or maybe next time, I'll have my throat cut".

The doctor confirmed that my nose was broken. Of course during the following days with my bruised face, one black eye, one purple eye and a stitched lip, everybody was asking in horror what had happened. I lied that Mike had braked suddenly to avoid a dog and I was thrown full face into the dashboard. I even told the same story to my sister. A couple of days later, he left for Sudan. I returned to Tiwi.

The first time I accompanied Mike to Bor, in Sudan, was not bad. I went for one week. Mike was one of a team of friendly workers from Holland. They lived in a camp, where they had built a dozen houses. There was also a little club-house and tennis court, where I played tennis daily. I spent most of the day driving around the wetlands, photographing and watching birds. I am sure we all have frustrations at missing out on special photographs – well the first of my three such frustrations was on the wetlands of *Bor:-* I was driving back to the camp in a hurry as a huge storm started out of nowhere. As I was slithering and sliding, I saw, right beside the road, a Saddlebill stork, standing next to a Shoebill! *Can you even imagine?* I was unable to stop due to the muddy condition of the road. That was the only Shoebill I ever spotted!

Mike arranged for the children and I to fly to Sudan to join him for Christmas 1980. We flew on a Sunbird Air Charter from Wilson Airport. We were not there for very long.

57. ENTER THE GERMAN

Jeni and Andrew knew everybody along Tiwi Beach, and all the comings and goings at the campsite. One afternoon I watched from the verandah, as they stood at the top of the beach in earnest conversation. They came up to the verandah holding hands. Jeni gave Andrew a shove towards me, "You tell her!" she instructed.

"No!" he hissed, backing away. "You tell her!"

"Tell me what?" I queried.

In unison, they replied "We've found you a new boyfriend, mummy!"

"But I don't want a new boyfriend!"

"Yes, you do. Uncle Mike's horrid! And our friend lets us use his frying pan to make pancakes in the sand!"

"Okay". I laughed. "What's his name?"

"He's called Hans" they informed me, excitedly.

"Oh no! 'Hans' sounds German and I don't like Germans!"

"But why mummy?"

"Because all Germans are pigs!"

After that, whenever I told them off, the children would take off down to the beach with the words "We're gonna see Hans, he's our friend!"

I did get to meet this Hans person, of course. He was tall, blond and long-limbed with warm, gentle eyes. His English was quaint, to say the least! Apparently he learned to speak English via a Danish sailor, whilst working on yachts in Spain. The result was broken English with German grammar, spoken in a typical Danish accent, which had me in stitches.

He told me he hated cold weather. He said he had been skippering a German millionaire's yacht around the Med during the week, sailing into whichever harbour the boss's "party" was being held at over the weekend. He said in winter months he sailed out to sunny islands, happily living like a Nature Boy until he received a message to meet the boss back in Majorca, Ibiza, or wherever. Apparently, at the end of one season, having expertly guided the rather large yacht perfectly into a space directly in front of the Ibiza Yacht Club without once using engines, Hans was puzzled as to why the ladies and gentlemen on the patio were staring at him in open-mouthed delight and stupefaction over their pink gins. Until he realised that he was stark naked!

Hans was in Barcelona when it started to snow, whereupon he hot-footed it to the nearest Travel Bureau and ordered "Dee sheepest ticket to dee sunchine". Thus ending up holidaying on Tiwi Beach.

Hans told me he had left Germany because he was anti-National Service. He told me he had Russian friends and could not imagine joining the Forces and being told to point a gun at a Russian. He said when the Authorities had called at the family house with the "papers" his father, who had suffered terribly on the Siberian Steppe during the war, had lent him the money to leave the country quickly, which he did. This sounded very honourable to me. But of course this caused the problem that he was unable to visit his home and family again because his name was on the "wanted" list.

58. MIKE THE MONSTER

As usual, I was at Tiwi when Mike returned to Kenya for a fortnight. He called from Nairobi, saying that I should meet him there before returning to the coast together. After the sale of my house was completed, we would stay at the Hurlingham Hotel on visits to Nairobi. I met Mike at the Thorntree. He was seated alone at a table, with a beer in front of him. As I walked over to him, Mike stood up and smiled with his lips and teeth, pulling a chair out for me. He beckoned a waiter, ordering a vodka and lime for me and, oddly, three beers. When the order came, he sent two beers across to two heavily made-up young African ladies at a nearby table.

Stunned, I said "They're prostitutes!"

He kicked my shin under the table. "Shut up!" as he handed me the drinks bill.

He must have been fed-up that it was taking me so long to learn how to behave. That evening, we were sitting side-by-side on a bench-seat in the nightclub of the Swiss Grill, when Mike started his game of making obvious signs to two heavily made-up hookers at the next table. I may as well not have been there at all, he was so engrossed in this, one of his favourite past-times, where he would raise his eyebrows and wiggle his nose in what was supposed to be a provocative manner. They were giggling at him. Fed-up at being left out and looking like a fool, but not wanting to cause a scene, I thought the best thing to do was to act as if I was joining in the game. Mike's beer glass was empty, just a tiny residue of beer in the bottom. I picked up the glass and, laughing, trickled the drip of beer onto his head. The women laughed with me, amused. I am sure they would have done at least that, had they been in my place!

Absolutely livid, Mike drew his arm across his chest, then drove his elbow into my ribs with a crack. I doubled over in agony, temporarily finding it difficult to breathe. The hookers looked shocked. He stood up, gripped my arm and forcibly dragged me out to the car. "Who the fuck do you think you are?" he said through clenched teeth. He dropped me off at the Hurlingham Hotel then drove straight out again, wheels spinning. He returned in the early hours, smelling of booze and sickly cheap perfume. The next morning, he took off alone for Tiwi, in my car, saying not a word.

> *"The bandage makes me sweat*
> *So I have prickly heat, too*
> *And I think of you*
> *Each time it itches.*
> *Waiting for rib to set,*
> *All black and blue*
> *I picture you*
> *With the campsite bitches"*

I caught a flight to the coast. Dad was wondering why Mike had turned up on his own. Dad did not like Mike at all. It was not because he knew how weird and psychotic Mike was; it was mainly because dad would not accept anybody being with me. Mike returned Dad's dislike, mainly because Dad got in the way of Mike achieving his dream. We were now living in the beach house I had built, next to Dad's little cottage.

I don't know whether Dad recognised a sadistic streak in Mike, in a manner of speaking having a very slight one himself. Many a tourist would complain when Dad roamed the property with his air rifle, shooting a tumbiri (Vervet monkey). This did not bother me as much as it should have, because Dad was an excellent shot and a monkey fired at by my father dropped dead in an instant. This would keep the thieving little beasts away for some time. Many was the time we would return to the beach house to discover that a troupe of timbiris had visited in our absence. They would open the refrigerator, stealing the contents, leaving papaya and mango skins, spaghetti and, worst of all, streaks of squidgy smelly money-poo down the walls and across the bed-sheets. Tourists would not listen when we instructed them not to feed the Vervets. Luckily, very few were bitten by the vicious little beasts. I was frightened of them and had to threaten one with the air-gun when it had chased Jeni. It took off at speed.

59. DANGEROUS SUNSHINE

I was a mad sun-worshipper. I loved the sun and loved to be tanned. I would deride "whiter than white" bodies on the beach. When back in Nairobi I spent as much time as possible at the Impala Club swimming-pool. When the weather was no good for sunbathing, I would use a sun-lamp. That is, until one day in 1981, when I was visiting Dr Landra for something unrelated. I happened to mention a little scab on the back of my hand that never healed; I would pick it off and it would soon be back again. Landra told me this was "solar keratosis", pre-sun cancer, and that I must never sunbathe again, should wear gloves when driving and always wear a hat when outdoors.

Dad was waiting for me in the car-park. I asked him, "What would you say is my favourite past-time?" After a very short pause, Dad replied "Basking in the sun!" "Yes" I said, "But no more". I kept to my word.

I was a frequent visitor to Dr M. I. Patel, a dermatologist, who prescribed Efudix Cream, which seeks out and destroys the damaged cells. I first applied the cream to my back. As per the doctor's instructions, I slept in a "plastic bag" so the sweating would make the cream work more thoroughly: I used the plastic bags that Dry Cleaners put over jackets and shirts, which were ready-made for the purpose. After a couple of weeks I had raw weeping patches all over my back. OhmiGod! By evening, when it was coming up to shower-time, my skin would be itching violently, driving me crazy, until I entered the shower and washed all the cream off, which soothed everything for half an hour or so. After that, my skin tightened and became so sore that I had to apply the cream as quickly as possible, to loosen up again. When treating my back, Mike would assist in applying the cream. When he wanted to teach me a lesson, he would delay applying the cream to "punish" me; sometimes he would refuse to apply it at all. When my back had healed, leaving white patches where the sores had been, I treated my arms, then my legs.

I have used Efudix cream many times over the past thirty-five years, even very recently, because even after staying out of the sun for such a long time, the solar keratosis keeps cropping up. I have had a few hundred lesions burned out with liquid nitrogen and a couple of dozen "baddies", such as Bowen's Cancer, excised. I have white patches and scars all over my body!

And I showed Landra the "little scab that never healed" ha ha! I have more than a hundred worse than that, even as I write this.

60. FAREWELL MONSTER

In May 1981, after a particularly bad altercation with Mike, the reason for which is too awful to relate here, I wandered into the kitchen and saw there was about half a bottle of vodka left. I had a couple of sleeping pills remaining, which I downed with the Voddie. Although I was a pretty hardened drinker and pill-popper by now, I doubt whether I walked in a straight line to the beach. But I managed to get the windsurfer into the water. It was a particularly high Spring Tide, the waves crashing over the top of the beach and flooding the turtles' casuarina tree. But the sea was as calm and flat as a giant's mirror, as is often the case at Spring Tide.

I zoomed out to the reef, then way over it and beyond, at fantastic speed. Then the sea changed its mood. On the way back I became a real cropper! I managed to get back on the board a few times, noticing Mike sitting on the beach, watching. I soon gave up trying to stand on the board and sat exhausted as I drifted towards the coral rocks beneath the Purdy's cottage. I didn't care.

I was to witness a pantomime in slow motion! I observed my dear old dad stumbling along the beach as fast as his poor legs would carry him, gesticulating madly at Mike. Mike stood up and walked up the beach. I then had a clear vision of Hans, my children's friend, running along the top of the coral cliffs, his beautiful legs carrying him along in huge great strides. I lost sight of him and was surprised when he suddenly reappeared about a hundred yards in front of me, swimming towards me with huge, powerful strokes. He must have dived straight off the cliff into the crashing waves, wow!

Then I heard his deep, kindly voice asking "Need help?"

"I'm fine!" I said stupidly.

Ignoring me, he was determined to get both the board and me to safety. There was no beach where we were heading, just towering coral cliffs with one set of broken cement steps beside "David's Pool", a bombed-out hole in the coral so-called because a gentleman by the name of David Petrie had fallen into the hole one night after imbibing in an access of alcohol at Twiga Bar. The Germanic madman first climbed onto the jagged coral, then lifted me up onto the steep steps. He proceeded to unceremoniously push me up the steps, before turning back to haul up the surfboard, which he shoved towards me. I turned on him in astonishment and disbelief, calling out "Leave it!"

"Take dee fookin' board!" he yelled.

"Your English is appalling!" I didn't want the stupid board anyway.

Thus, unaided, he saved the board, the mast and me. Leaving the board, mast and torn sail safely on the cliff top, a panting Hans walked beside me, ruefully informing me that he had probably missed out on the roast lamb dinner he had been invited to, at a nearby beach cottage. When the cottage came into view, I told him to go and eat his roast lamb. I sat on the ground leaning against the wall of the outside loo.

After a while, Harkon, a Norwegian friend who had also been eating roast lamb, walked back down to the beach with me. Upon reaching our cottage, dad came and put his arms around me, almost sobbing, telling me that Mike had refused to go out to assist me, and that he did not have the strength to swim out there himself! He had told Mike that he "didna want tae see hide nor hair of him again!"

212

Mike's bags were packed. The next morning he returned to the house, spittingly furious with my father. He wanted to purchase a ticket to England, but could not because there was not enough money in my bank account. I asked dad if he could lend the money temporarily and dad, delighted to be getting rid of Mike, wrote out a cheque immediately. Mike wordlessly took the cheque, put his bags in my car, and drove away.

I never saw nor heard of him again.

Not ever.

Sixteen years later, when I started writing this narrative as "self-therapy", I tried to track Mike down. I tried through parties who had contacts with Interpol. I gave them the phone number for Mike's flat in England, also a collection of photographs. I gave addresses of people who knew Mike, including the name of the young Mexican girl who lived in his flat. Mike had proudly told me that he had had a sexual relationship with the girl since she was a twelve-year-old schoolgirl.

The only feedback we ever had, was that he was imprisoned in Germany after killing a young child he had assaulted. But we never had this verified. If he is indeed in a German prison, I would really like to visit him.

61. GETTING TO KNOW THE GERMAN

The following Sunday, in high spirits, dad drove my children and I to "Nomads", a popular restaurant-cum-bar at Diani Beach, renowned for its Sunday curry lunches. When we returned home, I discovered that my surfboard had been returned and placed at the top of our garden. Having being drinking voddies with my lunch, I had a few abortive attempts at clambering onto the board, but the stupid thing kept slipping away from under me. It was then that I noticed Hans standing in the shallow water watching me, amused. Saying nothing, he walked over to the board and held it still until I managed to balance sufficiently well to sail out to the reef and back. Hans pointed out that the sail was in need of repair. He announced that he would return to repair it for me, "In dee next dayz".

In fact, he was back dee very next day. Returning from the morning school-run, I discovered Hans sitting cross-legged on our verandah, intently stitching up my torn sail. The children were very happy to have him around, and he gently but determinedly became part of our lives. Horrified upon discovering he smoked cannabis, I accused Hans of being "no better than the campers". Late one Saturday morning, Hans arrived in time to discover me swallowing a multi-vitamin with voddie whilst cooking brunch. He silently removed the voddie from my hand, saying it was too early for vodka, "but skrumbled ecks okay!" He continued, amused, "Cannabis bad but fodka breakfast okay, eh?"

He returned that evening at Sundowner time and joined me for a "Blackjack" (voddie and coffee liqueur). Dad brought his Black-and-Tan over and joined us for a while. Eventually, very late, I told Hans he might as well stay the night, as I had a "houseful of beds". In the morning, Andrew came through for a Sunday morning cuddle. Upon seeing Hans, he beat a rapid retreat, whispering loudly to his sister, "Jeni, come quickly, *he's still here!*" They walked back together, holding hands. Andrew gazed up at Jeni, intently, waiting for her to speak. "Hans", she asked seriously, "are you going to marry our mummy?"

After three weeks, Hans suggested we "try anuzzer zree veeks!" I never expected him to stay. Later, quite astonished that he was still with us after three months, I reminded him that he must book his return flight to Spain, as his ticket was due to expire.

"Lost dee ticket!" he replied, simply.

Twenty-three years later, Hans still blamed it on the Blackjacks! He maintained I lied very convincingly about having a houseful of beds whereas, in fact, we ended up "sharing". Many a time, when somebody remarked on how the children naturally referred to him as their "dad", he was heard to comment "Yes. Years ago I thought I was moving in with a wealthy landowner, but it turned out to be a package deal!"

The main problem with Hans moving in, was my dad. Having seen the back of John, then successfully seen Mike off, he was now determined to protect me from all men forever. Dad always rose at 6 a.m., taking a walk either up on the cliff top or down on the beach. The children would check it out, then come back and tell Hans "Grandad's up the back", whereupon Hans would rush down to the beach and disappear. Should they report that "Grandad was on the beach", Hans would vanish across the adjoining wall between our cottages and Twiga campsite.

The three of us returned from a great night out at "Tradies" (Tradewinds) weekly disco, my father escorted Hans to the edge of the property, shook his hand, and bade him Goodnight. Then dad proceeded to sit it out with me until 3 a.m., his head bouncing up in alarm every time his chin dropped onto his chest! I eventually suggested that dad go to bed, as he would be pretty tired the next day. I saw him to the door and waited for him to walk back to his cottage. But no, he stood and waited for me to close my back door. I explained I intended to take a walk across the campsite before retiring. Dad instantly agreed that a walk would do us both good! By this time Hans had fallen asleep beside a campfire, unable to sit it out any longer!

Dad had taken on the task of driving the children up the road to await their school lift. At around 8 a.m., Hans would nonchalantly stroll up the path from the beach, call out "hello" to dad, and join us for breakfast. That was, until the day dad handed him the car-keys, with the comment "Seeing as you're living here anyway, you may as well drive the bairns up the road!"

I recall the day Hans was driving the little Suzuki along the bumpy track on the way to town, when Jeni's voice piped up from behind "Hans, where do you come from?"

"Germany!" he replied.

"OH NO!" A horrified gasp from behind. I turned to see my daughter putting on an act, with hands over mouth, eyes huge and round.

"Why?" he drawled.

"Coz my mummy says all Germans are *pigs!*"

Jeni's mummy tried very hard to make herself small enough to disappear under the dashboard. The German glanced sideways at me, before the deep sexy voice queried, "Oh yes? And vat else does your mummy say?"

Splutters from behind as Andrew squeezed his nose tightly in an attempt to stifle the giggles.

One memorable lunchtime, Hans and I were sitting on the verandah of the "Castle Hotel" in Mombasa town, with oil dripping down to our elbows whilst eating the delicious samosas that only the Castle Hotel could produce. An American naval vessel was in port. Prostitutes from upcountry and as far away as Uganda had flown down to Mombasa in plane-loads, bus-loads and taxies, always knowing well in advance when the next US Navy boat was due.

We gleaned much enjoyment from watching the American sailors, sprawled across the uncomfortable plastic chairs as they swigged down bottle after bottle of warm Tusker beer. The Hotel would order a truckload of beer direct from the brewery. A park would be kept available for the truck, right in front of the Hotel verandah. The Hotel waiters would haul down crate after crate, selling the beers to the sailors direct from the truck. The soon-empty crates were slung back onto the truck.

Hans was drinking beer and I was drinking Guinness. As I drew the little bottle of multivitamins from my bag, Hans asked to see the bottle. He examined the label closely and announced quietly, "Dis iz Speed!"

"What do you mean 'Speed'? They're multivitamins".

"I am telling you, My Dear, dis iz Speed – amfetmins!"

A little warning bell jangled in the back of my mind. The quaint Asian accent of my pharmacist. For "M'ft'mins", read not "Multivitamins" but "Amphetamines"! Jeeez! *Eight years on Speed* – and large doses of it at that! Speed belongs with Cannabis, Cocaine, and all that stuff!

"Wow!" said I. "So what now?"

"*Zo no more!*" matter-of-factly, as he put the bottle in his pocket.

"Okay, fine! No problem!"

No problem!

When we reached home, the contents of the bottle were poured into the loo. In accordance with the instruction "And all dee ozzers!" I emptied out my remaining supplies, even the sleeping pills. All the strong yellow pills, then all but two of the milder orange ones – which I hid 'just in case' – went into the loo. They sat there in a congealed mass for days, simply wouldn't go away; just sat there laughing at me whenever I went for a pee.

No problem she said.

Is it really possible to continue for a fortnight without a wink of sleep? I am sure I did. Occasionally I would start slipping into a troubled, sleep-like state, only to drift straight into horrendous nightmares. Mike. Monsters. Devils. Mike. Panic.

Do you know what panic attacks are? I do. Oh yes.

Hans was there all the time. When I awoke shouting and yelling, he was there for me. He never criticised me, was never angry. Not even when, late at night, I would consume a couple of voddies before stumbling down to the beach and collapsing under a casuarina tree. After a while, he would follow me down, pick me up, and take me back to the house.

I cannot understand how he put up with me through my 'drying out'. I once shrieked at him that he should go back to where he came from.

His response? "You gonna miss dee kidz!"

As time went on, KC Sunshine Band's "Please Don't Go" became our signature tune.

62. MY INQUISITIVE CHILDREN

My children were fascinated with everything. During our beach-walks, they taught me about 'sandworms', long polythene-like tubes that appeared to suck sand in at one end and excrete it at the other in long spirals of wet sludge which piled up in mini helter-skelters along the beach. They showed me that the green moss-like substance that appears to grow at the water's edge is actually continually moving; not moss at all, but millions of little living creatures.

My kids and I were walking along the beach, my boy intently stretching his little legs to walk exactly in footprints left by an adult, which took him up to the top of the beach and back, sometimes running, occasionally walking in a complete circle, stopping to examine a crab-hole because it was what *"that person"* had done. Suddenly Andrew shrieked "Ouch!" I went over to see what had caused my son to leap around holding his foot: he had trodden on a sharp piece of coral. Calming down, he glared at the offending footprint he had trodden in, and mused "I wonder what *he* did, then!"

Probably quite wrongly, I tried to keep my children away from the fishermen whilst the fish were being de-gutted. Nevertheless, in the same way I watched headless chickens running around, I would find Jeni and Andrew staring in morbid fascination as flapping fish were beheaded.

I once heard water rushing into the bath-tub as Jeni's voice rang out "Hurry up Andoo!" Andrew came to me with a tin of sardines from the store, asking urgently, "Mum, please open this tin for us!"

"Whatever for?" I went to the bathroom where Jeni was swishing the water around and around the tub, taps on full.

"Pleeeez put the fishes in, mummy. We want to see if they can swim!"

The children remembered a few of the Dutch phrases they had heard spoken by the young workers on the project in Sudan. There was a time that I was looking for Andrew, only to find him standing with hands in shorts pockets, chattering away to some Dutch Missionaries who had set up tents on the campsite.

I later asked him what he had been talking about; he replied "Oh, I told them I could speak Dutch!"

"What Dutch did you speak to them?"

"I told them *'kipperstrandt'*" he explained proudly. I thought to myself, "Oh dear, that means *Chickenshit!*"

"And I also told them *'Hootferdommer!'*" he was well pleased with himself.

All I can say is, I trust the Missionaries appreciated my little boy's linguistic talents.

63. LIVING WITH THE GERMAN

In those days, we still occasionally retired at night without locking the doors. One night I was woken by a noise emanating from the kitchen area. I shook Hans awake, "I think there are thieves in the house!" He leapt silently out of bed, grabbed my tennis racquet and climbed onto the top of the bedroom wall via the dressing table. Most the coast houses had high thatched roofs made from makuti, making it possible for fearless children and drunken adults to walk along the tops of all the inside walls, where a large gap was always left below the thatch to allow for air-circulation. Hans hissed "Lock the door. I catch one of dee buggers!" I recall the vision of Hans's bare bottom as he crept along the top of the wall wielding my tennis racquet! Of course, he was right; had there been intruders in the house they would hardly have been looking upwards for an attacker, and he would surely surprise them. However, as it turned out, it was only a stray cat licking out the dirty steak pan in the sink.

I have a ridiculous and unexplained phobia for toads – not cute little frogs, just toads and big, lumpy bullfrogs – and to a lesser degree for bats. There was a bat in our house whom we named Sebastian. Our loo was at the end of a long corridor and many was the evening that I would be sitting on the loo puzzling over a crossword with the door open, when Sebastian would fly Kamakazi-style at low level down the corridor towards me. I would crash onto the floor while he swooped, chortling, up towards the makuti roof. One evening, he returned to dive-bomb me as I was pulling my pants up; I tore through to the bedroom and lay underneath the bed until I heard him laughing at me from the roof beams.

After we had retired one night, he was hanging somewhere up in the roof, squealing horribly. I did not dare to move out from the safety of the mosquito net. Hans was sleeping through the racket; I shook him awake. "Sebastian's screaming at me from above the bed!" Hans picked up the 2.2 Air Rifle that was beside the bed, pushed it out underneath the mosquito net and fired a shot towards the noise. The noise stopped. "Okay now?" he asked as he went back to sleep. Upon hearing a drip-dripping sound, I switched on the bedside lamp. To my horror, I saw a spreading pool of blood on the top lining of the mosquito net. I shrieked to Hans "You've shot him!"

"Oh no!" he replied, before dropping back to sleep.

Poor little bat. Even in death he was taunting me.

Sometime after the incident with the "Speed" at the Castle Hotel, after a late night at Tradies Disco, I decided it was necessary to take one of the little orange pills I had kept for just such an occasion. After breakfast, the four of us set off to Mombasa for our Saturday shopping trip. I sat back in the passenger seat, looking up at the beautiful sky. "Wow!" I said excitedly, pointing at the heavens, "Just look at the silver linings around all the clouds!" I had never seen anything like it, it was absolutely amazing. Hans gave me a quizzical sideways glance.

When we were sitting on the verandah of the Castle Hotel, the children asked if they could go across the road to browse around a bookshop. I was beside them as they stood holding hands waiting to cross the road, when I realised all the vehicles were zooming past at tremendous speed, so fast I could barely make them out......buses, vans, saloon cars, all whizzing past whoosh whoosh at hundreds of kilometres an hour. I grabbed my children's shoulders in horror, pulling them back from the road. "Stop mummy, you're hurting us!"

Hans appeared and began unfolding my clenched fingers and prising them from Jeni and Andrew's shoulders. "No no!" I panicked; "Look at the speed of the cars!"

Hans told the children to cross the road carefully before steering me back to my seat. "Vat did you take dis morning?" he asked quietly. I sat bolt upright. "Oh *yes!*" I said.

That was the last one I took, ever.

64. OUR NEIGHBOURS ON THE BEACH

Though many of these places are not so pleasant to visit today, due to the influx of tourists and inevitable entourage of pestering beach-boys, Kenya's beaches are all stunningly beautiful; long stretches of palm-fringed brilliant white sand. Back in the 60's and 70's there were few high-rise hotels, only makuti-thatched bungalows which fitted in perfectly with the landscape. Now, tall hideous buildings have sprung up all over the place; sadly, this is called progress.

You were either a "South-Coaster" or a "North-Coaster". The coast north of Mombasa Island is more easily accessible, with a bridge across from the Island to the mainland. The route to the South Coast is more adventurous, with cars lining up for a ferry to take you across the Likoni Channel to the South Mainland. We have always been South-Coasters. The beaches to the south used to be less-commercialised than the north, and still are to a certain extent. As you travel further south, so the beach sand becomes softer. The beach nearest to Likoni Channel is aptly named "Shelly Beach", with large grains of sand. The sand on Diani Beach, more than twenty kilometres further south, is very powdery and tends to stick to the body; even the sea-water is quite murky. Tiwi Beach, in between, has the best of all. Here, the sand is in between the large granules of sand at Likoni and the talcum powder of Diani, and the water is crystal clear.

At Diani, the edge of the reef is much further out and not possible to walk to even at low tide; there is always shallow water with local dug-out canoes passing back and forth when the tide is out. At Tiwi, the edge of the reef is much closer to the shore and when the tide is out it is possible to walk all the way out to the edge of the reef, snorkelling in little rock pools on the way.

Growing up on an unspoiled Kenyan beach must have been quite idyllic for my children. On the other side of the coin, however, were the mounting numbers of drop-outs who were drawn to our beach by the easy-going way of life and easily-accessible drugs. The drop-outs included various titled people from the British Aristocracy. I recall harbouring one absolutely terrified nobleman, who had got into a brawl over a girl with one of the overlanders. Lord Johnny had galloped down the beach and ended up hiding under our upturned boat while the overlanders, armed with sticks and other weapons, searched up and down the beach, seriously after his blood!

Another member of "The Aristocracy" who was reported to be eighty-s*omething* in line to the Throne, squandered away his fortune on the beach. I was told that he had thanked an overland trucker for assistance he had provided, by giving him his Grandmother's priceless antique diamond ring. Provided he was not drinking spirits, this man was a tremendously likeable, warm-hearted person, blessed with a super-brilliant brain, which sometimes flipped. I can't remember what I had done or said to bring it on, but one evening when drunk, he suddenly leapt at me with an animal roar and, squeezing his hands tightly around my throat, tried to throttle me. A visitor jumped to my aid and prized the drink-addled aristocrat's hands from around my neck. In doing so, the noble visitor landed up in a cactus bush with vicious thorns that pierced into his elbow. Upon returning to England, he ended up in hospital to have his elbow operated on; one of life's amazing coincidences was the nurse who tended him just happened to be a visitor that I had introduced him to whilst he was holidaying at Tiwi!

The back-packers were always there, still trying desperately to sell their belongings in order to remain on the beach for a while longer, making deals with the beach boys, smoking dope and often drinking illegal local brews. There was an occasion when we had to take a quick business trip to Nairobi, leaving an overland friend to keep an eye on our house. When we returned late in the evening, our friend was nowhere to be seen. I searched the refrigerator for something to eat. There was only a jug of delicious coffee-smelling liquid which, luckily as it turned out, did not appeal to Hans or the children, who went straight to bed. I poured a cup of the coffee-laced liquid and gulped it down. I don't think I slept that night. I sat on the bed, in my mind solving all the world's problems: everything was as clear as glass.

Until today, I can remember flying horizontally back and forth down the corridor, hoping to God t*hat* neither of the children would open a door to go to the loo, as they would collide with me as I flew past their door. Somebody was calling outside our bedroom window; I walked to the window to see a person climbing up the wooden criss-cross bars. Later, I was to learn the jug contained, not iced coffee, but a coffee cake mix laced liberally with cannabis. I was also to learn our overland friend had returned, and was indeed calling from outside our bedroom window – but he assured me that he did not climb up the wooden bars! He had wanted to collect the cake mix his girlfriend had left in the fridge! Funnily enough, the girlfriend was the same nurse who, back in London, had tended the noble rafiki who fell into a cactus bush while defending me.

An English girl had set up her tiny tent on the campsite, right at the high water mark. She would hardly have noticed if the tide had swept away her tent with her

226

inside it, so stoned was she all the time. If I was walking along the beach, I would sometimes see her stepping out of her tent in a diaphanous white cotton dress; she would wander dreamily down to the sea, and keep on walking until she was floating. Then she would walk up out of the sea like a nymph and drift in a dazed fashion onto the verandah of the bar, the ultra-thin fabric of her dress, now soaking wet, clinging like wet tissue paper to every fold, bump and crease of her body. But she was really nice if you were lucky enough to catch her first thing in the morning.

One Sunday afternoon, dad and I were sitting at Twiga Lodge bar, surrounded by a group of Dutch back-packers. Standing beside me ordering drinks was a severely over-tanned girl wearing nothing but a long thin T-shirt with armholes torn out halfway down to her waist. The barman's mouth was wide open while his eyes were riveted onto the bare nipples that popped into view every time she turned to pass a bottle to the friends standing behind her. It was all I could do to restrain myself from grabbing her and pressing her arms down to her sides. Finally, to my intense relief, she moved away from the bar. Throughout this embarrassing episode, dad was giving the barman the full benefit of his chilling, unwavering stare. I had noticed one of the young Dutch men looking at dad with an expression of disbelief and horror. Dad, well aware of the impression he was making, continued unsuccessfully to engage the barman in a Battle of the Eyes. The traveller nudged me and pointed a finger at my father. I asked him what his problem was, although it was quite obvious.

The young man shook his head as if he wasn't seeing correctly and, staring at my father, said "The eyes! *Look at the eyes of that man!*"

Trying to play it down, I said "Oh, it's OK. He lives here and knows the barman well!"

The young man physically shuddered. "Never have I seen such a look of hatred!"

Well, yes. While the Dutchman had incorrectly read dad's look as one of "hatred", it was rather incredible. I didn't even try to explain that what dad was actually trying to do, was to will the barman to take his eyes off the young girl's nipples. My dad, having spent over thirty years in the country, knew how the behaviour of certain Western women made the Kenyans look down on them – even though they enjoyed looking! I mean, would *any* Afro-Kenyan man allow his woman to display her nakedness publicly, for Heaven's Sake? And, in those days anyway, would any Afro-Kenyan woman have been happy to do so? It would be beneath them. This would be impossible to get across to the uninhibited European youths crowding onto our beaches.

65. MY CHILDREN

The time came when Jeni was to spend the full day at school in Mombasa, while Andrew still finished at lunchtime. I frequently took the children to lunch at the club where my mother worked and, after dropping Jeni back at school, would spend the afternoon at the club swimming-pool with Andrew. On one such afternoon, I saw Andrew wander over to chatter to a young woman surrounded by a number of children. He was deep in conversation, every so often turning to point me out to his audience. I thought, "How sweet, Andrew is pointing me out to his new friends!"

When the lady packed her belongings together, I smiled and nodded as she passed me. Smiling back at me, she stopped and said "I just couldn't wait to meet a mother who can make a noise like an elephant!"

One afternoon we went to collect Jeni from school, to find her lying in the playground with a blood-soaked cloth tied around her leg. She had fallen from the climbing frame and ripped a deep, jagged eight-inch tear up her calf. I hurriedly drove to the doctor's surgery, as the wound clearly required stitching. We found the doctor leaving early, dressed in tennis shorts with racquet in hand. He looked briefly at Jeni's leg and said "Oh that's fine, it will heal up nicely!"

Jeni will always have the scar. A very noticeable jagged scar. I hope the doctor enjoyed his game of tennis.

Some years later, I watched Jeni regaling a group of tourists in our bar with a story that obviously fascinated them. Afterwards, one of them said to me "How awful for Jeni, to be scratched so badly by a cheetah!"

For some reason, I never liked having a "middle name", and never use it. Thus my children were given one name only. I remember the day I walked with Jeni across to the verandah of Twiga Lodge when a visitor said to my little girl, "Hello! Let me see if I remember it correctly: 'Jennifer Rachel Julia Stanley'. Is that right?" Jeni looked at me with embarrassment, worried about what I might say. I said nothing!

To this day, my daughter is known as "Jeni-Rache"!

66. BACK TO THE SHITTY CITY

At that time, we were yet to build a restaurant and beach bar. After putting final touches to a couple of chalets, Hans wanted to find a proper job. The money coming in from the chalets was insufficient to keep dad, Hans, the children and I, as well as paying school fees. Dad was still quite capable of looking after the bookings. We moved up to Nairobi, where we shared a bungalow with my sister. I was employed in a very pleasant office, working as personal assistant to an English gentleman.

The bungalow we rented was on Mukinduri Drive, opposite the Bomas of Kenya. There was a dear little one-roomed guest cottage on the compound, which we rented out to a couple who planned to spend their weekend visits to Nairobi there. It was while we were living here, that there was an attempted coup against the President, Daniel Arap Moi. At the time, Linda was visiting dad at Tiwi. With most people in the country sensibly staying in their houses, my sister decided she would hitch a return to Nairobi! She managed, somehow, to get through all the armoured vehicles at the roundabouts and arrived at the door unscathed.

The couple who were departing from their weekend retreat in our garden, were not so lucky. They were dragged out of their vehicle and made to lie in a ditch with guns pointing at them, before being permitted to return in the direction from which they had come. We spent a cosy evening together and it was only after a few vinos that the truth came out – the couple were not married: well, not to each other anyway, and their spouses knew nothing about the illicit affair. After this, their spouses were probably about to find out! Unfortunately the coup was put to an abrupt end by the Dictator-President, who acted as if he owned the country. In fact, on reflection, he did own a large percentage of it.

Our one mode of transport was Linda's Honda 250 motorbike. Hans would drop Jeni off at the school bus, come back to collect Linda and drop her off at her office. Then back for me. Amused friends would comment "I saw Hans driving around on a little motorbike, with a gas cylinder on the handlebars, a crate of beer on the carrier and a shopping bag behind him!" Hans cultivated a vegetable and herb garden and always had a meal ready for the evening. He thoroughly enjoyed attending ladies' "coffee mornings" and catching up on the local gossip. His English improved very quickly.

We found an old VW Beetle going for eighteen thousand Kenya Shillings. I asked my boss if he could lend the money, which he was quite happy to do, but he was going away for a couple of days. Two days later, the car dealer said that somebody else had offered twenty-three thousand shillings for the "Veedub", so that was now the asking price and, if we wanted it, we should give a cheque immediately to avoid losing it. I wrote out a cheque, knowing that my boss would be back before the cheque had time to clear.

The very next morning, the car dealer found his way to my office. He walked in and unceremoniously smacked the cheque onto my desk with "Refer to Drawer" stamped across it! My first "bounced" cheque....I wondered how he had managed it. I asked him to wait while I telexed my Insurance Company in England where I had a Life Insurance Policy I had been paying into since I was eighteen. It was due to mature in three months' time. I received back from them the exact amount I had struggled to pay every month for almost twenty years! I bought the car.

The Company that employed me was very good in giving jobs to Hans, in Somalia. He would disappear or a week or two or more, returning with a bit more money to spend. Then we would dine out, visit hairdressers, go to the cinema, and take a few days off work to drive to the coast to spend time with dad.

Linda, Jeni, Andrew and I – now of course with Hans – happily found we were renewing our relationship with Marianna. My sister would relate to me their escapades over various weekends, when she and Marianna toured Nairobi's party scenes on Linda's trusty Honda motorbike. They had great fun. Linda would comment upon how Marianna appeared to know everybody and they were able to get into discos at extra-special rates due to her connections. One particular morning, on the way home, upon passing the flat of one of Marianna's friends; they decided to pop in for breakfast. They sat down to a delicious crab soufflé breakfast – hilarious!

67. ANDREW AT SCHOOL

Mum was recovering from a broken heart, which had been caused by the sudden, nasty and extremely vicious dumping by the man she had fallen deeply in love with. This had aged her of course, but she was becoming "mum" again. She was now working as matron at Pembroke House Preparatory School in Gilgil, in the Rift Valley. We spent many a weekend visiting her. Andrew thought this school seemed like Heaven, with hundreds of boys having fun, wearing smart uniforms. We booked him into the school at the tender age of six, possible because mum was working there. My little boy was very excited and couldn't wait to attend this *fun-school*.

Remembering my own homesickness, I dreaded leaving Andrew at boarding school. At his first half-term, mother proudly announced he called her "Ms Brown", was treated exactly like any other boy and, in fact, some of the pupils did not know they were related. Jeez! How ghastly! Back in Nairobi that half-term, I was seeing my boy to bed when he asked seriously: "Mummy, this school isn't as nice as I thought it would be. Can I leave there please and come back home?" This wrenched my heart. I explained that he was very lucky to have the opportunity of attending such a good school, and in the future he would appreciate it.

"But I don't care how good the school is! I don't care if I don't learn anything! I want to live at home with you!"

"Tell you what!" I said. "Let's give it a couple of years and see how it works out!"

"Okay then" he sniffed.

Although he did not broach the "leaving" subject again, he was terribly homesick. As each holiday was coming to an end, he would become miserable and clinging; it was dreadful for us all. I loathed leaving him at school, where the poor little mite had to listen to the other boys making jokes behind his grandmother's back, and bear with it, even when they made a hole in the dorm floor above her bathroom.

Two years later, almost to the day, my then eight-year-old son reminded me "Mum, do you remember two years ago, when you said we'd give this school a try for a couple of years and see how it works out?"

"Yes, I do seem to recall something like that," said I.

"Well", he stated. "I am now eight and I still don't like the school. Can I leave now?"

68. VISITING U.K. and MY EX-HUSBAND

Due to expiry of visa and suchlike, Hans had to leave Kenya for a while. He went to England and stayed with his brother Herbert, in a flat on Priory Road, London. He told me that, though he did not have sufficient "qualifications" to be accepted for a job sweeping the streets, he was successful in applying for work with a construction company converting Victorian houses into flats; he soon became foreman of the site. I had saved up enough money to pay for a ticket to visit him.

When Hans and his brother had left for work, I washed a huge pile of dhobi in the bath-tub, as one does. As I was hanging everything out on a line in the garden, I noticed curtains twitching at the windows of the other flats in the block. When Hans's brother returned from work he was most embarrassed; he showed me how to work the washing machine and tumbler dryer. When it came to doing the ironing, I phoned my cousin Margaret in Banstead to ask how to use a steam iron.

I liked Herbert. He was a workaholic, quite the opposite of Hans. He told me he was very pleased that Hans had met me, because at least he was now settling down to "proper work"! One evening Hans telephoned his family in Stuttgart; his dad answered the phone. He chatted away for a while. I understood enough of the conversation to hear Hans tell his father that he had a girlfriend in Kenya, after which he asked quite abruptly if he could speak to his mother. Afterwards, I asked what his dad had said to upset him. Apparently his father's immediate response had been "How black is she?"

Herbert kindly lent us his personal car whenever we liked. I actually drove in it to Banstead to visit Margaret and family; to this day, it is the only car with an "automatic gearbox" that I have driven. Hans and I travelled to Scotland to visit dad's relatives, also intending to stop en route to visit John in Stranraer. We stayed for a night in a quaint little guesthouse nearby, purposely giving no warning of our visit as our plan was to call on John alone after Caitlin had gone to work. I phoned him in the morning to say we would like to visit; he was very happy. Shortly after we arrived, Caitlin came dashing into the house, admonishing us for giving insufficient warning...it had caused her great problems to take the day off work at such short notice!

However, in spite of planning to avoid her, we thought it generous when Caitlin invited us out to lunch at a famous Scottish Castle. It was indeed a beautiful Castle, but the food was nothing to rave about and was extraordinarily expensive. Hans whispered to me that perhaps we should offer to share the bill; I agreed.

When the bill arrived, Caitlin motioned for the waiter to pass it to Hans! He paid without a murmur.

69. TONY THE SCHOOL TEACHER

Back in Kenya, Linda had changed jobs. She was happy, but no longer in touch with Ray Cuthbert, her previous employer for whom I had worked on the couple of occasions when she was visiting Tony in England. She was in constant communication with Tony, who was now teaching in a nearby African country, hoping to be back in Kenya shortly. One lunchtime, I happened to bump into Linda's ex-employer, in "Marino's. He cupped his hand around my ear and said "I hear Tony's been flown back to England on a stretcher!" That evening I told Linda what Ray had said. We went back to my office and Linda phoned Tony's mother in Somerset.

Tony had indeed been flown back to England on a stretcher. He had died two days' previously. Linda cried helplessly "And he so much wanted to live!"

You still have not told us why why why, God? Please explain, in a way we can understand

70. MY BOSS'S UNRESPECTABLE BROTHER

When Hans returned to Kenya, he continued working with the same Company that I was working for. For reasons of work permits, this still meant working outside Kenya, but he came home frequently. One Sunday evening when Hans was away, I was sitting at the bar of Muthaiga Club after a hard afternoon's tennis. I was being strongly chatted up by my boss's extremely sozzled brother. Up until then, I had liked this man very much, and had always respected him. As he poured more triple shots of neat Johnny Walker Black Label Whisky down his throat, this gentleman was becoming less and less gentlemanly. It was time to disappear.

"I must go to the loo!" I exclaimed, as he lurched out to grab me. I walked in a very slow and controlled manner to the door; I opened the door gently and calmly, closing it slowly behind me. The instant the door was closed, I flew like a pursued fox across the main clubhouse, through the open French windows, leapt over a balcony wall and shot across the car-park with feet barely touching the ground. Panting as I neared the car, I pulled my car-keys out of my handbag.

My boss's brother was leaning nonchalantly against my car. "You weren't thinking of leaving me, were you?"

How the *hell* did he do it? There was obviously a shortcut. Panic! An extremely unpleasant struggle followed, this no-longer-a-gentleman pressing me backwards against the side of the car, an appendage akin to a steel bar poking into my body.

"See what effect you have on me?" he panted.

"But you know I am with Hans!" I blurted out.

"Hans?" he snorted. "Pshaw! He's nothing: nobody! I will look after your children, pay their school fees, and you will live in luxury!"

"But I happen to love Hans!" as I roughly shoved him out of the way.

As the non-gentleman stumbled to regain his footing, he threatened "Hans will find that he's out of a job!"

I drove home, terribly shaken up. When Hans returned a couple of days later, I related nothing about the unpleasant incident. He went straight to the workshop to report back. An hour later he arrived in my office, very miserable. "They paid me off" he said, incredulous, "for no reason!"

I gathered up all my personal items and left the office, never to return. Pity; I loved the job and truly liked my boss.

71. BACK TO THE BEACH

Through a friend of Linda's, Hans landed up in an interesting position with a transport company whose Headquarters were in Mombasa. I was given the job as Secretary to the Manager of Golden Beach Hotel at Diani and we moved back to live on our family plot with dad.

My previously strict, stiff-upper-lipped father had become somewhat of a beach-bum, never wearing a shirt before evening and even then only wearing his favourite ragged shirts with his favourite torn shorts – and rubber flip-flops on his feet. Over time, I bought him new shirts, sandals, smart shorts. A couple of days later I would see them being worn by Hamisi the gardener. One Christmas mum gave him a really nice shirt that she had bought for him in England. Two days later, I saw Hamisi wearing it in the garden!

But dad was happy. He walked a lot. He would drink two "Black-and-Tans" at eleven o'clock in the morning. He had two cups of tea at four o'clock, then any number of black-and-tans in the evening, before falling asleep on his verandah chair, chin on chest. We would wake him to join us for a light supper, and then see him safely to bed.

72. MY CHILDREN'S EUROPEAN EXPERIENCE

In 1984, Hans and I had saved up enough money for a visit to the UK, this time taking Jeni and Andrew. As Hans was unable to return to Germany, we arranged to meet up with his parents and a couple of his siblings in Zurich, en route. We changed flights at the airport in Brussels very early in the morning. The airport appeared to be one wide corridor, kilometres long; Hans said we had to run the whole length of it in order to catch our connecting flight! In the middle of this flat-out dash, I noticed the children were not with us. I stopped to look back and there they both were, hands cupped around eyes against a large plate glass separation, staring open-mouthed into an airport store. "Whatever are you doing?" I called out, "Hurry up, or we'll miss our flight!" They were watching a very boring scene – a large lady wearing head-scarf, overalls and apron, vacuuming the floor.

"Look mummy! *A white lady cleaning the floor!*"

In Switzerland, we met up with Hans's parents, and various members of his wonderful, happy family. We stayed in a hotel in Zurich, in a room where everything was white: brilliant white ceiling, walls and floor tiles, white curtains, bed-posts, bed-covers, blankets and sheets, carpets, towels, lampshades...I mused that they must have had to use a heck of a lot of bleach when doing the dhobi.

We drove to the Rhone Glacier, where I took some beautiful photos. As we were about to set off down the mountains there was warning of a severe snow storm, meaning we had to break our journey to stay at the "Hotel Glacier" en route.

We then spent a wonderful time in Geneva, as guests of my Swedish ex-boss Gunnar, his wife Brenda and their son and daughter. They met us at the airport together with their delightful Airedale dog "Bonnie". They had a lovely house overlooking Lake Geneva. Coincidentally, Andrew's Godmother, Pam, happened to live nearby. We surprised Pam by turning up at a Party she had invited Gunnar and Brenda to, on the very night that we arrived. One evening, Gunnar and Brenda took us across the "Border" to a Glogg Party in the French sector of Switzerland. It was very amusing that, on the Swiss side, the Border office building was immaculately painted, tidy and clean, with spotless loos. On the French side, the other half of very same building was scruffy, dirty, with distasteful loos and altogether more like home!

Brenda and Gunnar took us to a stunning resort in the mountains where, for the very first time, my children and I saw people skiing! Bonnie came with us in a cable car; she loved leaping and skidding on the snowy slopes.

I became sick two days after arriving in England, while we were staying with Sylvia and Ray in Norfolk. It turned out that I had hepatitis. I was admitted to the James Paget Hospital in Gorleston. Any time Hans or family visited me, they were made to wear fancy-dress: white cloth hats, face masks, gowns, aprons, gloves and protective covers over their shoes. We had planned to travel to Scotland to visit dad's relatives and then John and Caitlin. Hans took the children to Scotland without me.

When they returned to Norfolk over a week later, Hans commented that they would kill me if I remained in hospital! We decided we should return to Kenya, where hepatitis was viewed as a normal illness, rather than a dreaded disease. I set out to settle my bill at the hospital;

I was viewed with suspicion after continually asking for the Accounts Office. It turned out that there was no such thing. I had spent ten days in the excellent hospital.

What had previously been the "whites" of my eyes had now turned a brilliant golden-yellow. In order to hide this, I purchased a pair of extra-dark sunglasses to wear on the return flight.

Shortly after returning to Kenya, I elicited the help of Dr Mungai, to obtain Kenya Citizenship for Hans. This would enable Hans to visit his family in Germany whenever he wished, without fear of being arrested at the airport on arrival. In the Minister's office, we met with two Representatives from President's Moi office, to whom I paid the legal Citizenship Fee of thirty thousand Kenya Shillings, plus an extra one hundred thousand for the Man at the Top.

73. JENI AT SCHOOL

Jeni developed a very strong, dependable character, which was to a large extent attributable to "TAG" the Tigony Academy for Girls: Pat Kelly's excellent outward-bound style girls' secondary school. I had known Pat Kelly from the age of sixteen, when he would drive me in his Renault Roho to take part in tennis tournaments at Makuyu and Nanyuki Sports Clubs.

TAG girls climbed mountains; para-glided; camped in game-parks; ran and cycled as far afield as the Coast; in the school truck nick-named the "TAG-Wag" they toured the country staging musical theatre productions...

I shall remain forever grateful to Pat Kelly, in spite of his many odd traits. A student whose parents were late with payment of fees would be made to stand up in front of the whole school and ordered to contact the offending parents with instructions to cough up forthwith if they wished their daughter to remain at the school! Upon discovering that Jeni was taking scraps of food back to the dorm to feed a kitten that she had rescued from a pack of dogs, he threatened to "shoot the bloody cat" if she didn't get rid of it. Jeni phoned my sister in panic; Linda immediately drove out to the school to collect the kitten!

Now both Jeni and Andrew were attending boarding schools. The company that Hans worked for won a Tender for a huge aid transportation job in Ethiopia/Eritrea; there was also a position for me, running the administration side, from the Port of Assab. We would be amongst the first "foreigners" – apart from the staff with Church organisations and various "do-gooder" agencies – to work in this area since the Glorious Revolution twelve years previously. Now it was Linda's turn to keep an eye on dad. She agreed to move to the coast until our contract was over.

74. NORTH AFRICA

Before leaving for the North, Hans and his Company Directors were to meet at the Nairobi office of the Agency for whom we were to carry out the work. I bought Hans a suit and tie for this occasion. As I dropped Hans off, his two "bosses" arrived, also dressed up in suits and ties. I looked back to see Hans pointing at his two co-workers, laughing his head off at the sight of them properly dressed. They, in turn, were both pointing back at him, collapsed against each other in fits of hysterical mirth. I remember it so clearly...wish I'd had a camera with me!

The suits and ties turned out to be well worth it. Hans flew up to Eritrea a few months before me, to set everything up. He hired a plot of land in the desert next to an electricity transformer on the road to the "airport". He managed to reach me by telephone; I asked him what the beach was like. "Beautiful!" he enthused, "It's covered in land mines and it stretches inland for about two-hundred-and-fifty kilometres!"

These were the days when rebels were fighting against the "Derg", the Government led by Mengistu Haile Mariam. The Derg was backed by Soviet and Cuban troops, who were to be found in every corner of Ethiopia and Eritrea. I wasn't very fond of the Cubans after learning they would drive into donkeys, so they could pick them up – dead or dying - and take them to eat.

I flew to my new home in the desert via the capital of Ethiopia. The name Addis Ababa had always had a romantic ring to it, a "Beautiful City eight thousand feet above sea-level". I recalled Haile Selassie's visit to Kenya in 1964; Dr Mungai, my Minister boss, got along well with him. But now! How can I describe my shock and disappointment? The buildings were really scruffy. There was a dusk-to-dawn curfew; armed soldiers were absolutely everywhere. Gigantic posters of Lenin, Marx and Engels adorned every square and prominent building. "Long Live Utilitarian Proletarianism!" was emblazoned on banners stuck to every wall and shop-front. I stayed overnight in The Raj, a well-built Colonial-style hotel, which must have been beautiful in the times of Haile Selassie. It was not beautiful now, in November 1985. I was the only guest in the enormous wood-panelled dining-room, which must have seen some great banquets in days gone by. The food was disgusting.

The next morning, as passenger in the jump-seat of an RAF Hercules aircraft, I flew away from that sad, dejected city. We soared over mountains, lush green valleys, then barren deserts, dropping off loads of food aid en route to Assab. When we arrived, the RAF pilot did not want to leave me there! Hans met me at the windy desert airstrip. En route to the excuse of a Hotel where the Kenyan contingent was staying, Hans pointed out "our" plot. Just after that, we drove past a patch of land where hundreds of white-gowned men kneeled with their heads on the ground and bottoms in the air.

Foreigners were not permitted to stay outside approved establishments. The Manager of this particular establishment must have thought he had died and gone to Heaven when the Kenyan contingent arrived. In 1985, the Company was paying forty-five US dollars per night each, for us and our sixteen Kenyan drivers and mechanics. The door of our room did not close. The mattresses were lumpy, smelly and itchy; there were no pillows. There were no curtains at the windows, no panes in the windows and no carpets on the uneven floors. There was a shower of sorts, cold water only, which trickled in green slime down the wall. The trick was to cup your hands under the trickle and wet your body, soap yourself all over, then stand against the slimy wall to try to rinse the soap off.

Mealtimes were an experience! One had to purchase a ticket, join a queue, and then move forward slowly, one at a time, as a seat became vacant at a table. Hans and I rarely managed to sit at the same table. My first meal was an introduction to what was to follow: I was motioned to a wobbly chair to share a dirty table with two scruffily-dressed local gentlemen balancing AK47's across their laps. The one item on the Menu was "Spaghetti in the Oven" (as in Al Forno). A plate with a completely solid lump of baked spaghetti covered with bits of dried tomato paste was dumped onto the table in front of me. The spaghetti lump slid off the plate onto the filthy table, whereupon the waiter picked it up with his hand and placed it back on my plate. I asked for a knife to cut the solid mass.

"No knifes!"

"Then a fork, please".

He pointed to a used fork on the fly-covered table. Declining the fork, I picked up the cake of spaghetti and managed to break off a piece with my fingers. It was hard and crunchy. A residue from the Italian times: spaghetti, tomato paste and garlic were always to be found, even in shacks in the middle of the desert.

Oddly enough, the wine was good! And, with the local naturally-sparkling spring water "Ambo", it made an excellent spritzer. Ambo came in very valuable glass bottles, and we were to discover that there was *no way* a new bottle of sparkling water could be purchased without return of an empty bottle.

Every morning we would drive to the site on the airport road, where we had plugged into the nearby electricity transformer. This ran lights, welding machines, even an air-conditioner and, most important, my telex machine. My office was a container perched upon two other containers, and the entrance was via a wooden step-ladder propped against one of the lower containers.

ASSAB 1986

My office was a container perched upon two other containers

We were nearly a month into this way of living, when all was suddenly in a state of frenzy due to President Mengistu Haile Mariam's impending visit to the Port of Assab. Now there was a problem because the President and his entourage of bodyguards would take over the whole of the town's only High-Class Hotel. Very apologetically, the Manager informed us that we would have to move out. Perhaps it would be an honour for him to have the country's unpopular leader to stay, but the establishment was collecting a lot of easy money from us. We pretended to make a fuss about this, acting as if it was a terrible inconvenience. But between ourselves, we said "Wow! Great!" We instructed our Kenyan staff to pack their bags as we were going to live in tents on our desert plot! I smuggled out six precious Ambo bottles in my luggage, without being caught; this was lucky, because people were imprisoned for such heinous crimes.

I do not know why Mengistu did not visit Assab after all, but I did not blame him as he was extremely unpopular in Eritrea and maybe he had heard the rumours of plots to assassinate him. The Manager of the quarter-star hotel drove out to our site at high speed, to give us the good news we could all move back to the luxury of his establishment. Hans waved his arms around to show we were well settled-in. "Thanks, but no thanks" he said.

Vegetables were transported to our site weekly, from fertile mountain areas such as Dessie. We set up the best canteen in town. Top Ethiopian officials would wangle invitations from us, to sit and eat good wholesome food and watch the latest videos. The Assistant Commander of the Navy was a well-read and ultra-civilised gentleman. And I mean *truly* civilised; after all, some of these wonderful people should be able to trace their family trees back to David the Shepherd Boy. His English wife having taken their children back to UK for schooling, he was one of our most frequent visitors and he became a good friend. Being so high up in authority, he did not have to worry about driving around at night, but others who over-stayed were very happy to sleep on mattresses we laid out for them; anybody found moving around after midnight risked being shot and the sound of gunshots after curfew hour were a regular occurrence.

Initially, our shower was a hose-pipe around the back of a water tanker parked at the edge of our site. The first shower I had was quite interesting: having switched off my torch, the watchman kindly shone his spotlight for me so I could see where I was soaping! Our loo was a long-drop, consisting of a box over a hole dug in the only semi-soft soil available on the site, encircled by a wall of nailed-together crates. Many was the time I was sitting on the loo, peering through the slats as 150-ton cranes were turning in the yard, within metres of the little box.

Daytime temperatures were into the high forties. Night-times were very hot. One night was just too hot to bear and we carried our camp-beds outside to sleep under the stars. That night was the one-and-only time we saw rain for the extent of our contract! I returned to the tent while Hans pulled a sheet over his head and continued to sleep. In the morning, the desert was abloom with colourful flowers. Incredible!

Having spent the last eight years in Kenya under the dictatorship of Daniel Arap Moi, where we dared not mention the name "Moi" in public (plus having had a visiting German acquaintance imprisoned in Mombasa for committing this sin) something we eventually became used to in Eritrea was the fact we could say the name openly without looking around in trepidation that we may be heard! By the way, when our German visitor was locked up, he was hideously obese; when he was very fortunately released in an "amnesty" after forty-seven days, he was quite skinny and looked almost respectable! The first time our Naval Officer friend in Eritrea asked me

"What sort of a job is Moi doing - in running Kenya?" I literally cowered in fear, arms over head, in anticipation of being dragged away and locked up!

75. THE CHILDREN'S VISITS

Back in Kenya, Linda would put Jeni and Andrew on a flight to Addis. It would take the kids two or three days to reach us. In Addis, they would be met by our "minder"' Elsa, spending one or two nights with her before Elsa found one or other means of transport to deliver them to us in Assab. Lovely Elsa had to stick regimentally to the Communist-style rules. On the children's first visit in December 1985, Hans and I went to Addis to pick them up. We stayed in the "Ghion", the second-best hotel in Addis after the Hilton. Elsa dined with us. There was a vase of white arum lilies in the centre of the dining table. Hans pulled the vase of flowers towards himself and cupped a lily in his hands like a microphone; looking around furtively, he whispered urgently into the flower-head "Ivan? *Ivan, come in....*" Elsa, amused but horrified at his audacity, admonished Hans "Stop it, you cannot do that!" Along the corridor to our rooms the children, quickly catching on, bent down to the non-functional electrical outlets where vacuum cleaners used to be plugged in all those years ago when such appliances were used in Addis, whispering "Come in, Ivan Ivanovich!" This hotel still had a functioning swimming pool, albeit extremely murky, which Jeni and Andrew enjoyed. One day a body was discovered sucked against the outlet vents. It had been there for some time.

After one night in Addis, we set off for the desert. The children enjoyed staying with us in this unusual environment; I hated seeing them off when their holiday was over. Their departure from the local "airport" was like something out of a TV Comedy. Until it was time for the children to board the Twin Otter, a gun-toting bespectacled official made us stand a couple of metres apart, on either side of an imaginary line; the left lens was missing from his spectacles, which he wore completely squiff – up on the right side of his nose and down on the left. He had a large belly protruding from an open button-less shirt; he wore wide khaki shorts and, best of all, a two-foot high bright green hat made from plaited banana leaves and shaped like a pyramid. Jeni and Andrew looked at us in disbelief that we were actually allowing this weirdly-attired individual to keep us apart! But he was the local Airport Official, wielding immense authority.

We watched the Twin Otter taking off in a strong crosswind, seeming to stand in the air without moving, then shooting straight up at a ninety-degree angle, battling its way against all odds over the nearby escarpment, before disappearing from sight.

76. DESERT LIFE

We were quite happy living here. It was hard work. We had forty trucks that transported bags of food aid to all borders, through a tremendous variety of landscapes. There were huge areas of grassy fields where cattle, goats and sheep were grazing; and flourishing plantations of papayas, mangoes, bananas and every type of vegetable. We watched happy, well-dressed people driving donkey-carts to the distribution points to collect their sacks of "food-aid". A few times, our trucks returned from desert areas displaying bullet holes. It was pure luck that only one of our drivers was shot dead. Hans would often drive the leading truck in a convoy, sleeping on the hot bonnet through the cold desert night, watching the bullet tracers zooming across the skies like firework displays. If there was indeed any famine in the country, it would be largely due to the failure of crops brought about by the Civil War.

Many was the time we would be gathered in our little canteen at night, listening to the gunshots when end-of-the-month executions were carried out. At each shot, our locally-employed watchmen would moan loudly in unison, "aaaaah!"

Our Kenyan drivers and mechanics found it quite an experience. One evening our Kenyan workers ventured into "town" to watch a film at the open-air cinema. It was an old black-and-white film starring Fred Astaire. One of our workers did not return that night, or the following morning. Apparently a number of people leaving the cinema had been press-ganged and held in preparation to go to the front line to fight the good fight. I donned the only dress I had brought with me and drove into the town in our little Datsun pick-up to negotiate the release of our worker; I succeeded. En route, I was pestered by a jeep full of Russian soldiers, who zigzagged around and in front of me, taunting me to see if I would drive off the road: I didn't. They were collecting recruits, and I watched horrified as mothers screamed, trying to cling onto their young sons who were torn from their grasp and thrown into the Russian jeeps and driven away to be sent off as cannon fodder.

Ybetal "Jackie" Demissie, one such "recruit", managed to fall from a Russian truck as it wound its way past our site. He rolled into a ditch until the convoy disappeared, then turned up asking for employment, gingerly supporting an arm that had broken in his fall from the truck. Jackie worked for us until we finished our assignment there. These Russian convoys were a constant source of amusement, as tanks frequently stopped and had to be *push-started!* The trucks ran on petrol and consequently every tenth truck in the convoy was a petrol tanker.

The Russian doctors reputedly practised "military surgery", chopping off or cutting out the offending limb, or ear, finger, toe, piece of stomach or whatever. I had a daily "dispensary", helping out with simple medications such Aspirin for headaches, and iodine, plaster and bandages for wounds, and so on. The Desert people had a great sense of humour; when I told one man suffering from bad migraine he should go to a proper doctor, he slid his finger across his throat and said "Me no go Rooskie doctor for headache. Rooskie doctor cut off head!"

Staff from the UN and certain Church Organisations and Aid Agencies drove around in modern four-wheel-drive vehicles. Some of these people criticised us for "making money out of delivering food to the starving", while we were living in tents and driving around in a little Datsun pick-up. There was the time somebody came rushing in to tell Hans that a UN vehicle was in serious trouble on the beach. Suspecting that the vehicle had met with a land-mine, Hans set off in a lorry with a winch-cable. He discovered the Land Cruiser was indeed in trouble. A couple of UN officials had been racing each other along the beach when one became stuck in the sand. By the time Hans reached the scene, the tape-recorder was still blaring out at full volume, and the incoming tide was creeping up over the seats of the vehicle. "I can't get it to budge" shrieked the excited UN expert. Hans waded into the ocean pulling the winch-cable behind him. As it turned out, he did not require the cable; he clambered into the cab of the Land Cruiser, engaged four-wheel-drive, and drove the vehicle out of the sea and up the beach to safety.

"Four wheel drive???" exclaimed the UN official.

I used to travel to Addis to collect our orders of luxury items from Nairobi, such as tins of baked beans and UHT milk. I had trouble finding my little consignments amongst the generators, washing-machines, television sets, electric kettles, irons and hair-dryers flown in for the UN families! Hardship post, you see, and we were the greedy capitalists.

We had great fun visiting the "boom-towns" in the desert, where Hans joked that one could purchase anything from a paper-clip to an aeroplane! Commodities were brought in across the border from Djibouti on camel-back. The two main towns of Bure and Manda, consisted of shacks built out of cardboard, corrugated-iron and straw. At Christmas-time, politicians and wealthy Ethiopian gentlemen would risk their lives by travelling to these desert shack-towns to purchase Levi Jeans, French perfumes and expensive teddy-bears. I was amazed to discover in one shack, bars of my favourite "Fresh" soap, which was not even available in Kenya!

Reaching these shanty-towns from Assab meant driving down tracks winding like helter-skelters round and round mountains and up and down valleys, hooting on bends in case a truck was coming in the other direction while we were gazing down three thousand feet over the edge that was inches from our tyres. Then across the "Danakil" – a vast salt desert, below sea-level, stiflingly hot – one of the lowest-level expanses of land on this planet. Throughout the flat desert areas there were rocks built into piles, each with a helmet placed on top. Men with AK47's lay behind these piles of helmet-adorned rocks.

One of our trucks jack-knifed on a bend on an infamous "Death Hill". When Hans reached him, the driver was paralysed with fright, sitting in the cabin at a right-angle in open space two-thousand feet above the ground beneath, but luckily the trailer with container was still on the road. Hans climbed along the chassis and into the cab, then carried the driver back along the trailer to safety before towing the whole contraption back onto the road.

77. ENTERTAINMENT IN THE DESERT

Our main source of evening entertainment was watching videos. It was incredible in this dictatorial-run State, that there was a huge trade in pornographic videos, as well as every Chuck Norris movie ever screened, and really up-to-date videos of Madonna, Mister Mister, Fergal Sharkey and so on.

Our weekend's entertainment, if not visiting the boom-towns, was often a Sunday afternoon drive around the Port. We would pass through the forbidden gate to the far end of the Port, holding handkerchiefs over noses to keep out the nauseous stench of rotting wheat from the aid cargo that had been kept waiting for too long while the ships carrying Soviet and Cuban tanks and arms were off-loaded. I had sympathy for a certain celebrity who, so the rumours went, had paid more to charter the ships to carry in the wheat than it would have cost to purchase the ships outright.

I sadly recall spotting a Ford Transit van sitting at the far end of the Port in a shroud of dust, on four flat tyres. There was an inscription on the side; I walked over to the van and wiped off the dust, to read "A Gift to the People of Tigray, from the Villagers of Wrexham, Surrey". I could visualise the Councillor or whoever in that beautiful little far-away village, together with kind old folks who had given up their winter central-heating money for a worthy case, poignantly sending the van off on the High Seas, totally ignorant of the fact that they had consigned it to the very people that the Government of the country was fighting against.

Although UN "experts" and Russian soldiers were always in evidence (many had brought their wives with them, but the wives were hidden away) Hans, our "second-in-command" Ian, and I, had virtually no inter-action with other mzungus. There were a couple of Europeans apparently languishing, forgotten, somewhere in the desert port having got on the wrong side of the authorities some years previously. We used to laugh about one such Italian, who could be seen walking around Assab in the evenings, dressed only in a pink bath-robe, wrapped around kikoi-style!

Paul, a visitor from Europe who was to purchase our two-hundred containers at the end of the project, paid us a visit in Assab. He was brought along by Chris Hughes, another employee of the Company, who usually stayed in a compound with the "bosses" in the relative civilisation of Nazaret, a little town south of Addis. Chris came with his lovely girlfriend, who was visiting from Kenya. It had been months since I had met up with a female that I could sit and talk to, and laugh with. We went completely bonkers that night, all of us, standing under the shower drinking bottles of Ethiopian wine.

Paul was delighted to have arrived at the Port on a day many thousands of sheep were being herded onto "ro-ro" roll-on-roll-off vessels for export. While the country was crying out for donations of food for the "starving", the Government was happily shipping thousands upon thousands of sheep-on-the-hoof out of the country! The one and only Main Street through Assab was blocked to traffic all day while the poor animals were brought into town from far and wide, some literally on their last legs. Every inch of road-space was crammed with tightly-packed dirty white-bodied, black-headed sheep!

The one & only main street through our town was blocked to traffic for many hours....

Just over a year later, the project was successfully completed. Hans and I flew to the UK, to look for a school for Andrew because Hans, for some reason, was determined that Andrew should continue his schooling in the UK. We also opened an HSBC bank account, which turned out to be a good move. We visited a number of Public Schools in England, looking for a small, friendly institution. We found one, "Reeds School" in Cobham,

Surrey. I often joke that Tim Henman's claim to fame is that he went to school with my son!

I was to fly back to Kenya while Hans returned to our desert site for a couple of weeks to organise the shipment of our two-hundred containers from Assab to the UK. The forty trucks had already been driven back to Kenya in convoy via Moyale. Hans' and my flights happened to depart from Heathrow within half an hour of each other. As he walked through the barrier, Hans waved and called out "'Bye Love. See you in about two weeks!"

Ha ha! For "two weeks", read "five months"!

78. ADJUSTING TO LIFE BACK HOME

After returning to Kenya, I met Andrew's art teacher when picking him up from school at the end of term. She explained that at the beginning of each term, she began class by giving the pupils a large piece of paper, asking them to draw a picture of "something that happened in the holidays". She wondered if Andrew's vision wasn't "rather far-fetched".

She showed me a wonderful drawing. There was my container office, sitting atop two other containers. A huge hot sun was searing down. In the background was the ocean, with explosions going off in all directions from a little island not far from shore. On the beach, soldiers in uniform paraded, one staring down at a land mine. Directly in the foreground was our workshop full of trucks, swarming with mechanics. To the right was a vacant plot, with tanks taking part in target practice. On the left-hand-side was the graveyard with dogs lurking around digging up bones. Overhead, aircraft were flying in one direction with bomb doors closed, others returning with bomb-doors open.

"No", I said. "It's not far-fetched at all. In fact, I think he's summed it all up pretty well!"

In spite of having just spent a busy week in the UK, Hans had been with me. I now found it extremely awkward to be back home in Kenya amongst so many mzungus congregating together, and living "normal" lives. One particular Sunday, I plucked up courage to go to lunch at Nomads Beach Restaurant, which was frequented by local Kenyans. I found that I was too nervous to walk across the restaurant to the loo in front of all those white Kenyans, and instead took a long journey around the back of the building, over pipes and manhole covers!

Here, I have to say a special "thank you, Rosie" to a lady who became a good friend at this difficult time. She helped me, not only to "fit back into society" as it were, but I could call on her to discuss my fears about Hans and the danger that he could be in.

79. HOSTAGE IN THE DESERT

As Hans so aptly put it, "the Government expected every bag of relief food to be donated together with the truck it was sitting on!" Top Party Officials in Assab were indeed unamused that our forty trucks had managed to escape their grasp to successfully return to Kenya. But, they still had our two hundred forty-foot containers in their Port. They were not about to let them out of their grasp as well! Party Officials fabricated all sorts of reasons as to why they should hold onto our containers, keeping Hans hostage meanwhile.

After his "arrest", without too much negotiating, Hans was allowed to live on the UN compound in the Port. From here, he was able to telephone me weekly. Having arranged to pay US Dollars to an Ethiopian Shipping Line to transport the containers to UK, Hans needed to go to Addis to sort out the paperwork. But the local Officials were not letting him out of their sight. He could not walk anywhere without the accompaniment of at least one AK47-toting guard. Finally, a friend named Mohamed literally put his life on the line by covering for Hans, broadcasting that Hans was spending the night at his humble residence, whilst arranging for Hans to drive to Addis and back in an ambulance. For some weird reason, ambulances were never stopped at the roadblocks. Hans faithfully promised Mohamed that he would be back within twenty-four hours.....some drive! This was one of the nights when Hans was to have phoned me. When I answered the phone, I was surprised to hear Mohamed's voice. He spoke very cagily, in a loud harsh whisper, telling me that Hans was in Addis; I wondered what the heck was going on.

Twenty-three and a half hours later, having successfully dealt with the "paperwork" in Addis, Hans – to Mohamed's intense relief - walked into Mohamed's office.

At the sound of people hammering on the door of the flat, and shouts of "We hear that the prisoner has escaped. Where is he?" Mohamed went to open the front door before they succeeded in breaking it down, as Hans went to sit in the chair behind the desk. The guards burst in, to find Hans sitting with feet up on the desk, nonchalantly smoking a Cuban cigar. He asked calmly, "Good Morning. Did you want to speak to me?"

Over the years, we had become friends with a correspondent with a UK-based Media establishment called Mike who, together with his family, was a regular holidaymaker at our Tiwi plot. He booked into one of our beach cottages. On the second day of their holiday, I watched from my verandah as he walked down to the beach with his wife and children. Then he turned and strode purposefully up the beach towards my verandah. In the way reporters do, he had heard somewhere along the grapevine that Hans was being held "hostage". He sat down, said nothing at all, but signalled with his hands for me to "speak"! Not wanting to prejudice the sale of our containers, or Hans' safety, I could not tell him anything. "I'm really sorry" I said, "but at this moment a reporter is the very last person I would speak to!"

"OK. But remember, sometimes reporters can help! Here's my direct number!" Less than two weeks later, Hans phoned to say that the containers were on the High Seas, out of Eritrean waters. "Wow!" How on earth did you manage that" I asked, amazed and delighted. He later explained it to me thus:-

As per usual, the town of Assab closed down for the Christmas holiday, at the beginning of January. While the top Party Officials disappeared to the boom towns, the gun-toting security officials went on drinking sprees, as one does. The UN employees flew home for the break, leaving Hans, the trusted hostage, to look after their compound full of trucks. Under cover of night, Hans drove trucks to the Port, until he had loaded each and every one of our containers onto the Shipping Line carriers. The Shipping Company was only too happy for the vessels to set sail. Hans lined the trucks up neatly back in the UN compound. The next morning, all hell was let loose. Back from their holiday, Party Officials accompanied by hung-over guards, were jumping up and down in rage.

"Where are the containers?" they bellowed.

Hans walked the Officials out to the edge of the pier. Casually shielding his eyes from the morning sun, Hans pointed out to sea. "Over there!" he said.

Now Hans wanted to get home. When we next spoke on the phone, I asked "Can I go to Press?"

"*Yes!*" he said. "*Anything!* I don't intend to spend the rest of my life walking around in a pink bath-robe!"

I immediately telephoned Mike, my reporter friend, and told him that I would be driving to Nairobi the following morning. He asked me to come straight to his office. Of course, when I related all the interesting experiences we had in Eritrea and Ethiopia, there was no Big Scoop for my friend: reporting on the antics of certain UN Officials and NGO's, not to mention rumours of a certain Celebrity's trucks being held in Port for months due to non-payment of Port fees, also that huge consignments of food were rotting at the harbour entrance to allow shiploads of arms to be offloaded first, would be quite contrary to the news he had been relaying thus far.

BUT, he did call in Rolf, the German News Agency Representative, to whom I described Hans's plight. Rolf instantly telexed the German Embassy in Addis, asking for news of this "German", who was being held hostage in Assab. As it turned out, within an hour, Hans was summoned to the office of the Party HQ in Assab, where two Party Leaders were perusing a translation of Rolf's telex, together with a message from Government Officials in Addis who wanted to know what it was all about, and instructing that Hans be flown to Addis forthwith.

The two Party leaders were having a heated discussion in their local language. Hans, realising they were discussing how their clever scheme appeared to be doomed for total failure, had taken the precaution of switching on a little pocket memo dictation machine that he had hidden in his shirt. He was put on a flight to Addis, accompanied by two armed guards. He joked that there wasn't much point in sending the guards, as he was not likely to jump out of the aircraft! Upon arrival in Addis, he was taken directly to the office of a Senior Party Official, where he was questioned at length by two Officials, as to why he had been held hostage for so long. With pressure being put on by the German Government, the Officials were anxious to avoid an international scandal. Hans played his tape to them. This appeared to contain some pretty damning evidence against the Assab Party bosses; therefore, having been handed their scapegoats, they were happy to release Hans to the confines of the Addis Hilton.

Finally, Hans was free to leave. He was booked onto a flight leaving for Nairobi at 6 a.m. the following morning. By hook or by crook, he was determined to be on that flight. That night, he went to the Hilton Manager's office to settle his bill by Credit Card. "Uh uh!" the Manager shook his head sorrowfully from side to side. Only cash would do. Apparently the Hotel had had its "fingers burned" when various do-gooders had lived it up on champagne parties, then refusing to pay their bills asking "Haven't we brought enough money into this country?" This is when our short visit to the HSBC Bank in UK paid off. Our Bank Manager was very polite when the Hotel Manager of the Addis Hilton telephoned him at 3 a.m. GMT to obtain clearance for Hans's Credit Card. Then Hans took a taxi to the airport.

Linda picked Hans up at Nairobi's JKI Airport, while I drove up from Mombasa. We met at Alan Bobbe's Bistro for lunch. I had not seen Hans for nearly half a year. It took him a long time to settle back into conventional life, which is hardly surprising considering how neurotic I had been upon my return; and poor Hans had spent many months longer, under not-so-pleasant conditions. He let me take over the wheel of the car and drive everywhere. I was absolutely astonished that he left me to drive the five hundred kilometre stretch back from Nairobi to Mombasa, something hitherto unheard of.

It transpired that Rolf, the German Newsagent whom I had met in Mike's Nairobi office, had flown to Addis and was booked into the Hilton. He met Hans at the bar, where they had a few drinks together. But he did not tell Hans why he was there, or that he was directly responsible for his release! I never had contact with Rolf again, but would have liked to thank him! Nor did I meet up with Mike again, though I spoke to him by phone twenty-one years later, when he visited Kenya at the time of the so-called "Post-Election Violence". I still hear him on radio and occasionally see him on telly. Thank you, Mike.

80. TRAVELS THROUGH NEIGHBOURING COUNTRIES

In May 1988, Hans and I undertook a memorable journey that lasted for two months. Working for the same Company we had worked for in Eritrea, we accompanied a few trucks from Mombasa, through Tanzania, Zambia and Malawi, then back through Tanzania to Kenya. The first night was spent in a disgusting dump on the border between Kenya and Tanzania. The second night we stayed in a nice hotel in Tanga. My last visit to this Tanzanian coastal town had been with mum, dad, Linda and Bessy, when we stopped off to visit my Groundnut Scheme friend Anne and her parents, on our way from Morogoro to Kenya, in 1952.

We then spent a week in Dar-es-Salaam, where I had ridden in rickshaws en route to Morogoro, thirty-six years previously! We passed through our old home-town of Morogoro where, sadly, I couldn't spot our little house on the mountainside. Then through Iringa and Mbeya on the way to Zambia. Passing trucks on a fast tarmac road which cut through the centre of Mikumi Game Reserve, I asked Hans to stop when I saw movement in a huge water-filled trench left by road-builders, beside the road. We watched amazed as two hippos wallowed around in the mud, a few feet from speeding vehicles on the main road! A Greater Kudu was watching us from a distant hillock.

Being held-up by ridiculous paperwork, a polite Immigration Official in the border town of Nkonde allowed us to sleep on his office floor for the night. The next morning we set off for Lusaka, the capital of Zambia. I was constantly amazed by Zambia: the roads were excellent, such a contrast to the appalling roads of Kenya and the even worse roads of Tanzania. Zambia was so wonderfully under-populated. We would drive for miles and miles without spotting a single soul. Heaven! We drove through the "Copperbelt"; although the buildings were sadly neglected, it was obvious how beautiful these places must have been all those years ago, with English-style housing estates and tree-lined streets. We spent a few days in Luanshya with Sue Stampe, a dear friend who used to stay with us at Tiwi. In Kitwe, we met up with friends who also used to visit Tiwi Beach. We stopped in "Chililabombwe", a little town on the border with Zaire, which means "place of croaking frogs", then back to Chingola.

Whilst driving through Chingola at night, we were waved down by three armed men in uniform who leapt onto the back of our vehicle, one man lying across the roof of the cab with his gun at the ready. They ordered Hans to follow the car ahead, a pick-up with a tarpaulin tied down over the back. I said to Hans "You can't do that!" to which he replied, pointing upwards "that AK47 on the roof tells me that I can!" When the vehicle we were following stopped at a hut next to the bridge across the Kafue River, the men jumped from our vehicle and rushed over to the pick-up, jamming their rifle butts with great force into the tarpaulin. Screams and yells emitted from beneath the tarpaulin which erupted into a seething mass of bodies, following which, people began clambering out of the pick-up and attempting to run off. Hans did a quick U-turn and drove away, the sound of gun-shots ringing out.

On a stretch of road between Luanshya and Lusaka, we were stopped by Police who went ballistic when they saw that I was making notes of mileages between towns. They held onto our Kenya Passports for nearly an hour before Hans managed to convince them that we were not South African spies.

Our last night in Zambia was spent camping at Mulungushi Dam. There were two days of Public Holidays in Zambia and it appeared every white person in the country was camped there, to witness or take part in the water sports on the Dam. Or just to get drunk. I cut Hans's hair short because the following day we were to cross the border into Malawi, where men were not permitted to display women's hair-styles!

So to Malawi. Now that I was in Banda's country, he had the say, so I did not wear a mini-skirt. Neither did I wear trousers, as women were "Banda-d" from wearing men's clothes. Lilongwe, which for some strange reason was the so-called "Capital" of Malawi, was like a model town, with well-maintained empty roads and buildings, few cars and hardly any pedestrians. The lamp-posts were adorned with enormous portraits of President Banda. After a few days as the only guests at the Ridgeways Hotel in Lilongwe, we drove to Blantyre. As in Zambia, the roads were excellent. It was surprising to see pigs wandering around freely, the way that goats and sheep do in Kenya. In fact, on the way to Blantyre, we stopped to allow a jet black pig to cross the road; it must have been the largest pig I had ever set eyes on, it appeared to take up half the width of the road! What a wonderful drive, the road was high above Lake Malawi and the views of the lake were stunning. Along the roadside, people were selling barbecued mice skewered on sticks.

We did not stop to purchase any.

The contrast between Lilongwe and Blantyre was beyond description. Whereas Lilongwe appeared to be a ghost town built in the middle of nothing, for no reason, practically devoid of people or activity, Blantyre was heaving! Loads of people: black, brown and white. Back-packing tourist girls wore kikois wrapped around like long skirts.

A couple of days later on the way to Limbe, Hans got out of the car so I could take a photo of him "in Mozambique". The road was, of course, in Malawi: to the left of the road was Malawi, but from the very verge on the right-hand-side of the road was Mozambique! Upon reaching Limbe I spent a really enjoyable evening playing darts at Limbe Sports Club.

On our return journey to Tanzania, the border guards confiscated all the South African magazines we had bought in Malawi...welcome back to East Africa! In Zambia, we had bought a beautifully carved chest made out of old railway tracks; we packed it full of our clothes etc., and managed to convince the border guards that it was simply our "suitcase"! I still prize that chest.

81. HOME AGAIN

Mum's job at Pembroke came to an end. We all turned up on speech-day; we even took dad along, expecting from the Headmaster at least a mention of our mother leaving. But, after a long speech in which he said "Goodbye" to another long-standing member of the staff, he did not so much as *mention* mum's name. OK, she could be difficult, but come on.....after a decade of dedicated service to the school, most of the parents were not even aware that she was leaving. All through the Headmaster's speech, mum sat there with a little smile on her face. My heart ached for her. To begin with, mum moved into my sister's rented house in Lavington, Nairobi.

At "TAG", Jeni sat her O-levels. Not wanting to be held responsible for our daughter failing her exams, Pat Kelly wrote us a letter pointing out she was most erratic, and whether she passed or failed in any subject depended entirely upon what mood she was in on the day of the exam! Kelly had stated loudly in front of the school that if Jeni passed any O-levels, he would "eat his hat"! The day the results were due out, our Tiwi telephone was out of order: surprise surprise. Therefore I drove Jeni to Shelly Beach Hotel at Likoni to telephone the school. Jeni was a bag of nerves. Finally we managed to connect and my trembling daughter asked to speak to the Headmaster.

She listened for some minutes before stating loudly, with a huge grin, "Well Mr Kelly, I guess you'll just have to eat your hat, won't you?"

Twenty-three years after this, I was to become a regular visitor to Pat Kelly, at Nanyuki Cottage Hospital. He had virtually lost his eye-sight, but he never lost his sense of humour. Unable to read, he asked me to bring along the draft of My Story to read to him. I took the first few chapters along on the morning of 27 January 2013. I was a bit too late. He had passed away that morning. Straight-away, I called Jeni to tell her. On the table beside his bed were two bottles of Guinness I had left for him; the staff told me he hadn't drunk them, because he was waiting for me to come and drink with him.

The old rogue will surely be drinking Guinness with my dad now.

We had booked tickets for Jeni and I to travel to England to visit various Art and Drama Colleges. However, all of a sudden, my young daughter became drastically ill. A week or so before, she had been horse-riding at Diani and been thrown off a particularly obnoxious horse, apparently dislodging a kidney stone we didn't know she had. Although she appeared to overcome that, I did wonder whether it had anything to do with her sudden illness. She ended up in Mombasa Hospital on a drip, with temperature continually raging around forty degrees and above. The doctor said the medical fraternity were baffled by her illness; he did not reassure me one bit when he told me "all we can do is pray". Meanwhile, a twenty-eight year-old woman down the corridor died of Measles, which astonished me, I had always considered that to be a children's ailment.

I slept beside my girl on the high, narrow hospital bed oblivious of the fact Hans and my sister were making arrangements for us to be medevacked to the UK. Luckily, before this came about, our doctor had called in another physician for an expert opinion. As this doctor was complimenting her on a pair of earrings that I had bought to cheer her up, he noticed a rash behind her ears. MEASLES! Now, at least the demon had a name. We discovered later, that whilst we were in the Outpatients Department waiting to have her kidney pain diagnosed after being thrown from the horse, we were sitting amongst a group of patients who were victims of a measles epidemic.

82. MY CHILDREN IN ENGLAND

One month later, Jeni was back to normal. She and I were in England, staying with Cousin Margaret in Banstead, while we visited Art and Drama Colleges. We had not been there long, when I noticed my girl, immediately she woke in the mornings, would sit up and examine her pillow closely. "MUM! My hair's falling out!"

"Don't be silly!" My daughter was prone to exaggeration. Then I noticed she was in fact sweeping strands of hair off the pillow. I washed her hair, hiding the fact I was grasping handfuls of hair as it clogged the plughole, depositing them quickly in the waste-paper-basket. We visited hair-dressers and doctors; apparently it was an after-effect of the measles and all the medication. A bald patch began to appear at the back of her head, and all this just when Jeni wanted to look her most beautiful while attending interviews at colleges. She began to wear a scarf all the time.

I took Jeni into Selfridge's Department Store in London. Saying nothing, I led her purposefully through the departments until she saw the sign "Wig Department". She froze and squeezed my arm tightly. "NO! NO!"

After much persuasion, and a lot of sympathetic support from the wonderful ladies in that Department, we finally chose a wig that looked great on Jeni. She wore it with gay abandon, and it never became dislodged, even when she was screaming her head off on roller-coasters and hanging upside-down on magic wheels.

We booked her into ALRA, the Academy of Live and Recorded Arts, in South London. She was to come back to Kenya with me for a few weeks before returning to commence at ALRA. On the return journey, the Kenya Airways flight broke down in Cairo. Jeni and I, amongst a score of other fed-up passengers, sat around on uncomfortable plastic seats drinking warm sodas from paper cups; none of us had any inclination to speak to each other. As dusk fell, we drifted towards the bar.

All of a sudden, it dawned on me we had sat doing nothing for hours, in *Egypt,* the Land of the Sphinx and the Pharaohs! I jumped up and called out to the other pissed-off passengers, "Let's ask them to take us to Giza"!" Everybody perked up. We suddenly all became friends. I spoke to the ultra-stressed Egyptian person who didn't know what the heck to do with this unwanted cargo of miserable Kenyans. Eventually, after handing over our Passports in case we were overcome with sudden desires to defect to Egypt, a trip to Giza was organised. At 9.30 p.m. we were driven in a coach through streets teeming with seemingly millions of people, past an amazing statue in the middle of a highway, which the guide told us was of Ramses, and was five thousand years old. Thence out to the Sphinx and the Pyramids. It was fantastic! The breakdown was worth it!

Back at the airport, we Kenyans all sat together, chatting happily, until we were ushered onto a coach at three o'clock in the morning. Driving across the tarmac to our repaired KA plane, I became self-appointed Guide. I stood up and, throwing out my left arm, said "To our left is Cairo Airport, where we intrepid Kenyans were lucky to sit for seven hours on plastic chairs before visiting the Pyramids at Giza. Then I threw out my right arm "To our right is an aeroplane belonging to Kenya Airways, the Pride of Kenya! We are crossing our fingers that this aircraft will finally deliver us safely home to Jomo Kenyatta Airport, Nairobi!"

It did.

Sometime after returning to Kenya, Jeni's hair began to grow back. But something really strange is that, instead of the mass of blonde curls she had for the first sixteen years of her life, it grew back almost straight, and dark brunette. To this day, I cannot brush Jeni's hair vigorously; she cringes and places her hands over her head.

We had purchased a little second-hand Ford Fiesta in England, which was garaged at my cousins' house in Banstead. Cousin Margaret and her husband Bernie graciously acted as "guardians" to Andrew whilst he boarded at Reed's School, which was conveniently close-by. Their home became our "second home". Apart from being a fantastic gardener, Margaret just happened to be a Nursing Sister. Apart from being a Scout Master, an avid stamp-collector and a motorbike nut, Bernie just happened to be a Metropolitan Police Officer.

We saw the children every holiday; either I would fly to England to be with them, or we would fly them home to Kenya. They would frequently bring school-friends with them, to holiday on Tiwi Beach. Andrew occasionally spent half-term holidays with Hans's family in Germany. Sometimes I would travel back via Germany after visiting my children in England. I loved Hans's family. On one of these visits, Hans's older brother told me that the reason Hans had been unable to visit home, had had nothing to do with skipping National Service, but something to do with money .... Oh well, I had obtained a Kenya Passport for him, so-be-it.

The money we had made in Eritrea just lasted through Andrew's High School and Jeni's College, before running out!

In 1990, on one of my visits to UK for my children's holiday, I took Jeni and Andrew to the hospital in

Scotland where John, their biological father was living, plugged into a kidney dialysis machine. He was truly happy to see us, and very positive about waiting for a donor kidney. It was terribly sad leaving him like that. We never saw John again. On 17 June 1991, his mother phoned to tell me that he had died, aged only sixty.

Was that really fair, God? Really?

I arranged for Jeni and Andrew to take the train to Scotland for his memorial.

83. MINILETS

Hans and I had been busy building up our Beach Resort at Tiwi: we called the enterprise "Minilets". We had a few really happy years running our business. We had three beach cottages plus six chalets on the cliff. We built a beach-bar, which was always packed.

We had live music at our beach-bar on weekends. On one holiday from school in England, I was astonished to see my studious son asking the entertainer, Ben, during a break, if he could borrow his guitar. A few minutes later Andrew was strumming away on the guitar and singing "Wild Thing" as if he had done it all his life! This was the first time I came to know that my son could sing *and* play the guitar!

We built a beautiful restaurant-cum-bar on the cliff-top. We were lucky the atmosphere created meant that while the beach-bar would obviously be filled with women and men wearing bikinis and swimming-shorts, every person who came to our top restaurant just happened to dress properly. There were no rules, but that is how it happened.

Being an early-morning person, Hans would be up at six o'clock to oversee the breakfast shift; he would normally be in bed by ten o'clock at night. Whilst I, on the other hand, believing there was only one "six o'clock" in the day, and that was at sundowner time, would stay up for the evening shift, which sometimes lasted until the early hours of the morning.

We were renowned for our Tequila shot parties, which were handy for me behind the bar, as I could get away with pretending to join in whilst drinking plain water. Golly, I could give many examples of fun-times at our top bar, such as Richard Hewitt doing his "Dance of the Flaming Assholes" but I won't....oops, sorry Richard!

After one particularly boisterous Tequila Party I unusually handed over to Newton, the head barman nicknamed "Newtonius", before crashing out at about two-thirty. There were only half a dozen people left in the bar. We were woken at three o'clock by Newton shouting "Hans! Hans! Come quickly! Aaron is dead!"

Hans shouted back "Well if he's dead, what's the hurry?"

It turned out that one of the Kiwi overlanders had decided he was Tarzan. He jumped onto the bar and leapt up, amazingly managing to grab hold of one of the beams, planning to swing from one beam to another. There was no way this could have been accomplished by other than Tarzan himself. Aaron fell head down onto the mazeras stone floor. We drove him to Mombasa Hospital. He recovered. When I went to visit him a couple of days later, he was walking across the main road in his hospital gown, to buy a packet of fags from a kiosk.

We were lucky in that few prostitutes came onto our premises. One evening, a well dolled-up woman came to the top restaurant. She sat at the corner of the bar and took her time to drink a Fanta Orange. Nobody heard what she murmured to Hans, but everybody heard his reply "Sorry, but you couldn't afford me!" She left without finishing her Fanta.

The Perrets of Rumuriti brought their rescued cheetah cub to Tiwi. I have photos of this beautiful animal climbing our casuarina trees and playing on the beach with Jeni's dog. The next afternoon the cheetah vanished and we sent out search parties. A runner delivered a letter from the Dutch lady managing Tiwi Sea Castles at the end of the beach near the Tiwi River. The letter read "Dear

Wendy. We have a leopard in our swimming-pool. Is it one of your guests?"

TIWI BEACH

COUSIN MARGARET AT OUR
"TOP RESTAURANT" ON THE CLIFF

"DEAR WENDY... WE HAVE
A LEOPARD IN OUR POOL.
IS IT ONE OF YOUR GUESTS?"

We received a letter from Andrew's Housemaster at Reeds School, accusing Andrew of being caught "drinking down at the local Pub!" I framed the letter and hung it on the wall behind our bar at the top restaurant, where it was much admired.

At the very last Minilets' New Year's Eve celebration, we had over one thousand guests. As per usual on New Year's morning, Hans, wrapped in kikoi, wended his way between bodies lying around the beach bar and along the beach-front, handing out Bloody Marys with our compliments.

84. MOTHER, COMPLETELY SANE

I received a phone-call from mum in Nairobi; she was worried her pay-off from Pembroke House had just about run out. She asked if she could come to live with us at the coast, and in return she would live in her ex-husband's spare room and would look after him. Naturally we agreed.

It was great having mum there. She really did help a lot with looking after dear old dad, which was becoming more and more time-consuming, especially while trying to run a business at the same time. Mum had given up living in dad's back room, and had joined us in our cottage. Mum enjoyed sitting at the bar watching modern-day overlanders' videos of their amazing trips across the Sahara. I was so proud when mum regaled these know-it-all travellers with stories of her epic overland journey, taken forty-five years previously: they loved to listen to her experiences. But I began to notice my mother was finding it increasingly difficult to walk up the stairs to the restaurant. Mum had taken to joining in with get-togethers of local Kenyan holiday-makers at our beach bar. This was good for her because, unlike the restaurant on the cliff-top, there were no steps to negotiate.

She finally admitted she had emphysema. "I've had a good innings!" she would say, making me livid. I said she should give up smoking, but mum said it was already too late for that, and she may as well enjoy the couple of years she had left. Years, she should have had. For "years", read "months". This was 1992, and she should still be here today.

I lay in bed with a "bug" feeling sorry for myself. Then mum complained of an upset tummy; had she caught my "bug"? It was a Sunday lunchtime. Hans was tending to guests who had turned up for our traditional Sunday curry lunch at the top restaurant. I sat with mum on the verandah of our beach cottage, playing Scrabble. Mum finished smoking a cigarette then immediately lit another. This was perfectly normal. Then she did the oddest thing: she stubbed the cigarette out on the verandah table, completely missing the ashtray. Startled, I looked into mummy's eyes, and was met with a completely blank stare. She was staring straight at me, but was looking through me. I sent Hamisi up to the top restaurant to call Hans, while I insisted on helping mum through to the sitting-room, to lie on the sofa. Very soon she was OK again and sat up, protesting when I tried to prevent her from lighting up another cigarette.

Hans came rushing down from the top restaurant, bringing Claude who happened to be a doctor with Medicins sans Frontieres. Claude checked mum's pulse-rate and said we must take her to hospital immediately, as her pulse was erratic. Although mum complained about "all the fuss", she allowed us to lay her on a mattress in the back of the car. Upon arrival at Mombasa Hospital, the nurses hurriedly applied blobs of jelly all over mum's chest, to which they affixed jelly-covered plugs on the ends of wires. The wires were attached to a machine that drew row upon row of small mountain peaks of varying sizes, interspersed with straight flat lines. She was admitted as an inpatient with the diagnosis "atrial fibrillation". Mum seemed to be quite happy in her little room overlooking the ocean, especially after changing the pillow round to the foot of the bed so she could watch the waves. She kept insisting Hans and I should return home and cross the ferry before it became too dark. I telephoned Linda from the hospital and suggested she come down for a couple of days to visit mum. She said she would try to come the following day.

The next morning I popped into the doctor's surgery on the way to the hospital. The doctor said that apart from atrial fibrillation, mum's tests showed she had malaria. I was really surprised, as she had shown none of the recognised signs of malaria. However, I was extremely relieved, because just about everyone I knew had contracted malaria at least once in their lives and all were cured, especially under a good doctor in an excellent hospital. The doctor said he had put mum on the new drug Halfan, but she had responded badly, so he had to change to a quinine drip. Even I, naive as I was, was aware of the effects of Halfan on people with heart problems- there was even a warning on the packet; and mum had been admitted with an irregular heartbeat for Heaven's sake. A few days ago, an eighteen-year-old camper had died in hospital after being administered Halfan. I gasped "*Why Halfan*?" He assured me it was an excellent new drug, showing excellent results.

Unfortunately, though, it had not been excellent for our mother. Mum was not nearly as chirpy as the previous evening. She told me with a shaking voice that she had not had a good night. Coming from mum that meant she had had a dreadful night. She complained they kept insisting that she lie with her head at the top of the bed. I helped her to turn around so she could watch the waves. Monday 18 May 1992, turned into more and more of a nightmare as the hours went by. Apart from the times I ran downstairs to use the telephone, I lay stretched out beside mummy on the hospital bed. Her legs ached and I massaged them continually; "Oh, that's lovely!" she would say. I had brought some ready-mixed dehydration salts, which she really enjoyed. But there was no way she would eat anything. I also took an inhaler spray that she had been using at home, which gave her great relief. She kept insisting she needed to go to the loo; she did not like the idea of a bedpan but she had no choice. I guess her poor kidneys were giving up. To cheer her up, I mentioned Linda would be coming to visit her; mum said "Oh, that's not necessary. I'm not *that* sick!"

As the day progressed, her speech became jumbled. Initially I understood her with difficulty, then I could catch a couple of words here and there, but eventually she was talking only gibberish. A friend later told me it might have been an idea to give her a pencil and paper to jot down what she wanted to say and, to this very day, I regret not thinking of this at the time. I frantically called the doctor's surgery. I tried to call Hans but, our phone being out of order again, I called Kirsten, a friend along the beach, and asked her to please send a message to Hans to come in as mum was deteriorating badly. I phoned Linda's office again, to learn she had left for the airport.

I cannot describe how relieved I was when the doctor finally managed to pop in, but all too briefly. He said he had to go to visit a patient with Meningitis. I grabbed him and said mum was trying to talk but she couldn't: her speech was jumbled. He said she must be dehydrated, and instructed the nurse to place some ice in her mouth. *For God's Sake!*

At about six o'clock, mum tried unsuccessfully to prop herself up on her left arm. She waved her right arm around wildly, her eyes beseeching me to understand. I shouted for the nurse. Two nurses rushed in and lifted her up once again to the top of the bed; mum did not want to be that way round. She gave a horrible, hoarse, gurgling moan of protest and resignation; I shall never erase that sound from my memory. Freaking out, I asked "Why are you turning her?"

"Madam, she has to be near the instruments!" They acted quickly, putting oxygen tubes into mummy's nostrils. Her eyes were closed and she looked peaceful, though she was pasty white. When I gently hugged her, she felt sticky and sweaty. A nurse had a syringe in her hand and asked me to leave the room.

Where was my sister! Rushing down the stairs, I almost bumped into the doctor who tore past me, ignoring me. I turned and climbed slowly back up the stairs as if in a dream. It was twenty minutes past six. Slowly I walked along the corridor to see the doctor close the door of mummy's room. He moved towards me. "I'm sorry!" he said.

"Sorry?" I must have shouted, because he pulled me into a small office and asked me to keep quiet, otherwise I would "upset the other patients!" The little office overlooked the hospital car-park. As I looked down, a taxi pulled up, and out stepped my sister; she walked towards the hospital entrance, bag slung casually over her shoulder. I began to walk down the stairs to meet Linda as she was walking up. She was smiling until she saw my face. She looked into my eyes and shook her head from side to side, pleading with me to deny it. Hans arrived at that very moment. Linda leaned against him, saying "She didn't even wait for me".

Our mother was young in years and young at heart. She would have been seventy-two in ten days' time. From the hospital, I telephoned my young Aunt Sylvia in Norfolk, and Jeni in London, asking her also to get a message to Andrew. As we walked out through the hospital doors, a Kenyan friend who had kindly lent me his handkerchief earlier on, called out to us "God be with you!"

My sister stopped. She turned around and looked straight at him. *"GOD??"* She blurted out.

I know you were there, God. So please, please, explain WHY?

85. MOVING DAD

Though Dad was physically extremely fit, his memory was almost non-existent. We were actually at mum's Memorial at the Mission to Seamen Chapel, when he commented to me "That person said he is sorry your mum has died. I don't understand what he's talking about?"

It was so wrong that mummy, at the young age of seventy-two, with all her faculties and a brain as sharp as ever, left us because her body was giving up. Yet there was dad, nearly eighty, striding out as active as ever, but unable to recall what he had done that morning. He could still remember events that had occurred decades ago, but his short-term memory was gone.

Hans and I were now living in a flat above the new offices that Hans had designed and built, behind the restaurant on the cliff-top; the best place I ever lived in, facing out over the ocean to the east and the Shimba Hills to the west. We couldn't leave dad in the cottage on the beach. We moved him into one of our new rondavels which was very close to us, on the cliff-top. He was very happy here, and walked around the gardens many times a day, popping in to greet the guests, whether they wanted his company, or not!

Dad had already suffered a minor stroke that he appeared to recover from quite successfully.

Then came the day I found him sitting on his little verandah quite early in the morning, bent over with his head in his hands. I asked him "What's up?" He didn't reply. In fact, he was unable to stand up without assistance. A few of us managed to carry him to the car. He was immediately admitted to Mombasa Hospital and I slept on a bench in his room. After a couple of days on drips and medications, dad was much better and speaking coherently. In fact, when the doctor called in to sign him out of the hospital asking "Hello, Mr Brown, how are you today?" Dad answered "I'm nae sae bad. And Yoursel'? Still chasing the lassies on the beach, are you?" Bloody man! I was surprised the doctor could not see through this: he actually believed dad recognised him!

Certain friends would visit dad and drink with him on his little verandah. Afterwards they would tell us how mean we were, not allowing him to drink whisky after three or four black-and-tans. *They* didn't have to put him to bed; *they* didn't have to wash his sheets in the morning. A particular couple would insist he "always recognises us" yet, when they had left, dad would say "That was a nice couple. Who are they? They really acted as if they knew me!"

He did realise he was becoming forgetful. To this day, we often repeat his "Och, it's just my awful memory, ye ken!" But he was so clever at covering up. He would come out with his well-worn joking phrases, such as "Well, hello there! Haven't the Police caught up with you yet?" Our guests were fond of dad and would smile when he said "Oh dear, no rain today!" when it had been pouring all night.

However, it was not so easy to take care of him. I advertised for a "carer" as I would not give his sheets to our dhobi-man to wash. Unfortunately the only lady I would have taken on, was asking far more than we could afford. Meanwhile, my good friend Rosie had moved upcountry to Nanyuki, to take up the position of matron at the Nanyuki Cottage Hospital, which had an "old folk's wing" attached. Further, and most important, Andrew was now living and working in Nanyuki. After much deliberation, we made the decision to book dad into the Cottage Hospital, under the expert care of Dr Butt.

We had a few laughs on the way to Nanyuki. Never knowing what dad would, or would not, remember, I pointed out Donyo Sabuk, asking him "Do you know that mountain?" He looked at me as if I was going round-the-bend. "That's Donyo!" he answered, as if *I* was losing *my* memory!

It was tough leaving dad, but he soon came to believe that Rosie was family. He would walk around the hospital grounds for hours. Andrew visited him regularly. We visited him as often as we could, and he never failed to recognise me. I have a photo I took in 1994, of Andrew and dad beside a small Chorisia tree in the hospital grounds. When Andrew and his girlfriend visited us in Nanyuki in 2013, I took a photograph of them in front of the same tree. You should see the size of the tree trunk, nineteen years later.

Andrew & Dad, Nanyuki

Andrew & his girlfriend ~
same place ~ 19 years later

The Hospital staff were good with dad. I made sure
he always had a supply of Black and Tans. Initially, dad
would walk around the gardens two or three times a day.
As time went on, he walked less and less. Eventually he
did not walk at all, and spent the day-time hours in a
wheelchair. I went to stay with Rosie in the hospital
grounds for a couple of days in January 1995. Dad's eyes
shone with recognition when I walked in, but he did not
speak at all. Not a single word. I cut his hair and trimmed
his beard, and pushed him around the garden in the

wheelchair. He must have been waiting for my visit, because he died just after I had left the following day, aged eighty years and six months. Oh dad! Hans hugged me and said "Well, I guess that makes us the *wazees* (old folks) now!"

86. TEMPORARILY IN NAIROBBERY

A couple of friends who had been successfully managing a cottage business slightly north of us, asked if we would be interested in renting out Minilets to them. I was definitely interested. Unfortunately, and much against my better judgement, Hans decided we should hire our business out to a visiting Englishman. This turned out to be our first really bad decision.

Meanwhile, Jeni, who had attended Dance and Drama College, and whose first position upon returning to Kenya, was Guest Entertainments Manager at Diani Reef Hotel, had totally changed roles: she became Operations Manager of a local airline! She worked in the desert post of Lokichoggio on the Sudan border, at a camp owned by Heather Stewart "All Weather Heather" of "Wings Over Africa" fame. Heather kindly flew me up to Loki to surprise Jeni on her Birthday.

I was lucky to be asked by Heather to briefly manage her Camp; Jeni happened to be away. Living and working in Loki was quite an experience. Rescued Oribi antelope and Grants Gazelle would find their way to the camp. The birdlife was amazing: beautiful Abyssinian Rollers with their long tail feathers, Brown (Meyer's) Parrots, trees full of White-Billed Buffalo-Weavers; a one-legged Shikra would come to drink from the bird-bath. The late Rory McGuinness was working there and at weekends we would attend discos at a canvas construction on the U.N. compound, jokingly referred to as the "U.N. Hilton". A wildlife veterinary officer lived next-door to the Camp. A young lady who worked at the Camp, kept pet turkeys. One day a turkey was bitten by a Forest Cobra; she frantically called the vet. The vet came dashing into the office asking "Where is it? Where is it?"

I told him that the poor thing was lying in the run with the other turkeys. "No no, not the turkey: where's the Cobra?"

Jeni still manages the operations of an airline, at Wilson Airport, Nairobi. Her knowledge of aircraft is mind-boggling. A strange noise from the sky and she will say "that's a 'so-and-so'", which means b.....-all to me. In her spare time, Jeni takes part in – and directs – local musical theatre productions. If Jeni happens to be in the restaurant or club where Andrew is playing, he calls her up to sing with him.

Hans and I were offered an interesting managerial position in Nairobi, temporarily taking over and running the Karen Blixen Coffee Garden for the very special Frank Sutton. Attached to the main building at the Karen Blixen Coffee Garden is "Swedo House", a quaint little cottage that was built by Karen Blixen in 1912, to house her Coffee Manager. Andrew did a painting of the cottage, which I printed out on the front of our menus. Andrew was becoming quite well-known as an entertainer: singing, playing guitar and harmonica. He sang at the Coffee Garden a couple of times a week. Whenever dear old Frank walked in, Andrew would play the opening chords to "Old Man River". Frank would stand up there next to Andrew, singing along in his amazing double-bass.....

SOCDO HOUSE '97

He calls her up to sing

It was while we were working at the Coffee Garden, that a major "ethnic cleansing" operation at the coast – as I described in a previous chapter as being politically instigated - began in earnest. Due to the rioting, tourists fled the country and so did the person Hans had entrusted

299

with our business. This "gentleman" renter unfortunately left staff wages unpaid and a pile of unsettled utility bills for us to deal with, as well as owing us a substantial sum in rent. I faxed him a few times, asking what he intended to do about his debts. He finally replied, accusing us of "carrying on an ostentatious lifestyle", which would have been quite amusing in happier circumstances! His message ended very rudely with *"Put a lid on your fax"*. My sister needed her share of dad's land, but she wanted money and not land. So we started making arrangements to sell the place, together with our business. Needless to say, this was another mistake: one of the greatest mistakes of my life to date. It would have been better to have borrowed money from the Bank.

Hans never used his German surname, he used mine, and just about everybody believed that "Stanley" was his real name. When our job at the Coffee Garden came to an end, we decided to leave Nairobi and move upcountry to Nanyuki, where we set up "Stanley's Safaris" operating safaris countrywide.

87. SAFARI FUN

I don't know how many others feel the way I do, when leaving game-parks, reserves and ranches. Since I was a toto, whenever we were driving out of a "wild game area", my heart would sink lower and lower, the closer we got to the exit. I had the same feeling, just last week, when driving out of a game ranch in Laikipia.

I feel at home in the wild parts of Kenya: I love the animals; the trees and plants. Overall, the bird-life is my favourite. Linda is the same. I recall one visit to a game park when Linda and I had been sitting with binoculars trained on a magnificent Steppe Eagle. A car-load of Japanese tourists came hurtling towards us, pulling up in a cloud of dust. "Lion?" they yelled out, excited, *"You see lion?"* My sister looked down her nose at them. *"No!"* she said emphatically, before turning back to her binoculars and the eagle. They drove away with puzzled expressions on their faces, tsk-tsking and tapping their foreheads.

I will always remember one interesting example of animal behaviour. Jeni and I were leaving Nairobi Game Park via the Langata Gate, when a male lion ran across the road in front of us; then we noticed he was being chased by a couple of buffalo. We stopped. The lion came right round to the side of the car and sat there as if for protection, panting, with foam pouring out of his mouth. The buffalo turned around and we watched them walk back to where a zebra was lying in the grass, clearly brought down by the lion. "Look what they're doing!" Jeni exclaimed. Having seen the lion off, the buffalo were nudging the zebra, obviously trying to make it get up. We watched them for some time! How cool is that?

A MAGNIFICENT STEPPE EAGLE

PANTING, WITH FOAM POURING
OUT OF HIS MOUTH..

Elephants are like people! We were staying in a little lodge built on stilts, on the edge of a water-hole, in the Shimba Hills Game Reserve on the South Coast. Standing on a walk-way that was strung between beautiful Bamba Kofi trees, we were watching a long line of elephants walking beneath us and along the edge of the water-hole into thick forest. When the elephants were trailing out of sight, a youngster decided that he wanted a swim; he left the herd, ran back, slithered down the bank into the water, and began to swim around with great joy and abandon. His mum and dad re-appeared from the forest, attempting to persuade their mutinous child to follow the rest of the herd.

The water-hole was not very deep and junior would swim-walk to the bank on the far side where daddy stood throwing his head up and down, ordering the youngster to "come here NOW", whereupon the naughty child would toss his head rebelliously, swivel around and come over to where mum was now waiting, just below where we stood on the rope-bridge. In no uncertain terms, mum would motion for her offspring to "get out at once", whereupon junior would throw his head back as if to say "make me!", before spinning around and swimming back to dad again. This was absolutely hilarious and continued for a good twenty minutes before the youngster decided he had had enough fun, and clambered up the bank in the safe space between where mum and dad were standing, before careering at speed past dad into the forest, with little trunk and ears flying, quickly followed by extremely irate parents. We were really laughing out loud; I only wish I could describe just how amusing it was to watch!

After a safari that had ended at Malindi on the North Coast, Hans and I were driving through Tsavo East Game Reserve, towards the Galana River. This is one of those typically long roads, with no side tracks or alternative "ways around". You drive all the way to the river, then follow the road left or right alongside the river. About one hundred metres ahead, in the middle of the road, stood a large lady elephant. Hans continued to drive towards her, until she started tossing her huge beautiful head around, trunk waving, to show us that this was her road, she was not moving, and we were not allowed on it.

I grabbed Hans's arm and said urgently "Go back!"

"Back to where?" he asked, "the only other way is a round trip of about one hundred and fifty kilometres!"

So we sat and waited. After fifteen minutes or so, Mrs Elephant appeared to bore of the game and moved off to the left-hand-side of the road. Hans started the car engine and began to move forward. She was instantly back in the middle of the road, waving her head and trunk around and saying "Oh no you don't!"

"Go back! Go back!"

Another ten minutes must have passed. Again, the ellie walked off to the side of the road, out of sight. As soon as we started to move, it was the same story all over again; what fun she was having! Eventually, the time came when Hans started up the engine and Mrs Elephant did not rush triumphantly into the middle of the road. Phew! As we began to advance slowly, we noticed her trunk flicking back and forth from behind a bush at the road-side. She was hiding in the bushes waiting for us; waiting to take us out.

"Go back!"

Hans was becoming fed-up with this game, fed-up with me, fed-up with everything, and determined not to turn back and drive the long way round. I pointed out that it was all very well for him; the ellie was on *my* side of the car. *I* would be the one to cop it. *Hans* would be the one to get free drinks while regaling friends and visitors as to how his woman was taken out by an elephant in Tsavo East.

After a while, the trunk-swinging stopped, and even I considered it safe to continue on our journey. Hans put his foot down hard. Indeed, Mrs Elephant had given up this fruitless game and was wandering off away from the road-side. As she saw us speeding past, she spun around very fast and hot-footed it after us, absolutely livid, trumpeting like fury, her great feet thundering along the road behind us. But she didn't catch us.

Since then, our family has always referred to elephants as "Go-backs".

Ingrid, a special friend from Germany, joined me on a number of safaris, both working safaris and also when we simply wanted to get away into the bush. Four of us: Ingrid, my son, my sister's partner, and I, made an exploratory trip to Chololo, an isolated cattle-cum-game ranch in Laikipia. I had brought along four little dome-tents, which we erected side-by-side, approximately ten feet apart. Ingrid took an end tent, a couple of feet from a large boulder.

We camped beneath a magnificent rock that towered above us, with a troupe of loudly-protesting baboons sitting along the ridge, hollering down at us. My friend Sam, the owner of the ranch, came by that evening for a few beers and regaled us with animal stories. He pointed at the boulder beside Ingrid's tent and said that was where a leopard would sit and roar at the baboons until one would fall off the rock in fright, "straight into the leopard's mouth!"

After a barbecue dinner, the two men soon retired. Ingrid and I sat beside the campfire drinking wine and chatting until nearly two o'clock in the morning. I drifted off to sleep to the sound of Ingrid's snoring. At around four o'clock, I was woken by an impossibly loud, impossibly close, animal noise, which I was unable to identify. I sat up in the tent counting off on my fingers, all the sounds that were familiar to me. "Not an antelope; not a zebra; not a baboon; more like a cat but definitely not a lion....oh heck! Of course! It has to be a leopard!" Right there amongst us, making a sound I can only describe as a rasping intake of breath, followed by an extended "sneeze"; in-out, in-out, in-out..... Very excited, I waited for one of the men to unzip their tent to shine a torch on the animal. Nothing doing.

The sound continued for some time until Ingrid's snoring suddenly came to a shuddering halt. I thought the leopard had finally woken her! But no, Ingrid's bladder had decided she needed a pee. As soon as it heard the sound of the zip, the leopard shut up. As Ingrid went behind the tent, I waited with baited breath, hoping the men were ready to rush out to her rescue. Then I heard her return to her tent and zip up the flap. Two minutes later, the night was once again filled with the sound of her snoring! No more leopard sounds. At six o-clock in the morning, the two men were checking out the leopard pug-marks around the boulder next to Ingrid's tent. Until she saw the prints, Ingrid thought we were teasing her!

It does not occur to most people brought up in the wilder areas of this country, to be frightened by the sound of animals in the bush, provided we are protected by a sheet of canvas. A rather special friend, nick-named "Nuts", used to tell the story of the time he was stranded in a little tent, completely surrounded by lions. It was cool at night, and he was able to sleep. As the sun rose higher, the tent was becoming hotter and hotter. Fed-up with this, Nuts eventually cut a hole in the floor of the tent with his pen-knife then, sticking his feet through the hole, proceeded to walk the fifty or so metres to his vehicle *between the lions*, safely under cover of his tent! He made it.

My own lion story involves a safari in the Maasai Mara Game Reserve, once again in our tiny dome tents, once again taking Ingrid along; this time catering for a group of Spanish TV stars filming an episode for the "Paz Padilla" series. We set up the stars' dining and living area around a huge camp fire. At night, Maasai moran patrolled the camp for us. As this was in a private area outside the Park boundary, my son Andrew had been able to take various of the stars and crew out on nightly game drives to spot lion, jackals, hyenas, and so on. On the last night, with the filming over, the camera-man in charge of the operation now wanted a chance to go out with Andrew "to look for lions". I crawled into my tiny tent and fell asleep. Then I was woken by a one-hundred-plus decibel sound that filled the heavens. The leopard had nothing on this! I knew, of course, that it was a lion, very nearby, but still....I called out *"What was that?"* Ingrid's voice rang out, full of laughter, "You know very well what it is!"

A short while later, I heard the Landie being driven back into the little staff compound, then my son's voice, "So *that's* why we didn't find any lions; they're all here!" Apparently, as they drove into the staff camp, Andrew and the camera-man could clearly see nearly a dozen pairs of green eyes in the car's headlights. The next sound was the excited voices of Maasai warriors as they scrambled into the back of the Landie. "Oh no!" I thought, "I'm missing all the action!" I hurriedly pulled my khanga around me, unzipped the tent and began to put my feet into the flip-flops I had left in front of the tent.

A bright spotlight from the Landie was aimed full onto me. Embarrassed to be wrapped only in a khanga in the glare of the spotlight and in full view of everybody in the vehicle, I motioned to my son to move the light away. He paid no heed. Sighing with resignation, I stood up, preparing to run to the vehicle before I missed the fun. My son always manages to act very cool, calm and collected. As I was about to make a dash for it, with the spotlight shining on me unwaveringly, my son's voice came across very calmly but with great conviction, *"Mum!....don't.....run!"* I temporarily froze before walking very slowly, half-naked but in as lady-like a manner as I could muster, towards the Land Rover.

It was only when I reached the vehicle, that everything became clear. Andrew had not been shining the spotlight on me at all. He was shining it into the face of the lioness walking about ten feet behind me, screwing up her beautiful face against the glare of the light.

Thank you, Andrew, that's My Boy. No fascinating story to recount around the bar: "I once had a mother....."

"With the spot light shining on me unwaveringly, my son's voice said very calmly but with great conviction "Mum! Don't... Run!"

For the uninitiated and ignorant, I must explain that a "khanga" is a brightly-coloured piece of cloth, usually bearing a Swahili proverb, worn by most of the East African ladies living in coastal areas, and by many colonial ladies in bed at night or around the home. A "kikoi" is similar, a slightly thicker piece of material, not so brightly-patterned and without the proverbs, with the frayed ends twisted and tied into neat little knots along the edges; they serve the same purpose as khangas. Many men wear kikois tucked around their waists skirt-fashion; better than shorts at night as they help to keep the mosquitoes off the legs. I think they look very smart. Kenya-born men frequently wear kikois out at night, even to special occasions.

Beer-bellied men do not look so smart in kikois.

Although it was indeed lucky Andrew was there when the lioness was fancying me for dinner, I felt guilty I had called him away from another camp to help with this one. We had been setting up and running camps for an edition of the US "Survivor" series and Andrew had been running an isolated camp at Il Ngwesi, up north, for those entrants who had been dropped from the Series and had to be hidden away from the prying eyes and ears of the media until it was over. One of the lady contestants had struck up a good rapport with Andrew but, instead of accompanying them to the coast at the end of the programme, I asked him to come to help me with this camp for the Spanish TV stars. Each time they show a replay of that particular episode of "Survivor", and I see the lady referred to, I wonder what she is doing now, and if Andrew would have been in the US with her, had I not called him away!

A while ago, a gentleman whom I gathered must be one of the creators of the Survivor series, was being interviewed on an international chat show. He was describing the five-star hotel he had stayed in during the latest filming. He went on to explain how different it was to the African series, where even HE had to sleep in tents, *shower* in tents, and even *use tented loos!* The pretty face of the Hostess of the show was contorted with disgust as she exclaimed "Tents! Ugh!" I would have liked to call her to let her know that our tents were as good as five-star accommodation!

Some of our most memorable safari experiences were the few years when we spent the first three months of the year transporting students from one campsite to another over most of Kenya. The students, from Universities across the Atlantic, were on full Study Courses, ending with examinations and all the works; they came with a full Faculty of Professors. For some reason, the students were always ninety-percent girls, and numbered anything between twenty to sixty-plus pupils; I often wondered whether these visiting students appreciated the fantastic experience, in *my* country, as much as I did!

Since I was a child, I have always preferred the North of the country, as far as animals are concerned. For some reason, the animals and birds in the more arid, northern regions, are brighter and more vivid than those found further south.

Take, for instance, the handsome Reticulated Giraffe of the North, with vivid white patterns painted onto a rich dark brown background, as opposed to the more common Maasai Giraffe found in the South, patterned with pale brown splodges on an off-white background. The beautiful thinly-striped Grevy's Zebra of the North, with large ears and altogether more like horses, in contrast to the Common Zebra of the south, which have thick black stripes and resemble fat donkeys. In the north, the rusty-brown Defassa Waterbuck with two brilliant splashes of white on their hind-quarters: quite different from the drab, grey Common Waterbuck south of the equator with pale circles on their backsides making them appear as if they have been sitting on freshly-painted toilet seats! The auburn-coloured Jackson's Hartebeest of the north, unlike the pale brown Coke's Hartebeest of further south. There are also different animals found in the North, such as the Gerenuk, a giraffe-necked antelope that stands on its hind-legs to reach the yummy foliage.

Of course, the contrast between the animals in the different areas would probably have been lost on these students, who had never been to Africa previously, and who naturally found one giraffe as exciting as another.

On the way "up North" we would travel for hours along dusty roads in searing heat, aiming for a little dot on the horizon; this little dot was Mount Marsabit, the "Mountain in the Mist". We would drive through the scruffy little township of Marsabit and start climbing the Mountain: driving cautiously through swirling swathes of mist, very conscious of the thousand foot drop down to the aptly-named Lake Paradise on one side of the road, occasionally spotting a gigantic elephant with huge tusks lolloping towards us, suddenly appearing from nowhere, *straight out* of the clouds of mist. Indescribable. After a couple of nights camping in Marsabit, we would drive across the Chalbi Desert, a sparkling white desert of pure salt. We would set up camp overnight in Kalacha, a tiny little trading centre in the Chalbi Desert.

Prior to the arrival of the students, Hans and I did a recce over many of the planned areas, to find the most suitable campsites, establish fees, etc. When we reached Kalacha, we did not stay where we would set up a large camp for the students. Instead, we were permitted to put up our tent next to a little maize and bean plantation. That evening, we followed a scrawled sign indicating "Swimming pool this way" and stripped off to dive into a little cement water storage tank that was used for irrigating the nearby vegetable patch! Lovely!

On Mount
Marsabit,
we would drive
cautiously
through
swirling swathes
of mist

We would drive
across the Chalbi
Desert, a
sparkling white
desert of pure
salt

Lake Turkana,
the "Jade Sea".
An enormous
turquoise lake
surrounded by
black rocks

Caution!

Those swimming in this water tank ...

... do so at their own risk!

Thence on to Lake Turkana, the "Jade Sea". From miles away, you can look down at the unbelievable spectacle of an enormous turquoise lake surrounded by black rocks. One evening Hans and I sat by the lake watching a Turkana couple erect a windbreak of black lava stones, while their young son caught a fish on a length of baited string. He used a tiny piece of wood to light a weenie little fire and held the fish over the flame: this was their evening meal before kipping down for the night behind the windbreak!

Funny old Kenya: even way up there, where unspoilt people are living the most basic of lives, the next morning, upon departure, we found ourselves up against corrupt officials who man-handled Hans and threatened to lock him up if he did not pay extra "Council Tax" on top of camping fees! Our visitors were totally bemused at being witness to such bizarre bureaucracy "in the middle of nowhere"!

With the students, we camped high up on Mount Elgon, near the Uganda border, where the water froze at night. Here we saw Giant Forest Hogs and black-and-white Casqued Hornbills. With the forest growing right to the edges of the narrow winding tracks where it would be almost impossible to turn the Land Rover, it was quite scary when spotting an elephant stealthily walking right alongside the track, practically hidden by thick foliage.

In Kakamega Forest we spotted brown-tailed monkeys, the Great Blue Turaco and the rare Blue-Headed Bee-eater. We climbed hills and looked across to the Nandi Escarpment. At Lake Bogoria we swam at night in warm water from the natural springs; we spotted the Silverbird and Jackson's Hornbill. At Lake Baringo we photographed Jackson's Golden-backed Weaver and other birds we would never see anywhere else. Sometimes the lake would have receded so far, that it was possible to walk nearly all the way to the nearest island; at other times the water flooded three-quarters of the campsite. In the Maasai Mara, in spite of the inevitable invasion of mini-buses, we saw golden jackals, a rufous-bellied heron and lions climbing trees. To my mind, the only advantage of the Mara, is that you don't just see one or two animals....you see hundreds of them; but whether that is more fun, is debatable.

At the coast, we visited holy Kayas, drank madafu (green coconut milk) and scuba-dived with whale-sharks and dolphins. On the final student safari, we temporarily "re-opened" Minilets, where the Faculty had the luxury of the bandas. The students stayed in tents that were erected at the top of the beach. Esther, the daughter of one of my Scottish cousins, happened to be visiting us at the time. She was in the same age group as the students, which was great. Then came the night when Esther told me, wide-eyed and horrified, that the young students were inviting beach-boys into their tents at night. I took this information with a pinch of salt thinking they were probably just having a few drinks and getting to know the local people. Then, on our last night at the coast, I saw our dish-washer Hassani appearing from behind some coral rocks with one of the students. Apart from the fact that Hassani was recently married, he did not speak a word of English; but I guess speech-communication was not required. The Professors that I mentioned this to, simply did not believe it. Especially as the girl concerned was one of the favourites, very quiet and shy!

Whilst over-nighting in Nairobi, a Professor – against our better judgement – unadvisedly took a bus-load of students to the City Centre, where they had jackets and wallets stolen. We had hired mini-buses from a well-known Kenya company and took everybody along to a gig where Andrew was playing, at Psy's Bar near the Carnivore Restaurant. Esther told me that the students had been bonking the mini-bus drivers in the car-park; she had even witnessed a couple having it off over the bonnet of a vehicle!

I was finally taken seriously when, at the end of the safari, Hans and I took one of the Professors and his wife to Nairobi's JKIA Airport; they had become good friends, and always stayed a few weeks longer. We had thought all the students had left on earlier flights, but one pretty young blond had obviously stayed on. Hans and I noticed her, crying her eyes out while leaning against a post, kissing and cuddling Dennis, one of the casual workers I had taken on as a kitchen-helper at Minilets. Dennis, a coastal man with wife and family, had never been away from the coast prior to this all-expenses-paid trip to Nairobi. This was his first very memorable experience of the eye-boggling so-called "civilisation" of the metropolis; let alone bonking an overseas student who "fell in love" with him, as evidenced by her distress at having to leave him! We pointed out the devoted couple to our Professor friend and his wife. Apart from a few *"Oh My God's"* they were absolutely speechless!

88. VISITS TO AUSTRIA

Over the years Hans naturally met many of my friends, who also became his friends. One such friend was a gentleman who just happened to be Chairman of "AMREF Austria". He had an idea he discussed with Hans: the prospect of taking a group of Kenyan athletes to partake in the annual "half marathon" in Salzburg. In 2000, this became a reality. Thereafter, Hans and I would annually accompany the selected team to Austria. Some of the athletes who assisted were well-known names such as Patrick Sang and Paul Tergat, both great people, and wonderful ambassadors for Kenya. On one trip, the tragically late George Saitoti came along and delivered an excellent speech at the end of the race.

Most competitors were hitherto unknown, chosen because they had achieved good results in long-distance runs marked on the Kenya calendar. I particularly remember a young man who came because he had achieved first place in the "Nairobi Road Race"; I was sure he had never been on an elevator, let alone an aeroplane or cable-car! Cordon-bleu-style dishes were not for him. I recall searching the markets of Salzburg for dried maize which had to be ground to make "posho", Kenya's staple diet. This provided great entertainment for the expert Austrian hotel Chefs!

The first year, we stayed in a wonderful small hotel where Mozart had lived. We were really comfortable there, in the gracious old building with uneven wooden floors, so much nicer than the following year when we were accommodated in a large, modern, typically sterile "high-class" hotel.

Annually when we were in Salzburg, Hans's mother travelled by train to join us. She was usually accompanied by other family members. This was wonderful: I loved his mother and was particularly close to his extra-special sister-in-law.

Yet another "Sue", a very dear friend who was a regular visitor in the Minilets days, coincidentally lived on a farm not far from Salzburg and I was able to spend a lot of time with her. I frequently accompanied her to the farm where she lived. I came to know Sue's hairdresser, the shop where she bought delicious fresh rye bread – both of us being wheat-intolerant. Together we toured the beautiful old, and not-so-beautiful new, sections of Salzburg.

Sue joined us when we took the Kenyan athletes by cable-car to the top of the Untersberg, a massif of the Berchtesgaden Alps. We swung up through amazing scenery, excitedly catching sight of incredibly agile mountain goats, eventually dining at a little rustic restaurant at one thousand eight hundred metres above sea-level. There were stunning all-round views, and we felt as if we were at the top of the world! It was funny to think that Nanyuki town is as high above sea-level as the summit of the Untersberg!

THE UNTERSBERG
"FELT AS IF WE WERE AT
THE TOP OF THE WORLD"

On the day of the marathon, Sue stood with me on the balcony of the Glockenspeil Restaurant, waiting for the first runners to come in. I cannot describe the feeling of immense pride when the first sprinters to appear from around the corner were always our marvellous Kenyan athletes!

Our annual visits to Austria had become one of the main highlights of the year. I was so looking forward to our next visit, at the beginning of 2004.

But, sadly, it was not to be.

Not for me, anyway.

89. MY CHEATING BLUE-EYED GERMAN

A week before Christmas 2003, when Hans and I had spent five years running our Safari business from Nanyuki, life changed suddenly and drastically. Out of the blue, Jeni received a phone-call from a Kenyan man, advising her that "her dad" was seeing a local "Malaya" (hooker) called Jeannie and that, if we wondered where Hans's money was going, it was being spent on her. Jeni called me immediately, suggesting that I speak to a good friend and shop-owner in Nanyuki, who "knows everything going on in Nanyuki", and that I should also speak to our mutual friend Gordon.

I drove into town and spoke to my friend at the duka. She practically laughed out loud, saying Hans and I were one of the couples who were happy in Nanyuki, and I should not believe it because she was sure Hans would never cheat on me.

After dinner, sitting in front of the fire, Hans asked me what was wrong. I asked "have you been having sex with somebody else?"

His eyes were really disturbed as he replied, "Well, when you put it like that, yes I have!"

"Someone called Jeannie?"

"Yes. Who told you?"

Incredibly, I kept myself together. I had been through all this before. John had started an affair with the American woman on the night that Jeni was born, and Mike used to meet up with prostitutes. There was obviously something wrong with me that made my men go after other women. "Jeni had an anonymous phone-call. Why did you do it?" I asked him.

"I don't know why; something is wrong in my head!"

You knew what was wrong in his head, didn't you, God?

I asked how often he had been meeting up with her. He told me they had only "been together" about three times. Well, that wasn't so bad, I thought. Then I gasped, as the horror of AIDS suddenly loomed very large. I asked if he had "used protection".

"Yes!" he replied.

"Shit! Thank God for that!"

He went to bath. I sent a message to Jeni stating "I'm afraid it's true". She phoned me, crying so much she could barely speak. She made me promise not to do anything stupid. She was so disappointed in her "Dad".

"Mum", she said "You are a strong lady. You have been through a lot and you will get through this!"

I finally managed to collar Gordon and, wondering whether he was also party to Hans's treachery, asked him if he knew what was going on. Gordon said awkwardly he had heard rumours via a mutual friend. Gordon was of the opinion that if a guy wanted to "get a leg over" occasionally, that was fine; but he agreed with the "mutual friend" that, to continue with such an odd relationship when he had a perfectly good wife-cum-business-partner at home, was beyond comprehension. I asked Gordon why he hadn't said anything to Hans about it, if he disapproved. Gordon explained that he was good friends with both of us, and he didn't like to "take sides". *Take sides* for Heavens' Sake! Sides with whom, I wanted to know – the choice was between the tart and me, not Hans and me!

Hans had to go to Nairobi the following day. He met with Jeni. Poor Jeni. She told him she had always looked

322

up to him, had always compared her would-be boyfriends with him, and they seldom matched up. She rang me and related all the details of the conversation to me. She added Hans had cried, and swore he still loved us all.

I learned Jeannie sometimes had a "day-job" braiding African ladies' hair, in a shop owned by a friend, Nazmi. Coincidentally, Nazmi's husband owed us money for a camp I had recently arranged for him at "Lewa Downs". Nazmi called me to say she would leave the money at the shop for me to collect. I said simply "Just make sure Jeannie is not there at the time".

Sounding relieved I had broached the subject, Nazmi said "Wendy, I am so sorry about all this! We just don't know what to do. Jeannie used to live on our compound and when we noticed Hans was coming to pick her up in his car, we kicked her out! But I only keep her on here because she is really good at braiding afro-hair". I went to Nazmi's shop and, firmly believing Hans's story he had slept with her only three times, I decided to get shot of her for good. Whilst signing for the payment, I asked the girl behind the desk "Is Jeannie here?" The girl stuttered, "Yes, but she's busy!" Why the stammer? Good Lord, she obviously knew who I was and what was going on.

"OK!" I said. "In that case I'll just have to speak to her in front of her client".

"Oh no!" Panic! "Please come to the office and I'll call her". I waited in the office.

While I was waiting for Jeannie, a short, fat, extraordinarily unattractive person *slopped* in: hair sticking up at all angles, extremely petulant, matchstick sticking out of corner of mouth. Eventually it dawned on me. Surely not? Hans would not be attracted to a woman like this in a thousand years! Astounded, I asked, "Are you Jeannie?" She must have heard the shock and incredulity in my voice.

She moved her head up and down, her mouth jiggling the matchstick about.

"Hello. I am Wendy, Hans's wife". I was very controlled and dignified. She stared at her feet.

"I just want to tell you. If I ever hear you have so much as tried to contact my husband again, you are *fucking dead meat!*" And I walked out like a lady.

Actually, I was shaking as I stepped out onto the pavement. Coincidentally, Ingrid was walking past the shop door. She asked me whatever was wrong. So I told her. She couldn't take it in; it was "so unlike Hans to do something like that!"

I drove home. As I walked into the house the phone rang, and it was a friend, "Mouse". "Oh, thank Goodness you're home!" she gasped. "Hans burst into our workshop telling everyone that you had beaten up some girl and were being held at the Police Station, so I was just going to get you released!"

What on earth?

A few minutes later, Hans came storming into the house as if he was possessed by a demon. "I've just had a call from the Police Chief!" he shouted. "It was reported to him that you went around town threatening people and I had to stop the Police from coming to pick you up!" He warned me I could not go around *threatening* people and I had just ruined any chance of us getting back together. He walked out in his dirty shorts and flip-flops, climbed into a Land Rover, and drove out at speed.

This was Christmas Eve. I was certainly in no mood to drive to Nairobi to celebrate Christmas with the family. Now, of course, Andrew, my sister Linda, and everybody had to be told. As planned, they congregated at Jeni's house that evening for Christmas Eve drinks. Jeni told them. Andrew immediately rang and told me he and his girlfriend were packed and about to drive the two-hundred-and-thirty kilometres from Langata to Nanyuki. I persuaded him not to; it would just be too unfair to Jeni and her wonderful partner Anthony, who had prepared a Christmas party, and already Hans and I were not going to be there; so Andrew agreed to wait until Boxing Day.

Jeni later told me that she had walked into her kitchen on Christmas Day to find her brother sobbing. "Oh Jen!" he cried, "I love dad so much!"

Mouse and her husband invited me to their home on Christmas Day. With the help of amazing Happy Pills prescribed by our wonderful local doctor, I discovered over the next few days that, after bouts of bawling my heart out, I became totally, quite comfortably, numb....thank you PF.

My staff spoke earnestly to me. "Mama, this woman is very evil; we hate her. She must have been given some strong dawa (medicine) from a Mganga (Witchdoctor) to change Mzee so much". I was very annoyed that none of them had told me about her. Peter the askari (watchman) told me Hans had threatened to shoot him with a little gun, if he told me anything. Peter described perfectly the flare-gun that Hans kept beside the bed. Of course, as I mentioned previously vis-a-vis the case of Caitlin's friend Chuck, I knew that Witchcraft existed, but if I hadn't been so devastated, I would have found their assumption amusing....as if a mganga's medicine could have any effect on a person as strong as Hans.

Having been pretty shaken up to learn from Hans on Christmas Eve that I was on the verge of being taken away in handcuffs, I decided on 27 December, that my next step would be to visit Nanyuki Police Station to discover what sort of complaint Jeannie had filed against me for "beating her up". I spoke personally to the Police Chief, who confirmed there was no such "case" filed against me. But he and his Deputy knew Jeannie fairly well from the times she had been brought into the Police Station; they quoted her as being a real "trouble-maker". They were distressed Hans had taken up with such a woman. The Deputy referred to her diplomatically as a loose woman who "followed men – mainly British Army Squaddies – for their money".

What these women did, was to first stick their hands through the fence to grab five thousand shillings from a Squaddie, then they would stick their backsides through the fence.... Imagine. At that time, our house-girl was very happy at being paid eight thousand shillings per month. All Jeannie had to do was to stick her backside through the fence once per day, and she would be bringing in one hundred and fifty thousand shillings per month! Do it two, three, four times or more: the mind boggles.

The Police Chief and his Deputy advised me I had every right to threaten Jeannie and were surprised that was all I had done. They said they would give her a warning but I asked them not to do this. They said they would try to meet up with Hans for a drink, to put him right about this woman. The Deputy later told me they had met up with him but when they tried to reason with him, he became extremely abusive and they backed off.

90. JUJU

The Crime Boss's Deputy very interestingly told me Jeannie was from his home area of Siaya, and he alleged that even men from that part of the country tended to avoid some of their women, because they delved deeply into witchcraft! He went on to say that a Mganga would give these women a concoction that would make a chosen man follow her anywhere, crave sex with her, do anything she wanted, even to the extent of – quote "handing over all his money!" Not sure quite how to take in this information, I telephoned my sister and relayed what the Policeman had told me. Linda had a good friend who also hailed from that part of the country. My sister, a total non-believer, would enquire whether there could possibly be any substance to these "witchcraft" stories.

Later I received a brief text from Linda: "F...... Hell! I spoke to Susan who says the spell can only be lifted by a Church person!"

Andrew reminded me that Oscar, a friend in Nairobi, was studying "Witchcraft among Kenyan tribes". Upon returning to Nairobi, Andrew called Oscar who straight away put him in touch with an Afro-Kenyan friend called George who, apart from being a Church Preacher, was a psychic, and also possessed other amazing gifts. First, in order to find out whether voodoo *was* involved in our case, George asked Andrew to bring along a photograph of Hans. George studied the photograph and confirmed that something was "definitely going on". Andrew arranged to meet up with George the following morning, 30 December.

George placed a bowl of water, a packet of soap powder and a cloth on a table. He put a small amount of soap powder in the bowl and asked Andrew to swish his hands around in the bowl until the water was really bubbly, then George placed the cloth over the bowl. George was leaning back against the wall....he later explained to me he has to do this, in order to stop the juju from attacking him from behind! After a while, he sat up and jiggled the bowl; "Yes, there is something here," he said. He removed the cloth and they could see something in the water. He removed it; it was a small package wrapped up in bandages. George cut open the bandages, which contained bits and pieces of hair, animal skin and stuff. George explained that Jeannie carried this around in her handbag; he said it had to be disposed of completely. He gathered a pile of leaves and twigs in the garden, which he set light to, then placed the odd little package on the fire and made sure that it was totally burned.

The next day was New Year's Eve. Hans called in and was very pleasant and friendly, almost like his old self. On New Year's morning he drove out, returning with some groceries, saying he would be back later. As he was leaving, I must have looked unhappy, because he said "Don't make me cry!"

"What have you got to cry about?" I asked. "You're the one who's all right!"

"I'm not all right" he said, as he drove out.

He did not return, nor did he phone. He moved out of our lovely little home into a dirty dilapidated shack with Jeannie. Looking back, and knowing what I know now, Jeannie must have panicked upon discovering that her little package was no longer in her handbag, and she would have returned to the Mganga to get a replacement.

On 30 January 2004 I made a note in my diary that I had met with Hans briefly. I asked him why he was staying in that hovel, to which he replied that he preferred to stay with her "for the moment". When I asked him why, he said he did not know. I asked him how he would have felt if I had brought a prostitute to screw me in our bed every time he was away, to which he replied "Not very good". He was obviously under great stress.

Since those days I have frequently experienced, and been witness to, a variety of Black Magic applications: it is very, very real. Juju works much more effectively on those who refuse to accept it: that is, those who say "Huh! I don't believe in witchcraft. Pshaw, what rubbish!" All I can say to such pig-headed people is: "you cannot not believe in something that exists all around us!"

People who are aware, are far better-equipped to deal with it.

91. FAREWELL MY BLUE-EYED GERMAN

At the end of it all, I have to say that, in the twenty-three years spent with Hans, there were only one-and-a-half occasions when he was horrid after boozing. From my experiences of the male gender, this is beyond amazing.

Friends and acquaintances would relate to me stories that Hans had made up as to why we had separated; many believed him and some still do. Hans is a bull-shitter *par excellence*. People have always tended to be totally taken in by his over-the-top stories, which is one reason why our businesses flourished when he was behind the bar, recounting his fabricated narratives. He is very plausible. I must say the local people around Nanyuki are not taken in by his stories; many of them knew what Jeannie was all about and I have been told on many occasions that, upon discovering that she was pregnant by one of the many British Army squaddies she served, she set out to find a "white" father for the baby as soon as possible. Well, if Hans believes the brat is his, so much for telling me he had "used protection"!

One of the worst outcomes of Hans's betrayal was the total cut-off from his really special family; his lovely Mother and his exceptional siblings: over the years they had become our family; "Oma" was Jeni and Andrew's Grandmother. We had visited them often and a number of them had spent great holidays with us in Kenya. Of course he will have given many stories as to how "Wendy had left him". Although I am still in occasional contact with his sister-in-law, I have to admit that, to this day, I am still very hurt on behalf of my children and myself that the rest of them chose to believe him, without trying to hear the other side of it.

One day, close family.

The next day, out of our lives forever.

All that we did and went through together, just wiped out with one great big whoooooosh!

A few months after Hans left us, I met up with a friend whose husband had died suddenly and tragically in a fluke accident, when a tree beside the road fell onto the car he was driving. My friend said "Wendy, you have had it worse than me. I know my husband loved me above all else right up until the last moment. The man you loved for all those years betrayed you and you still see him around; that is unbearable". Imagine her being able to say that. What a wonderful lady.

So much for our signature tune. Whenever KC Sunshine Band's "Please Don't Go" is played on the radio, I wonder whether Hans is listening, and if he has any feelings at all. It is only very recently I have been able to hear his name mentioned "out-of-the-blue", without feeling myself almost leap up in shock that anybody can simply come out with his name as if he were a regular human-being.....as if it is Okay for him to strut around in my space; in the space occupied by normal people.

George kept a constant check on what Jeannie was up to. Every single time George removed her latest juju, Hans would call round and be friendly. Then the Malaya would go back to her Mganga and Hans would be off again. Suffice to say after a few weeks, I gave up fighting, thus leaving my man to his new and very different way of life.

And so I started out on my own new, and very different, way of life.

But I still have a huge scar which refuses to heal.

92. A HAPPY EVENT

The ceremony was to be held on the dry river bed

The seating was hay bales covered with Samburu "shukas"

Young Samburu men & women came to dance at the wedding and they presented Jeni with a beautiful Samburu necklace

A major event that managed to cheer me up immensely occurred one evening while I was sitting alone in Nanyuki. I received a phone-call from Jeni's boyfriend Anthony, who was on holiday with Jeni at the coast. He told me that he was thinking of asking Jeni to marry him, and what did I feel? I asked him if he knew what he was letting himself in for! He said he thought so. I asked if he was getting ready to polish his knee. When I disconnected, I leapt up off the sofa, threw my arms in the air and yelled "Y-e-e-e-a-h!" The dogs ran around barking, alerting the neighbours, who wondered what on earth was going on!

Apparently Anthony did indeed go down on one knee to propose, in front of a crowded beach-bar!

The Wedding was nearly a year later, on the site where Hans and I had our camp, on the banks of the Uasinyiro River in Buffalo Springs Reserve. Andrew set up a campsite for one-hundred-and-twenty guests, a dance-floor, and he even built a plunge-pool. The river, which had been a raging torrent not so long ago, was now completely dry. The ceremony was to be held on the sparkling white dry river-bed. For those guests who arrived a day prior to the Wedding we dug a big hole in the river sand, which gradually filled up with water. Later, we lounged around drinking wine in the pool of lovely clear water that had seeped in.

Much later, thirsty elephants gathered around our pool, delighted to find a pre-dug hole full of delicious water for them to drink.

The ceremony was wonderful. A dear friend whom we had known as the Chaplain at the Mission to Seamen in Mombasa some twelve years previously, flew over from UK with his lovely wife, to conduct the Service. John's niece Karen, who had been our little golden

333

flower-girl at our Wedding, flew over from England to attend the Wedding. The seating was hay-bales covered with Samburu "shukas". Young Samburu men and women came to dance at the Reception, and they presented Jeni with a beautiful Samburu necklace.

93. TOY-BOY

Some months prior to Hans's deception, a new family had moved to Nanyuki. Oreste, the father, took over a garage business and, after Hans took off, it was good to know that there was still a decent garage capable of looking after my remaining vehicles. I liked Oreste's wife; they came with their son and daughter. Sadly, the word around Nanyuki was that their marriage was yet another of those that appeared to be on the rocks.

Then, the story of Hans and I went to the back-burner, while a new story was circulating enthusiastically around the Nanyuki gossip-channels about Oreste having a "one-night-stand". His wife spoke to me about it, letting me know how discontented she was. Having suffered a broken relationship some fifteen months previously, I felt bad for her, and even contacted George. No juju was involved here. She asked me if I would try to talk to Oreste, with the aim of finding out whether he wanted to continue with the marriage. She confided in me that she would be happy to live somewhere in a little flat with their daughter. I figured out the best way to go about this was to call Oreste suggesting that, provided he had a shave first, he could come round to my house and I would trim his unkempt, overgrown locks!

He duly turned up, cleanly shaven, in a clean ripped T-shirt, clean shorts and flip-flops, picking leaves of rocket from my veggie patch on the way to the door. Whilst I was cutting his hair, we talked. He is quite a private person and it took a while to get him started. Finally, he confessed to being as discontented with their non-marriage as his wife was. Not long after that, Oreste and his wife separated. He and his son initially moved into what used to be Hans' and my office on a small site on the main road into Nanyuki.

I still puzzle as to how it came about that Oreste moved in with me; we are indeed the "most unlikely couple" from opposite ends of the Universe! Even much stranger is that, eleven years down the line, we are still together. We do share many of the same interests such as cooking, growing veggies, dancing, spoiling our pets, being amongst wild animals. On the other hand, apart from programmes like "QI", "Who Wants to be a Millionaire", "Would I Lie to You", we do not share the same interests as far as television goes. Whilst I will watch anything starring Judi Dench, Maggie Smith, Colin Firth, Hugh Grant *et al*, Oreste prefers watching glass-eyed men and robotic bikini-clad women toting flaming firearms whilst saving the planet from dinosaurs with flashing headlights as eyes.

Oreste at home with our newly-adopted menagerie 2015

The fact that he is normally scruffy and unshaven, is Oreste's only similarity to Hans. In contrast to Hans's ample stomach, pale-skin, thin blonde hair and pale blue eyes, Oreste is of lean build, olive-skinned, with a shock of jet-black curly hair and turquoise eyes. A true Kenyan of Kitaliani stock, Oreste was born and brought up in Kenya. He lived in Italy for a few years, where he completed his Military Service. He refers to himself as a "Wop", his late father being pure Italian and his mother French-Seychelloise.

Oreste is much younger than me. The age gap doesn't appear to bother him at all. A few years hence I shall be ancient and decrepit while Oreste will still be in his prime. Hans being twelve years my junior worried me greatly in our first years together; then along came somebody who really helped me with this problem. He was the camera-man filming "In the Shadow of Kilimanjaro". When filming was over, he and Irene Miracle came to relax with us at Tiwi Beach; every evening they sat on dad's verandah chatting over a few sundowners. This wonderful man really fixed into my brain that "age is only a number"; he told me that he had had a girlfriend twenty years older than him, which didn't bother him one bit. It was she who eventually ended the relationship because she could not "hack the age thing" whereas he would have stayed with her "until one of them left this world". These talks helped me a lot at that time. I wish I could find him again now for a few more such talks! But I am learning to take each day as it comes.

Ten years ago I was introduced to a lady who is a Psychic. I visited her regularly until she moved to Canada. I once asked Nadia why it was that Oreste, rather like John, sometimes had a change of character when drinking. She told me "It is all due to his extremely abusive upbringing". Sadly his father died when Oreste was only four years old, and his mother re-married, to a Seychelloise man, who became step-father to Oreste and his two older sisters. Thereafter, Oreste and his siblings suffered extraordinary abuse, which has been documented to a degree in a book written by one of their many cousins. We first heard about Belo's book when I went to cut one of Oreste's Aunt's hair, at his late mother's house. His mother said that Oreste should "sue Belo" for writing that she had "sexually abused her son, amongst others...." I was astonished and awaited Oreste's reaction. There was none, he just continued chatting normally.....until we were walking out to the car, whereupon he burst out laughing and said "So it took Belo to finally tell the truth!"

My cousin in Norfolk managed to order Belo's book for me; it is entitled "I Wish I Was Never Born".

I thought I had a large family. Well, Oreste has a *ginormous* family! Sometimes when he is driving, I joke "Be careful, mind that pedestrian, he's probably your cousin!" As one is never sure which particular family member is out of favour with whom at any specific time, it is best to steer away before becoming the subject of gossip. As I found out to my detriment a few years ago. The husband of one of Oreste's half-sisters told Oreste that I had been seen at a recent Wedding Reception "coming onto" the widower of one of Oreste's extra-special Aunties who had recently passed away: the Aunt whose hair I used to cut. This Auntie used to visit me in Nanyuki quite frequently; she was very special to me.

To explain my disgraceful behaviour at the Wedding Reception: - a visiting sister of this special Auntie danced together with me and the widower at the Wedding of yet another cousin's niece. This was in front of my son who, together with the son of the Auntie that was dancing with me, happened to be providing the music at the Reception. Sounds complicated? I am sure you get the gist.

Back in Nanyuki, when Oreste told me of this rumour, I put my hands over my mouth, laughter spluttering out between my fingers, until I realised that he was quite serious. "Yes!" I reassured him. "I am going to leave you for your bolshy old Uncle who happens to be co-habiting with a local Meru lady, who he was "with" whilst still married to your lovely Aunty!" Not everybody knew this.

As with Hans and his bullshit, I naively thought that people would not believe such ridiculous stories. Stupid me. People love juicy, hurtful gossip. As a result of this ludicrous story, even to this day, I remain Persona Non Grata in certain circles of this convoluted family.

Ah well, they say that worse things happen in Paradise!

94. MY WORKING LIFE AFTER THE GERMAN

After Hans left, I continued with the Stanley's Safaris but, on my own, the logistics were overwhelming. Looking after clients, doing the bookings, communicating with Tour Agents, planning menus and purchasing supplies, managing staff and vehicles, became too much. Oreste accompanied me to our campsite in Samburu and helped to dismantle the camp.

After many years of being self-employed, I went back to being an employee. I took on a number of temporary vastly varying positions. First was managing a quaint little guesthouse in a forested area of Langata on the outskirts of Nairobi. This job came to an abrupt end without any warning, when all bookings were cancelled due to the so-called Post Election Violence. I am still in contact with a couple of friends I made among the overseas visitors to this guesthouse.

I then managed the Giraffe Manor for the nicest couple anyone could hope to work for. It was very relaxed and the guests were made to feel as if they were visiting somebody's home rather than a "Hotel". The Manor had been built by a Scotsman; when driving in, if you visualised deer in place of giraffes on the sweeping lawns, it could well be a typical Scottish Manor House. The giraffes at the Manor were so special, each one with its own specific character. When I woke in the morning, I would open the bedroom window wide; this was the signal for giraffes from all directions to make their way towards the window. I have a photo of the nose of one youngster not quite tall enough to reach his head through the first-floor window, but he was having a jolly good attempt!

Kelly was a naughty youngster who loved to "mock-charge" people. When taking guests from the Manor across to the "Giraffe Centre" I would carry an umbrella. One time when I could see Kelly getting ready to charge at us, I told the guests to hasten towards the giraffe-barrier while I advanced towards Kelly, opening and closing the umbrella. Suspicious of the umbrella, Kelly spun around, legs flying, and took off; he was very close when he turned, and I was lucky not to receive a flying kick! But he was just having fun; I would stroke his neck whenever his head appeared through the breakfast-room window. The Giraffe Manor was sold to a commercial Safari Company, who did call me back occasionally as Relief Manager.

AT THE GIRAFFE MANOR

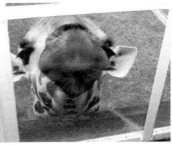

... not quite tall enough to reach his head through the first floor window...

Then I was taken on by a Committee of very caring ladies, to manage Harrison House, a Retirement Home for the elderly. At that time, there were eighteen lady residents; I had known all but two of them for decades. For instance, there was Kay, who had been a tennis friend of mum's. Kay was very special to me; when she was unable to sleep at night, I would sit up with her drinking cups of tea and reminiscing about the old days.

Then there was Gladys, a wiry little Centenarian. I was expected to visit Gladys every evening for a glass of sherry. If I happened to be late, she would stand in the corridor usually wrapped in a bath-towel, thumping her walking stick on the floor, yelling "Wendy! Wendy! Where are you?" whilst shaking off the carers who were attempting to control her! Gladys had retained her memory and we would sit putting the world to rights over a couple of glasses of sherry. Wonderful lady!

Jean hoodwinked the carers by pretending to be fast asleep. Somehow, even if I tip-toed, she never failed to recognise the sound of my footsteps when I walked along the corridor. "Wendy, Wendy, come and talk to me!" she would call out. Dorothy became a good friend; she was totally "all there", her main problem being that she suffered from macular degeneration and was losing her eyesight; so very sad. I had known many of her relatives for years; all lovely people.

I had also known polite, gentle June for a long time. She was a widow; in the past she and her devoted late husband used to holiday at Minilets. Robin, a well-known artist, had been my art teacher at Kenya High School. Denise had been an actress and in by-gone days, I had watched her on stage. She was still a performer and would entertain us all by playing the piano with great aplomb!

The grounds of Harrison were absolutely beautiful, with many trees and a variety of birds, including the occasional owl. I love owls; well, of course I do, being a devoted birder! It is quite understandable that most Kenyans maintain that "Owls bring Death". I have managed to convert a few, by explaining that they are not actually the "cause" of death, what they do is to warn people to be prepared when a death is imminent. When another special lady became sick, an owl perched on the roof above her room, hooting, for a couple of nights. The night she passed away, the owl was sitting on a post not far from her verandah door. The staff tried in vain to shoo it away. After Tinker very sadly died, the owl few off.

Another night, upon hearing an owl hooting, I walked outside with my torch hoping to spot it. I was angry when I found the askari trying to shoo it away from the roof of the servants' quarters. He told me "hi ndege ni mbaya sana, mutu ta kufa!" (This bird is very bad, someone will die!) Coincidentally, a young cook called Steve, had retired to bed with mild "homa" (this is in fact Swahili for "Malaria", but is used to describe any ailment from influenza to haemorrhoids!) After a couple of nights of noisy owl hooting above the servants' quarters, young Steve suddenly experienced difficulty breathing. We called the para-medics who turned up very quickly, but they were unable to save him. This was tragic, Steve was a really nice guy and so young. As soon as he drew in his last breath, the owl flew away. The askari gave me a knowing look, "I told you so!" How could I explain to him that it is well-recorded that owls predicted the death of Caesar?

The reason for my having to leave this job would take some believing, almost warranting another book! It started with a new Committee of businesswomen kicking out the old caring Committee who hired me. And so so so much more.

I then managed a camp on the shores of Lake Baringo. I lived in the chalet where, many years previously, a friend had spent a naughty night with a boyfriend. They rose before dawn with the intention of leaving early, only to discover that the lake waters had flooded the ground floor and there was a huge crocodile snoozing at the foot of the wooden staircase!

When the Lake was high, I would sit on the balcony watching hippos playing underneath.

I wonder if the croc is a descendant of the one that my friend found snoozing at the foot of the stairs!

I would sit on the balcony watching hippos playing underneath

I looked after a wheat farm near Naromoru, owned by a really nice family whose son had been at Pembroke

House when mum was matron. One boundary bordered Ol Pejeta Game Ranch and I frequently spotted elephants on the other side of the fence when driving around that area of the farm. Although reedbuck could be a pest on the farm, it was great to see huge herds of these animals; for some reason, I have rarely seen them elsewhere, and then never more than a couple at a time.

95. MY TOY-BOY

Oreste is the second person I have met, who has that special affinity with animals that Mervyn had, all those years ago. In fact, like Mervyn, he copes with four-legged animals far better than he does two-legged ones! When we holidayed at the coast, he made friends with a Sykes monkey that jumped onto our verandah wall. On that same holiday, Oreste was having his usual siesta and I was sitting on the bed doing a crossword puzzle, when a cupboard door banged in the next room. I dashed through, to see a tumbiri disappearing through the front door clutching a packet of Italian crackers. The next thing, Oreste was clambering over the roof after the little thief. What was so funny was that Oreste was as naked as – and nearly as hairy as – the monkey and, to this day, I regret not taking a photo. Kenyans (and other Africans) don't need much imagination to visualise how funny the photo would be!

ORESTE & SYKES MONKEY

On the ranch where he worked, Oreste kept a baby squirrel alive for many days by carrying it around inside his shirt, and feeding it "baby rice". He came to Nanyuki for a night, and put the little creature in the airing cupboard to keep it warm. In the morning I heard his "Oh no!" The baby had died. He was terribly upset. I would visit him on the ranch, where wild squirrels ate out of his hand and dikdik came to his verandah and let him touch them.

On one of my visits to the ranch, the head of security frantically radioed for Oreste to assist a convoy of vehicles unable to return to a campsite because a "rogue elephant" standing in the middle of the track would not let them pass. Oreste, in kikoi and flip-flops, shirtless and confident, leapt into the Land Rover. He roared down the track, stopped beside the elephant, opened the door and stepped out of the vehicle. Loudly (he is very loud) he asked Mr Elephant "What is your problem? They are not going to bother you. Let them pass!" While he was communicating with the ellie, throwing his arms around in typical Italian fashion, Mr Elephant tossed his head before disappearing into the bush and the vehicles drove safely past.

I had placed pots of herbs around Oreste's verandah. One evening I heard him yelling "Put it down! Put it down!" I went to the door and laughed my head off to witness his naked body chasing after an elephant trying to make off with its trunk wrapped around the stem of one of his precious rosemary plants! The pot was dropped and the chastised animal stood still, head down, taking a good scolding from this mad human.

The one animal that Oreste is wary of, is the unpredictable lone buffalo. He went to fix a water-pump on the ranch, and parked the Landie a few feet from the bushes surrounding the pump. As he jumped out of the vehicle and began to walk towards the pump, there was a crashing sound in the nearby bushes. He turned to see a buffalo charging straight at him. Within a split second, he slid under the Landie, closely followed by a buffalo horn that missed him by inches. His slide under the vehicle inflicted horrific grazes and bruises that lasted for a long time. But he survived!

96. RULES OF THE ROAD IN KENYA

Would-be "return" visitors to Kenya, be warned: in stark contrast to the good old days, the general standard of driving here has to be witnessed to be believed. The main Rule of The Road is "*Overtake!* Get in front, come hell or high water!" This means, pull out to overtake the vehicle in front, even if said vehicle has much more power than yours, so you end up driving side-by-side along the highway, making rude signs at the cantankerous driver who refuses to slow down to let you get in front.

It means, "*Overtake* the vehicle ahead, even if you are just about to turn left off the highway, bringing the car you have just overtaken to a screeching halt as you turn off". It means "*Overtake*, although cars speeding towards you will have to swerve off the road to avoid a head-on collision". You *must* cut onto the highway from an adjoining road, straight in front of an oncoming vehicle, although there are a few hundred metres of free road behind her/him, as this will put you *ahead* and save the hassle of having to overtake later.

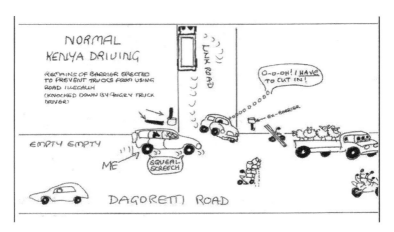

By the day, more and more Kenyan drivers are learning these Rules, as are newcomers to our country. Over the past few years, Kenya has had an influx of imports, for example white settlers who have escaped from South Africa, who are quick to catch on. They go charging around in their humungous four-wheel-drive vehicles, overtaking where it is impossible to overtake, cutting in and pulling onto the road in the path of oncoming vehicles. Of course, these recently-imported drivers of both sexes who have come here to show we silly Kenyans how to run our country, are totally ignorant of the fact there was a time in Kenya before the "matatu era", when the internationally-recognised Highway Code was adhered to. They probably think all Kenyans always drove this way.

I must explain here, a matatu is a dangerously over-loaded, road-hogging Public Service Vehicle, propelled by a rude, obnoxious, stoned, spaced-out, individual with a death-wish. "Boda-bodas" are as bad. Boda-bodas are motorbike people-carriers, so-named after the motorbikes that carry passengers from "Border-to-Border" between Kenya and Uganda. Boda-bodas *always* drive the wrong way down one-way streets; neither drivers nor passengers wear helmets. Permitted to carry only one passenger, they usually carry four, five, six or more – plus furniture, goats, chickens and very long strips of mbati (iron sheets).

I am not saying that no courtesy is ever shown by Kenyan drivers. To the opposite extreme, I frequently have to slam on brakes in the middle of a fast-lane highway, when the car ahead suddenly comes to a complete halt in order to graciously wave a waiting vehicle onto the main road from a side-road or lay-by.

The problem is, of course, our Driving Instructors cannot drive; they need instruction. They simply take money for handing over Driving Licences.

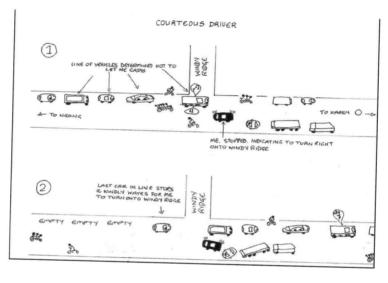

COURTEOUS DRIVER

① LINE OF VEHICLES DETERMINED NOT TO LET ME CROSS

WINDY RIDGE

← TO NGONG

TO KAREN ○ →

ME. STOPPED. INDICATING TO TURN RIGHT ONTO WINDY RIDGE

② LAST CAR IN LINE STOPS & KINDLY WAVES FOR ME TO TURN ONTO WINDY RIDGE ↓

WINDY RIDGE

EMPTY EMPTY EMPTY

97. A FEW PERSONAL CONTROVERSIAL VIEWS

There were "Research Students" on the ranch where Oreste was working. In a conversation with one of these "Researchers", I asked what her field of study was. She told me her thesis would be based on the interesting observation that "zebras stay on the grass plains rather than in the forests".

Yes.

One of the researchers, a whizz-kid on the subject of Wild Dogs, vehemently maintained these animals do not eat dead flesh. Quite why that was a good thing I did not understand as carrion-eaters are much needed. Once, driving from the Ranch, Oreste was horrified to witness a giraffe standing at the roadside, suddenly drop down dead like those elasticated toys we used to have about forty years ago. Later, whilst driving past the dead giraffe, he watched a number of Wild Dogs exiting from inside the carcass. He drove back to the Research Centre and asked the researcher to accompany him, as he had "something to show her". She was astonished and said she would never have believed it had he not shown her! Yet she, the expert, had been studying them for how long……

I am sure Oreste and I knew as much about these animals as she did. When I was growing up, this country's game parks were teeming with the infamous "Cape Hunting Dogs". We would drive into Nairobi Game Park hoping to see everything but these creatures. Annoyingly, they would inevitably appear, careering across the road in front of and around the car in packs of twenty, thirty, or more. These handsomely-marked animals hunted in packs. They didn't bother about unimportant things like killing their prey first; they would eat a beautiful antelope that was still alive, simply tearing chunks out of its flesh while it struggled helplessly. They would eat a baby zebra or wildebeest while it was being born, the petrified mother fleeing in terror while a Wild Dog was literally tearing the baby from her womb as she ran.

Jeez!

A beautiful dikdik would wait at Oreste's verandah to be given peanut nibbles. She plus her family lived in the bush next to his house. There were very many dikdik on the ranch. Oreste asked the students whose research project involved trapping these little antelopes, not to touch those living near his house. However, after he left this job, the researchers grasped the opportunity to trap Mummy Dikdik and family; far less effort than attempting to catch those living right out in the bush. In the clumsy process they somehow managed to break one of Mummy Dikdik's legs. Consequently, the hyenas got her. Oreste found this out on a return visit to the ranch. The researchers weren't particularly interested when he berated them: "Natural culling of animals by animals" they said. "We must not interfere with nature".

Excuse me? Humans trapping animals and breaking their legs is not natural. I still want to cry when I look at our dikdik photographs.

There was a beautiful dikdik that used to come to the verandah. . . . .

She and her family lived in the bush near his house

I still cry when I look at the photographs of Mummy Dikdik

If nature wasn't interfered with, malaria and the indescribably awful AIDS virus would cull humans. It is a well-known fact that human over-population is this continent's main problem. In the good old days, a nomadic herder would have ten children. Two would survive. Each surviving child would have, say, ten head of cattle. Plenty of room for all. Now, each herder has ten children, and all survive. And each of them has at least ten head of cattle. "Elephants, rhinos, lion, cheetah, leopards, in fact all wildlife, move out of our way – give room for our cattle. We don't sell them; we just keep them because the more we have, the richer we appear....."

Should I step off my soapbox and stop suggesting that Bill Gates *et al* should put their money towards building clinics providing proper family-planning education? Why don't the do-gooders get it into their heads that this is the one and only answer to Africa's woes? It is vital. The continent is becoming severely over-populated by humans who should be given the chance to attend sensible, well-run Family Planning Clinics, instead of struggling to survive in ever-expanding, revolting, disgusting, hazardous slums consisting of hovels and shacks. *They deserve better; they deserve a choice.* As it is, the end result will be billions and billions of unemployed humans living in foul disease-ridden slums.

Thus, no elephants. No rhinos. No lions. No cheetah. No leopards. No wildlife at all. Just desperate, starving humans.

What a future to look forward to.

98. TOUCHING VERY LIGHTLY ON POLITICS.......

I won't kid you, it was tough losing my job as Manager of the pleasant little guesthouse in Langata as a result of tourist cancellations due to the "Post-Election Violence" (PEV) in 2007-2008. I always refer to this dreadful episode as Pre-Election Violence, because it was all pre-arranged. Day after day, wananchi of *one tribe* were being slaughtered. Upon receiving news of the murdering of members of his tribe in Kibera, a really cool, hard-working young man whom Jeni helped out by paying him to deliver goods to her house by mkoteni (hand-drawn cart), rushed back to check up on his mum. He never reached home; he was *chopped up* en route. Words cannot describe. For us, this was tragic; but he was just one of thousands from this particular tribe.

Every single day, on telly, a female journalist on an international media channel was reporting on "Kenyans" being killed. Never once did she mention that it was members of *one tribe* that were being systematically butchered. To those of us living in Kenya, this was definitely the main issue. My family, friends, and I, were calling each other in consternation, trying to figure out why the situation wasn't being reported accurately. The said female reporter apparently posted a video of a totally unrelated event from an earlier period in Kenya's history, making it out to be part of the PEV.

We wondered why the targeted tribe did not truly fight back. As I remember it, the burning of women and children in a Church finally brought about a full-scale response. Women throwing babies out of the Church windows to save them from the fire. Dear God in Heaven. Well, retaliate, they did. And how! The said female reporter was then daily *naming* The Tribe that was fighting back; but she did not say they were retaliating; she simply reported as if that particular tribe was going on a killing spree. I understand that this reporter is no longer welcome in our country. Good.

And "The Hague"! Wanting to indict the Retaliator but not the Instigator? Get real.

99.........AND CORRUPTION

Our biggest problem second to population over-growth, is corruption. Our President is a nice guy, a businessman who did not intend to go into politics. Oreste was at school with him. He is surrounded by corrupt people. When a Kenyan applies for the issue or renewal of a document that is her or his legal entitlement by Law, it is normal procedure that the "file is lost" until such time as a wad of notes passes hands, whereupon the file is instantly and miraculously recovered.

It is common knowledge that the Traffic Police are actually instructed by the bosses, to go out and demand bribes from the public both to supplement their low salaries and to pass large percentages onto the "Top Brass". Apparently, those who do not come up with sufficient for the bosses at the end of the month, risk being "promoted" to unattractive posts in far-off desert regions. The most sought-after Police jobs are those on the roads. I have seen matatu drivers throw money out of the cab window at so-called Police Checks" without even stopping.

Meanwhile, we normal, careful, drivers risk huge fines and/or imprisonment for very minor traffic "offences", such as a dirty number plate after driving down a muddy side-track; or for fabricated speeding offences when we have not been speeding. Kenyans of my age remember the days when the sight of a Policeman made us feel secure. Now, the sight of a Policeman fills our hearts with dread.

Visitors emanating from an Eastern country reputedly pay enormous sums of money to Those In Power, in order to win contracts to re-build our roads and other ventures that can be far better accomplished by more sophisticated countries. They also use Kenya as a dumping ground for their over-expanding population, by bringing in their own people to oversee the projects. A section of the road we live on in Nanyuki was recently re-built by such people. The village dogs all but disappeared. I learned that they were sold to the road-builders, who eat them.

They eat them.

100. A KIND OF EPILOGUE

Is there a place for stupid sentimentalists like me? A few days ago, I stopped my car, in order to give room for a vehicle driving towards me to overtake pigeons that were pecking at grain on his side of the road. Instead of avoiding the pigeons, he drove straight over them. I screamed at him as he drove past me, gaping at me as if I was mad. Perhaps I am.

A friendly rhino lived on a nearby ranch. This wonderful animal *trusted* humans and followed the ranger around. We were told that he was painfully and horribly killed and his horn hacked out, the murderers having been led to the animal by the very person he trusted most of all. And all for bloody money. Because the inhabitants of the country where the road-builders come from believe that rhino horn cures cancer, and hang-overs, and gives them erections....

And I cry because somebody runs over a couple of pigeons?

Dear God, you have plenty of planets out there. Why did you place these heartless savages on the same planet as us?

In my mind, I had re-written the lyrics to Sinatra's song, thus: - "....regrets, I have thousands....but then again, too many to mention...." Then just the other day, quite unexpectedly, I had a breakthrough. I asked myself, "If you have done everything so wrong, how come you have the two most fantastic children in the whole world?" And the best son-in-law? And the best Grandchildren? I am not sure how much credit can be given to the men in my life, so I must have done something right?

LINDA LIVES IN NJORO WITH HER PARTNER, PET PARROT, ONE CAT AND TWO DOGS

JENI AND ANTHONY LIVE IN NAIROBI, WITH THE TWO BESTEST GRANDCHILDREN IN THE WHOLE WORLD, AND THEIR FIVE DOGS

ANDREW AND HIS GIRLFRIEND ELLIE LIVE IN NAIROBI WITH THEIR TWO CATS AND TWO DOGS

Linda lives in Njoro with her partner, pet parrot, one cat and two dogs. Jeni and Anthony live in Nairobi, with the two bestest grandchildren in the whole world, and their five dogs. Andrew and his girlfriend live in Nairobi with their two cats and two dogs. I know that bottled up inside them, my sister Linda, and my kids Jeni and Andrew, all have their own feelings about this amazing country. Do they match mine?

I love my country passionately: the brilliant white beaches; from the high mountains to the deep valleys; the barren deserts to the thick forests. I love my people. I have lived in townships and in the bush. I have lived with wild animals and with domestic animals. Unlike most mzungus, I have witnessed true witchcraft and the removal thereof. I have been loved and unloved.

Although in my own naive way, I rebelled against the Colonial regime, was I in fact *lucky* to have been brought up in this beautiful country during the Colonial era? Was I fortunate to be here to witness first-hand the transfer of power from the "Evil Colonialists" to the rightful inhabitants of the country? I now watch this wonderful country being run by open corruption, selfish greed and lust for power, and witness the *uncontrolled* population increase that is causing the devastation of our forests and annihilation of our wildlife, thus the destruction of the very core of our country.

Often I despair.

Roger Whittaker was at school with my husband, John. Why do tears pour down my face whenever I hear Roger singing "My Land is Kenya"? It is as if he is singing about a different place, on another planet. I am crying for the place he once knew. A place I once knew.

Dear God, will you please intervene in time to save the most wonderful country in the world from total self-destruction?

I recall a somewhat derogatory Colonial saying: "You can always take an African out of the Bush, but you can never take the Bush out of an African".

Well, let me assure you, nothing will *ever* take the Bush out of this African.

Me.

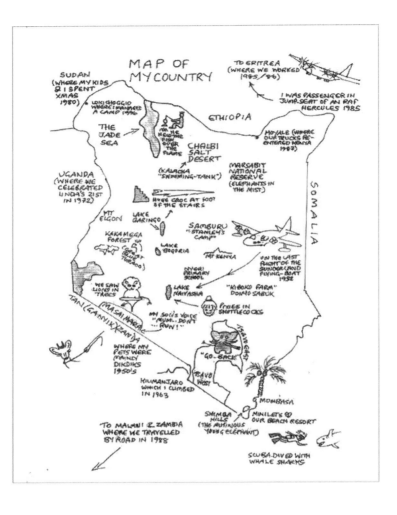

Dedication

I would like to thank all my friends who have continually encouraged me to "Get your book out!" The list is too long; but I have to say that I would certainly have given up if it were not for you special people, including many special "Facebook friends": Gerald Raath, Fenella Lockhart-Muir, Andrew Wright; far too many to mention. Not to forget the late Brian Connell, who gave me so much help and encouragement.

From my rafiki Brian Hartwick in Canada who, after reading the first draft years ago, was the first to say "Publish it!" to the best boss in the world Gunnar Schultzberg in UK who, each time we communicate, never fails to enquire "How's your book going?" And all those in between, including Mimi Shaw, who put me on the right track! Asante sana.

Thank you my most amazing children, Jeni and Andrew, just for being who you are; for all the fun times through the years, and for your everlasting non-judgemental support of your dotty mother through all the ups and downs.

A very special asante to my sister Linda, for always, unfailingly, being there for me, through thick and thin:- through the many good times and the all-too-many bad times.

Samantha Ford. Words cannot describe how special you have been. Without you, this book would never have been published.

Dear Ann Barnes, thank you so much for your assistance, your editing and continual encouragement, all the way from Oz..... Here's a little memory of Ann, from the late 1950's when, on her trusty Lambretta scooter, she would weave her way to work at Embakasi Airport, between sleeping lions..... If only the lions were still sleeping on the road to Embakasi these days.....

Love you all xxx.

*****

If you enjoyed reading this book and would like to share that enjoyment with others, then please take the time to visit the place where you made your purchase and write a review.

Reviews are a great way to spread the word about worthy authors and will help them be rewarded for their hard work.

Printed in Great Britain
by Amazon